D1457447

WEST BEND LIBRARY

The DARK Intrigue

The true story of a Civil War conspiracy

Frank van der Linden

Fulcrum Publishing
Golden, Colorado

WEST BEND LIBRARY

Text © 2007 Frank van der Linden

All rights reserved. No part of this book may be reproduced, stored in a retrieval system, or transmitted in any form or by any means, electronic, mechanical, photocopying, recording, or otherwise, without written permission from the publisher.

Library of Congress Cataloging-in-Publication Data

Van der Linden, Frank.
  The Dark intrigue : the true story of a Civil War conspiracy / Frank van der Linden.
     p. cm.
  Includes bibliographical references and index.
     ISBN 978-1-55591-610-7 (hardcover : alk. paper) 1. Northwestern conspiracy, 1864. 2. United States--Politics and government--1861-1865. 3. United States--History--Civil War, 1861-1865--Underground movements. 4. United States--History--Civil War, 1861-1865--Peace. 5. Government, Resistance to--United States--History--19th century. 6. Democratic Party (U.S.)--Biography. 7. Legislators--United States--Biography. 8. Vallandigham, Clement L. (Clement Laird), 1820-1871. 9. Clay, C. C. (Clement Claiborne), 1816-1882. 10. Legislators--Confederate States of America--Biography. I. Title.

  E458.8.V36 2008
  973.7'12--dc22

                                        2007033714

Printed in the United States of America by Malloy Incorporated
0 9 8 7 6 5 4 3 2 1

Jacket and interior design: Patty Maher
Cover image: The heavy toll of his wartime burdens can be seen in the lines etched into the face of President Lincoln in this photograph, but he has good reason for this unusual smile: Despite the "dark intrigue," he has won reelection and the bloody war is finally ending in a Union victory. This is Lincoln's last photograph. It was taken by Alexander Gardner on April 10, 1865, four days before the martyred president was fatally shot at Ford's Theater. The portrait is from the collections of the Library of Congress.

Fulcrum Publishing
4690 Table Mountain Drive, Suite 100
Golden, Colorado 80403
800-992-2908 • 303-277-1623
www.fulcrumbooks.com

973.7
V284

To the memory of
Margaret Lyn van der Linden McKay,
beloved daughter and scholar who faithfully served
in her country's defense as an analyst
of foreign intelligence.

Contents

Preface . . . . *ix*

Chapter One
"McClellan for President" 1

Chapter Two
Barlow Commands the Boom 7

Chapter Three
Stanton Smears McClellan 11

Chapter Four
McClellan's Fateful Letter 19

Chapter Five
"Little Mac Is Back!" 26

Chapter Six
"Plenty of Rotten Old Democrats" 33

Chapter Seven
Separate Peace Urged on the Northwest 38

Chapter Eight
Arbitrary Arrests 41

Chapter Nine
Democrats' Intrigue with British for Peace 47

Chapter Ten
"Treason Is Everywhere" 53

Chapter Eleven
"Don't Care a Damn" 59

Chapter Twelve
Lincoln Exiles Vallandigham 66

Chapter Thirteen
"The Great Dead Rabbit" 72

Chapter Fourteen
Bloody Chaos in New York 80

Chapter Fifteen
Antiwar Feeling Rises 86

Chapter Sixteen
Dahlgren's Fatal Raid 94

Chapter Seventeen
Confederates' Intrigue in Canada 99

Chapter Eighteen
Federal Spies Find Disloyalty in the North 107

Chapter Nineteen
Gold Gamblers and Shoddy Rich 112

Chapter Twenty
Vallandigham Returns 117

Chapter Twenty-One
Jubal Early's Raid Spurs Calls for "Mac" 122

Chapter Twenty-Two
Sanders, Rebel Agent, Woos Democrats 127

Chapter Twenty-Three
A Machiavellian Scheme 138

Chapter Twenty-Four
Lincoln Scents the Dark Intrigue .145

Chapter Twenty-Five
A Spy Exposes Plot for Revolt 151

Chapter Twenty-Six
Lincoln Fears Defeat 158

Chapter Twenty-Seven
Peace Democrats Oppose McClellan 166

Chapter Twenty-Eight
Mint Juleps and Sherry Cobblers .173

Chapter Twenty-Nine
"This Damned War Must Be Stopped!" 179

Chapter Thirty
Democrats Promise Armistice 187

Chapter Thirty-One
Seward Proves the Dark Intrigue .196

Chapter Thirty-Two
Pendleton and Belmont Assailed .205

Chapter Thirty-Three
Hood Moves North 213

Chapter Thirty-Four
"Treason" Trials in Indiana 217

Chapter Thirty-Five
Illinois Democrat Takes Rebel Gold 226

Chapter Thirty-Six
Rebels Betrayed in Chicago 234

Chapter Thirty-Seven
New York in the Balance 240

Chapter Thirty-Eight
Lincoln's Great Victory 245

Chapter Thirty-Nine
The Last Nail in Slavery's Coffin 252

Chapter Forty
Aftermath 257

Abbreviations 263
Notes 265
Bibliography 295

Preface

A FEW DAYS AFTER THE DEMOCRATS chose Union Gen. George B. McClellan as their nominee to run against President Abraham Lincoln in 1864, the *New York Times* came out with a blistering editorial headlined "McClellan's Military Adventures—Treasonable Intrigues with Our Foreign Enemies." McClellan's nomination, in the newspaper's view, marked the climax of a dark intrigue begun in 1861 by certain powerful men who were sympathetic to the South and carefully brought to fruition, by carrying out their antiwar schemes.

McClellan had been chosen by the "conservatives" as their champion three years before, when they were seeking by every means possible not to bring the war to a successful conclusion, "but to stop it altogether at any cost," it charged. "They were determined to have unconditional peace if they could, and were engaged in treasonable intrigues to procure it."

These were strong words indeed—*treasonable intrigues*—to stop the Civil War, not to win it. Were the charges justified by the truth?

The truth was, although Northern people generally supported President Lincoln in the war to restore the Union, many deplored it as a horrible waste of lives and yearned for some peaceful way to end the bloodshed. Others opposed the war because they saw it as an illegal use of Federal armies attempting to crush the secessionist Southern states. Some spoke out openly against the war, while others secretly opposed it, fearing that outright opposition would brand them as "disloyal" or even land them in prison.

By exploiting the public's dissatisfaction with civilian arrests, the Emancipation Proclamation, the draft, and the rising death toll, Democrats had made many gains in the 1862 elections: they seized control of the legislatures in Illinois and Indiana and frightened the Republicans with proposals for a compromise peace.

James R. Gilmore, a writer, reported that Northern people were so sick of war that they agreed: "There must be some way to end this wretched business. Tell us what it is and be it armistice, concession, compromise, anything whatever, we will welcome it as long as it terminates the suicidal war."

By mid-1864, the death toll had reached half a million and there was a universal cry for peace, and prominent Northern Democrats went to Canada and met secretly with agents of the Confederacy and discussed their own party's platform for the coming presidential campaign. This book discloses the incredible story of the Democratic politicians who risked their reputations—and possibly their freedom—by conferring with the enemy in wartime.

One hostile newspaper asked, "Do these peacemongers, who go to Canada to see how much they can get for selling out their country, reflect that they expose themselves, upon returning, to arrest as spies for holding correspondence with a public enemy?"

Although assailed as spies and traitors by many in the United States, the Northern Democrats who met with Confederate agents on the Canadian side of Niagara Falls did not consider themselves disloyal—after all, nearly all of the Confederates they met with were Democrats too. The Democrats in the North and South had been comrades in a common cause before the war, so why not try to patch up the family quarrel and bring peace at last to the tortured land?

President Lincoln, however, did not share with them their benign view of themselves as patriots. Instead, somehow he obtained a copy of a Democratic platform draft penned by C. C. Clay, one of the Confederates who met with Democrats in Canada. President Lincoln cited the paper as proof that the Democrats were in cahoots with the Rebels and that the election campaign was a struggle between his forces, who were fighting to save the Union, and the Democrats, who were working directly with the enemy.

How deeply did Northern Democrats succumb to the embraces of the Confederates? The printed records can supply only part of the story because the Southerners took great pains to destroy any incriminating evidence. Their chief commissioner in Canada, Jacob Thompson, had assured Confederate Secretary of State Judah P. Benjamin of his extreme caution in suppressing the records. "Indeed," Thompson wrote, "I have so many papers in my possession which, in the hands of the enemy, would utterly ruin and destroy very many of the prominent men of the North."

Thompson burned most of his papers at the end of his mission, as did Benjamin. But the identities of several Democrats who carried on friendly chats with Southerners can be found in the U.S. National Archives and Records Administration, the official records of the Union and Confederate Armies, and the official records of the Union and Confederate Navies. This book reveals the cast of colorful characters involved in the dark intrigue.

Most fascinating is the shadowy figure of George Nicholas Sanders, a behind-the-scenes operator in prewar Democratic politics who became a Confederate agent. He tricked President Lincoln and Horace Greeley into their "peace" fiasco in the summer of 1864. Also notable are several New York financiers and railroad promoters who sponsored McClellan—himself a former railroad executive—for the presidency.

The Southerners and their friends in the North came close to succeeding with their hazardous alliance, the Confederacy's last hope for independence.

Chapter One
"McClellan for President"

THE McCLELLAN FOR PRESIDENT campaign began almost as soon as the youthful general emerged as the first Union hero of the Civil War. The Young Napoleon rose to instant stardom when some Ohio and Indiana volunteers under his command routed Confederate troops in three small-scale battles in the mountains of western Virginia in June 1861. After the Federal Army suffered its first defeat, July 21 at Bull Run, and stumbled back across the Potomac from Virginia like a frightened mob, the handsome warrior was summoned to Washington July 26. The next day President Lincoln appointed him chief of the Army of the Potomac charging him with building the defenses of the capital and transforming demoralized soldiers into an army capable of defeating the Confederacy.

When the deeply worried president and the self-confident general met at the White House, they were a study in contrasts: Lincoln, tall, raw-boned, awkward, with long arms and legs and huge hands and feet, towered over the much shorter McClellan who was aptly nick-named "Little Mac." Lincoln, born in a log cabin in Kentucky, rose from his dirt-poor youth, educated himself, became a successful lawyer in Illinois and a one-term congressman who still felt ill at ease in society;

he was fond of regaling other men with funny, sometimes earthy stories. McClellan, the privileged son of a Philadelphia physician, excelled at the U.S. Military Academy, became a brilliant engineer and railroad executive, spoke French and mingled easily in high society, and was sure of his personal and intellectual superiority over mere politicians. Politically, the two men were far apart—Lincoln first a Whig, then a Republican, McClellan, a lifelong Democrat.

Graduated second in the legendary West Point Class of 1846, McClellan had proved his courage under fire in the Mexican War as an engineer on the staff of Gen. Winfield Scott. At age thirty, he was the youngest of three men chosen by President Franklin Pierce's secretary of war, Jefferson Davis, to go to Europe to study tactics of armies involved in the Crimean War.

Tiring of the peacetime military routine, McClellan gave up his commission and became chief engineer of the Illinois Central Railroad at Chicago; he then moved up to become president of the Ohio and Mississippi Railroad, with headquarters at Cincinnati. His connections with powerful railroad executives would become important in his later quest for the presidency. Now, at age thirty-four, the former captain found himself suddenly a major general, second in rank only to General Scott. The quick elevation went straight to his head.

"I find myself in a new and strange position here—the President, General Scott and all deferring to me—by some operation of magic. I seem to have become the power of the land," McClellan wrote to his wife, Ellen Mary Marcy, daughter of Army Captain Randolph B. Marcy. The couple had been married the year before, and she was in Cincinnati awaiting the birth of their first child. McClellan exulted: "I almost think that, were I to win some small success, now, I could become Dictator or anything else that might please me—but nothing of that kind would please me—*therefore*, I won't be dictator. Admirable self-denial!"

At a White House state dinner, the British ambassador assured a visiting French officer in McClellan's presence that McClellan would become the next president of the United States. McClellan responded with a smile. To his wife, he wrote:

> As I hope one day to be united forever with you in heaven, I have no such aspiration. I will never accept the presidency.

I would cheerfully take the dictatorship and agree to lay down my life when the country is saved. …

I feel that God has placed a great work in my hands. I have not sought it—I know how weak I am. I know that I need to do right, and I believe that God will help me and give me the wisdom I do not possess. Pray for me, darling, that I may be able to accomplish my task, the greatest, perhaps, that any poor weak mortal ever had to do—God grant that I may bring this war to an end and be permitted to spend the rest of my days quietly with you.

It is significant that McClellan proposed to "end" the war, not "win" it. That would become the major difference between the Democrats and President Lincoln in 1864.

Galloping around Washington, astride his stallion named Dan Webster, McClellan looked the part of the Man on Horseback. William H. Russell, a British war correspondent, described him: "He is a very squarely built, thick-throated, broad-chested man under the middle height with slightly bowed legs, a tendency to embonpoint. His head, covered with a close cut crop of dark, auburn hair, is well set on his shoulders … The brow small, contracted, and furrowed. A short, reddish mustache conceals his mouth."

In the general's dark blue eyes, the Englishman could see no trace of uneasiness. Noting that the commander liked fine cigars and sometimes a chew of tobacco, Russell, commented: "He looks like a stout little captain of dragoons."

McClellan labored night and day to weld his motley crew of raw volunteers into some semblance of a fighting force. By enforcing strict discipline, he cleared laggard soldiers and officers off the streets of Washington and out of the saloons, and inspired esprit de corps among thousands of recruits flooding into the city. He supervised the construction of a ring of forts to protect the capital from invasion, expected at any time. His soldiers hailed him as "Little Mac," "George," and "the Young Napoleon."

McClellan did not share the rigors of camp life with his men in their tents, however. His headquarters were in a mansion on Jackson Square. It was close to the White House—a fact observed by those who believed the ambitious warrior already had his eye on that residence. The gossip persisted although he was a year below the minimum legal age of thirty-five to be president. He would be old enough, his advocates noted, to qualify by 1864.

In early September, several Northern newspapers printed alarming stories indicating an imminent Confederate attack on Washington. The *New York Tribune* predicted that a gray-clad horde would cross the Potomac and converge on Frederick, Maryland, where pro-Confederate members of the legislature would vote to take Maryland out of the Union.

Under orders from President Lincoln, McClellan sent Federal troops to arrest the pro-secessionist legislators before they could convene at Frederick, September 17. Nineteen legislators were arrested, along with Baltimore mayor George Brown, two newspaper editors, and Congressman Henry May. Later the prisoners were sent to Fort Lafayette, New York, and to Fort Warren, in Boston harbor, where they languished for more than a year, until their release in November 1862. None ever had a trial. Their arrests and imprisonment were clearly violations of the Bill of Rights.

Maryland leaders insisted that there never had been any plot to take their state out of the Union. The legislature had already ruled that out in April 1861 when Lincoln had threatened to "bombard their cities."

The crackdown on the Maryland legislature typified the Lincoln administration's iron-fisted technique of dealing with dissent. Early in the war, a few brave—or foolhardy—souls dared to speak up and say it was wrong for Americans to be butchering each other over a political dispute. Their calls for conciliation were drowned out by the roar of cheers for victory.

After the Bull Run defeat, however, more antiwar protests could be heard, and the government began to deal harshly with newspapers and individuals daring to call for peace.

William Henry Seward, the secretary of state, who considered himself the "premier" of the Lincoln regime, became, in effect, the director of internal security. In a story that has made its way into the history books, Seward is quoted as boasting to the British ambassador: "My Lord, I can touch a bell on my right hand and arrest a citizen of Ohio. I can touch a bell again and order the imprisonment of a citizen of New York; and no power on earth, except the President, can release them. Can the Queen of England do as much?"

The *New York Daily News* printed so much antiwar copy that the government banned it from the mails. A crippled newsboy named George Hubbell was thrown into Fort Lafayette for selling the politically incorrect newspaper at a railroad station in Connecticut. His brother, a Republican Party worker in New York, protested to Lincoln: "George has been a cripple from his youth with a spinal deformity and is the sole help of his mother, who is in the deepest sorrow." It was difficult to explain how the imprisonment of this crippled newsboy promoted national security. Embarrassed by the blunder, Seward released the youth within a week.

James W. Wall, the leader of a passionate band of peace advocates at Burlington, New Jersey, wrote antiwar editorials for the *New York Daily News*. He charged: "The war has a four-fold object: first, power; the second, plunder; third, Negro equality; and fourth, southern subjugation." This was "treason" enough to land him in Fort Lafayette. After two weeks, Wall was freed. Upon his return to Burlington, he received a hero's welcome, complete with a torchlight procession to his home. Later, Democrats who controlled the New Jersey legislature elected him to the United States Senate, where his father, Garrett Wall, had served as an ally of President Andrew Jackson.

While Seward had the power of tinkling his little bell, he did not hesitate to arrest even men who had served with him in the Senate if they were suspected of favoring the South. One such former senator was Dr. William McKendree Gwin, a California Democrat and erstwhile physician who owned a plantation and slaves in Mississippi. With Calhoun B. Benham, California's district attorney, and a friend, Joseph L. Brent, Dr. Gwin sailed from San Francisco October 21, 1861, via Panama, for New York City. Upon arriving in New York, November 15, all three men were arrested under Seward's orders and lodged in Fort Lafayette.

"Gwin was known to be a sympathizer with the rebels and was believed to entertain the purpose of joining them in the insurrectionary states," the State Department claimed. Dr. Gwin denied charges that he sought to make California an independent state or to ally it with the Southern Confederacy. Eventually, President Lincoln intervened in the case and all three men were freed.

Former senator George Wallace Jones, an Iowa Democrat who had served as minister in Bogotá, then capital of New Granada (now Colombia), from 1857 to 1861, returned to Washington in the fall of 1861, had a cordial visit with his old friend Seward and a chat with Lincoln, and proceeded to New York. At his hotel there, however, he found himself arrested on an order from Seward.

Dr. Gwin was in the same hotel, having just been freed from prison. Jones recalled: "Mrs. Gwin entered hurriedly and threw her arms around my neck and exclaimed, 'Oh, my dear General, you're going to Fort Lafayette, from which my husband has just been released!'"

Somehow, the administration had intercepted a letter Jones had sent from Bogotá May 17 to Jefferson Davis, who had been his bosom friend for years. "May God Almighty avert civil war," Jones wrote to the president of the Confederacy, "but if unhappily it shall come you may (I think without doubt) count on me and mine, and hosts of other friends, standing shoulder to shoulder in the ranks with you and other Southern friends and relatives whose rights, like my own, have been disregarded by the Abolitionists."

Jones walked out of the Fort Lafayette prison February 22, 1862, after receiving his parole, promising "to give no aid or comfort to enemies of the United States." His two sons joined the Confederate army.

As the autumn days went by and McClellan's army showed no sign of going after the Rebels in Virginia, the Northern people began to complain. Correspondent Russell observed: "The people are beginning to think the youthful Napoleon is only a brummagem Bonaparte."

McClellan said he was handicapped by his obstinate superior, General Scott, with whom he feuded for months. Privately, Little Mac called Lincoln "an idiot" and wrote that Scott was "in his dotage." Sick and infirm at seventy-five, the once-mighty Scott retired, and on November 1, 1861, McClellan succeeded him as general in chief, while also keeping command of the Army of the Potomac, a dual load of responsibility.

"The supreme command of the Army will entail a vast labor upon you," the president told him.

McClellan replied, "I can do it all."

Chapter Two

Barlow Commands the Boom

McCLELLAN'S PROMOTION to supreme commander delighted a powerful New Yorker who intended to become his unofficial campaign manager and to catapult him into the White House. The mastermind of the McClellan-for-president boom was Samuel Latham Mitchill Barlow, a rich and influential Manhattan lawyer and a young man on the make. In 1861, Barlow was only thirty-five, just six months older than McClellan.

Born in Massachusetts in 1826, Barlow was the eldest son of Samuel Bancroft Barlow, a physician. His mother was the daughter of Jean Brillot-Savarin, an émigré who had fled France to escape the perils of the revolution. At sixteen, Barlow began working in a New York law office for a dollar a week. At twenty-three, he was admitted to the bar and soon became one of the city's most successful corporation lawyers. With his wife and two children, Barlow resided in a brownstone mansion at the corner of Madison Avenue and Twenty-third Street, where he entertained lavishly. He also loved to display his large collection of paintings and well-stocked library.

Behind the scenes, Barlow played a major role in corporations that expanded the nation's rail network during the boom years of the

1850s when railway executives increasingly influenced party politics. In that era, the railroads became the first large industrial complex, and their executives wielded great power in the legislatures and in the halls of Congress and manipulated political conventions. For instance, the New York State Democratic chairman, Dean Richmond, bossed the New York Central Railroad, while the leaders of the Camden and Amboy Railroad dictated the politics of New Jersey, one of the few strongholds of Democrats in the North.

In 1860, Barlow persuaded McClellan to become superintendent of the Ohio and Mississippi Railroad, which ran 340 miles between St. Louis and Cincinnati. Through their association in the railroad business, the two men became lifelong friends. It was quite natural for Barlow to become McClellan's most enthusiastic advocate for the presidency, although the general himself modestly disclaimed any desire to do anything except end the war.

In the first great wave of patriotic fervor after Fort Sumter's fall in April 1861, most Democrats joined Republicans in supporting the war for the purpose of restoring the Union. But partisanship reemerged as the war dragged on without victory, and the Democrats began to rebuild their shattered party. The strategy seemed clear to Barlow: McClellan would crush the rebellion, the Southern states would rejoin the Union if assured of new guarantees for the slave system, and the grateful American people would reward McClellan with the presidency.

Early in the war, McClellan felt confident that his policy of bringing the Southern states back into the Union without interfering with slavery represented the majority opinion of the Northern people as well as the policy of the president. Lincoln's orders canceling the decrees of Gen. John Charles Frémont in Missouri and Gen. David Hunter in South Carolina freeing the slaves of "rebels" in their regions bolstered McClellan's perception. Lincoln feared that Frémont's order would so enrage pro-Union slaveholders in Kentucky that the crucial border state would tip over into the Confederacy. Without Kentucky, the president believed, he could not win the war.

A week after assuming command, McClellan confided in Barlow his plans for ending the war with one tremendous blow. He asked Barlow and other influential men to help him achieve the original aim set forth by Congress by a nearly unanimous vote in July

1861—to defeat the rebellion and to restore the Union but not to interfere with private property, particularly slaves.

"Help me to dodge the nigger—we want nothing to do with him," McClellan wrote to Barlow. "I am fighting to preserve the integrity of the Union and the power of the govt." McClellan believed that the slavery issue must remain secondary, and he believed that Lincoln agreed with him: "The Presdt is perfectly honest and is really sound on the nigger question."

Barlow replied that, after a single decisive victory by the Federal armies, the South would be willing to return to the Union if the North made certain changes in the Constitution. Presumably, such changes would ensure the protection of slavery. Barlow and McClellan did not immediately realize that when the Republican-dominated Congress returned to Washington in early December, the radicals pushed Lincoln to adopt a tough new policy toward the South. The English journalist Russell was among the first to record this important change. He wrote on December 11: "The war which was made to develop and maintain Union sentiment in the South, and to enable the people to rise against a desperate faction which had enthralled them, is now to be made a crusade against slaveholders and a war of subjugation—if not extermination—against the whole of the Southern States. The Democrats will, of course, resist this barbarous and hopeless policy."

McClellan himself made politically unwise assertions to several Republican senators, stating plainly that "I am fighting for my country and the Union, not for abolition and the Republican Party." The senators interpreted these remarks to mean that, just as they had suspected, the general was fighting for the Democratic Party. If he had been a shrewder politician, McClellan would have spoken for "bi-partisan unity" and refrained from casting any aspersions on the Republicans. They controlled both houses of Congress, and, with the creation of a Joint Committee on the Conduct of the War, they would soon show their power and cause him plenty of trouble.

McClellan and Barlow believed they had a strong ally in Edwin M. Stanton, the former attorney general who had remained in Washington to build up his lucrative law practice. Stanton had a great reputation as a tough trial lawyer and a conservative Democrat. As one sign of their friendship, Stanton had once considered an offer to join Barlow's law firm in New York.

Barlow welcomed discord in Lincoln's cabinet. Lincoln had long been dissatisfied with Simon Cameron's mismanagement of the War Department that, overwhelmed by the demands of the war, had compiled a record of inefficiency, sloppy bookkeeping, and scandalous waste in contracts awarded to greedy profiteers. When Cameron angered Lincoln further by proposing to arm Negroes for combat, Barlow commented to Stanton that "such quarrels should be fostered in every proper way," and that McClellan "must, if possible, keep entirely free of them." "I think the General's true course is to mind his own department," Stanton replied, "and win a victory."

On January 14, 1862, Lincoln eased Cameron out as secretary of war and named him minister to Russia and offered Stanton the post of secretary of war. That evening, Stanton came to McClellan's house and said he would accept only if his friend "Mac" approved. McClellan urged him to accept and later recalled that Stanton pledged "all his time, intellect and energy to my assistance" in ending the rebellion. McClellan exulted to Barlow that Stanton's appointment was "a most unexpected piece of good fortune."

Barlow, too, praised Stanton as "a firm, consistent Union man, but as firm a Democrat as I know ... a man of strong mind and will— not afraid of anything or anybody—honest—not ambitious of political preferment and will have his own way."

McClellan naïvely believed that he now had a true friend in charge of the War Department. He did not know that Republican senators feared, at first, that Stanton was a "peace Democrat," and they delayed a vote on his confirmation until they could closely cross-examine him. After they had grilled Stanton in a closed session, Republican Senator William Pitt Fessenden of Maine commented: "He is just the man we want. We agree on every point. The duties of the Secretary of War, the conduct of the war, the negro question, and everything else."

Convinced that Stanton had really come all the way over to the radical Republican side, although still calling himself a Democrat, the senators confirmed him. Little did McClellan realize that Stanton, with his pathological penchant for deception, intrigue, and double dealing, would become a treacherous foe.

Chapter Three

Stanton Smears McClellan

UPON TAKING OFFICE AS SECRETARY of war, Edwin M. Stanton declared that the Army of the Potomac "has got to fight or run away ... The champagne and oysters on the Potomac must be stopped." Stanton deplored the lavish entertainments, which made many a wintry night merry at the McClellan home near the White House. The general's wife and their infant daughter, May—born in Cincinnati in October—had joined him, and "champagne and oysters" for high-ranking Union army officers contrasted sharply with the spartan fare of soldiers in their cold, damp camps in the capital's suburbs.

Republicans noted, with concern, that prominent Democrats visited the general's home and talked politics, confirming suspicions that these men were grooming him for the presidency. Navy Secretary Gideon Welles learned that S. L. M. Barlow had come from New York in response to an invitation from his dear friend, Little Mac, to attend one of the army's grand reviews. According to Welles, McClellan "said he did not wish the presidency, would rather have his place at the head of the army. ... He had no particular desire to close this war immediately but would pursue a kind of policy of his own regardless of the Administration, its wishes and objects."

New York Tribune editor Horace Greeley speculated that McClellan was delaying an attack on the Rebels in Virginia out of fear "that he would be likely to kill several thousand good voters, whom he would need in 1864 when he runs for president of the reunited and reinvigorated Democracy." "General McClellan is essentially slow," the Republican editor commented in his history of the war, continuing,

> But, in the high position to which he had been so suddenly exalted, it was also hard not to see that, in order to save both slavery and the Union, there must be little fighting and a speedy compromise—that fighting must be postponed and put off, and avoided, in the hope that financial embarrassment, a foreign war, or some other complication would compel the mutual adoption of some sort of Crittenden Compromise, or kindred 'adjustment,' whereby the Slave Power would generously condescend to take the Union afresh in its keeping, and consent to a reunion, which would be, in effect, an extension of the empire of Jefferson Davis to the Canada frontier, the perpetual interdict of all antislavery discussion and effort throughout the Republic. On this hypothesis, and on this alone, General McClellan's course while in high command but especially during that long Autumn and Winter became coherent and comprehensible.

This was, indeed, only the "hypothesis" of a partisan writer who distrusted McClellan, but it was shared by many critics who could not understand why the general repeatedly talked about an advance into Virginia but never made one. Greeley added: "During that Fall and Winter, his house was thronged with partisans of the extreme 'Peace' wing of the Democratic Party, who must have held out to him the golden allure of the Presidency as a reward of a forbearing, temporizing, procrastinating policy."

In response to repeated cries of "on to Richmond," McClellan decided to take his army down the Potomac to the Chesapeake Bay and to the peninsula between the York and the James Rivers and capture the Confederate capital through a siege, depending upon his heavy artillery and the aid of naval guns. Lincoln opposed this plan, fearing that it would leave Washington wide open to a Confederate attack. On March 8, Lincoln called McClellan to the White House to discuss a "very ugly" matter. The president said he had been told that McClellan had a "traitorous" scheme to leave Washington defenseless against an enemy assault. Shocked by this baseless charge, McClellan heatedly denied it and demanded a retraction. Lincoln said he was merely relaying reports from other sources; the most likely being Stanton and the new congressional committee on the Conduct of the War.

Gen. Joseph E. "Joe" Johnston and his Rebel army, after camping all winter at Manassas, quietly slipped away southward in March without any pursuit. On March 11, Lincoln relieved McClellan as general in chief, while keeping him in command of the Army of the Potomac. Although stung by the demotion, McClellan took it like a good soldier. "The president is all right," he told Barlow. "He is my strongest friend." But lobbyist Samuel Ward warned Barlow that McClellan was in disgrace with Lincoln.

With fanatical zeal, Stanton spread more tales against McClellan, seeking to have him kicked out as chief of the Army of the Potomac, too. He proposed to replace him with either Gen. Ethan Allen Hitchcock or Col. Napoleon Buford of Illinois or anybody.

Stanton also claimed that in 1860, McClellan had been initiated into the Knights of the Golden Circle, a secret order opposing the government; that Jefferson Davis, as secretary of war, had made young Captain McClellan, one of his favorites and "still had great power and influence over him"; that McClellan "would do nothing against the rebels which would be inconsistent with his obligations as a Knight of the Golden Circle." Once, when taking Senator Orville Browning of Illinois home in his carriage from the White House, Stanton said: "McClellan ought to have been removed long ago; that he could not free himself from the influence of Jeff Davis," and that he was "unwilling to do anything calculated greatly to damage the cause of secession." There is no substantial evidence to support any of these incredible claims, which sound like the ravings of a madman.

The intensity of Stanton's vendetta and the wildness of his charges against a man whom he called a friend caused many of his associates to express concern about his mental balance. Secretary Welles considered him "a hypocrite, a moral coward ... filled with panics and alarms … rude, arrogant and domineering towards those in subordinate positions … but a sycophant and dissembler with those whom he fears … by nature an intriguer." Postmaster General Montgomery Blair called him a dishonest double-dealer. George Templeton Strong, the New York diarist, wrote: "there is a good deal of evidence that his brain is diseased. … Stanton is certainly three parts lunatic."

Historians have recorded that Stanton became hysterical upon the death of his first wife and had to be dragged away from her grave and to be closely watched to prevent attempts at suicide. Noting Stanton's morbid fear of death, one biographer recorded that he "invariably carried" inside his vest, "a fine dagger some inches in length," apparently to protect himself against his many enemies. While it may seem incredible that a man with mental and emotional problems could efficiently run the War Department at the height of the Civil War, Stanton did preside over his kingdom as a despot totally dedicated to winning the war.

In April 1862 while McClellan and his troops were sailing down the Chesapeake Bay to a landing at Fortress Monroe at the tip of the Peninsula, Stanton made a decision that has been branded one of the worst blunders of the war. He closed all the army recruiting offices. Union volunteers were told to go home when, at the same time, the Confederacy was doubling its military strength by enacting a conscription law affecting men between the ages of eighteen and forty-five. One reason for the decree to send Federal volunteers home could have been euphoria; the hard-won Union victory at Shiloh in western Tennessee April 6, soon followed by the fall of New Orleans, apparently caused an erroneous belief that the war would soon be won, so the army already had enough men. Coming events, however, would prove that idea terribly wrong.

McClellan was already complaining that his force of about 150,000 men was inadequate to take Richmond. It was reduced by about a third when Lincoln and Stanton, fearing a Rebel attack on Washington, held back Gen. Irvin McDowell's army to protect the capital. Gen. William B. Franklin tipped off McClellan about the political motives behind the cutback: "McDowell told me that it was intended as a blow to you. That Stanton had said that you intended to work by strategy and not by fighting and that all of the opponents of the administration centered around you—in other words that you had political aspirations."

Reflecting Stanton's panic, Lincoln was displeased by McClellan's slow progress in pushing the Rebels up the Peninsula. Torrential rains had turned the ground into seas of mud, which bogged down McClellan's heavy artillery. "I think the time is near," Lincoln telegraphed McClellan, "when you must either attack Richmond or give up the job and come to the defense of Washington." On May 31, Gen. Joe Johnston led the Rebels in an attack at Seven Pines near Richmond. In two days of furious fighting, the Federal lines held firm. Johnston fell with wounds in his shoulder and chest, sure to disable him for months. His command passed to Gen. Robert E. Lee.

On June 15, a trusted McClellan aide, Colonel Thomas Key, made a curious "peace feeler" to the Confederates. Key met secretly with Brig. Gen. Howell Cobb, a fellow Democrat who had been President Buchanan's secretary of the treasury before going home to Georgia in 1860 to promote secession. The two officers met within Union lines at the Mechanicsville bridge across the Chickahominy River. To the War Department, Key reported Cobb's response to his proposal of a peaceful reunion was that "the invasion of the seceding states, with its consequent slaughter and waste, had created in the Southern mind such feelings of animosity and spirit of resistance that the war could only end in independence or extermination." Key replied to the bearded Rebel that the Confederate leaders must know the "hopelessness" of their fight against the far greater numbers and resources of the free states, the blockade of the Southern ports, and the failure of the South to win foreign recognition.

Refusing to believe their cause was "hopeless," Cobb said the Southerners would fight on. Although he personally opposed defending Richmond, he said, his superiors had determined to do so and the Yankees could take it only when the Confederates "saw fit to abandon it."

"Your people are fighting their friends," Key insisted. "Neither the President, the army or the people of the loyal states have any wish to subjugate the Southern states."

"We cannot now return without degradation or with security," Cobb fired back. "The blood which has been shed has washed out all feelings of brotherhood. We must become independent or conquered."

Key expressed the hope that "this wretched strife" could be ended soon if the Confederates would only "submit" and accept amnesty. The very idea of submission, of surrendering, was so horrifying to Cobb that it drew this hot blast from him: "No Confederate leader could openly advocate such a proposition and continue to live; that, uttered among soldiers or civilians, he would at once be slain."

So ended the peace overture by Colonel Key. He must have made it with McClellan's knowledge. With the overture to end the war without more bloodshed and to bring the South back into the Union rejected, McClellan pursued his plans for using his big guns to take Richmond by siege. "I shall make the first battle mainly an artillery combat," he told his wife. "I will push them in on Richmond and behind their works; then will bring up my heavy guns, shell the city and carry it by assault."

General Lee realized that McClellan, a fellow engineer, had achieved an advantage in artillery by hauling huge siege guns up the railway from his supply base at the White House almost to the edge of Richmond. Lee told President Davis that McClellan would take one position after another "under cover of his heavy guns and we cannot get at him without storming his works." So Lee devised a different scenario for the battles around Richmond which would be forever remembered as "the Seven Days."

Each army had about a hundred thousand combat-fit troops, but the Federals were divided by the Chickahominy River. Lee hurled about 55,000 men against the 35,000 troops led by Fitz-John Porter on the northern side of the stream. The Confederates broke Porter's line at Gaine's Mill and won a victory with heavy losses, a stunning defeat for McClellan. He did not bring up his reserves from the south side in time to avert disaster. Emotionally distraught and sleepless after about seventy-two hours of combat, McClellan sent this dispatch to Stanton shortly after midnight June 28:

> I have lost this battle because my force was too small. ... You must send me very large reinforcements and send them at once. ... I know that a few thousand more men would have

changed this battle from a defeat to a victory. ... I have seen too many dead and wounded comrades to feel otherwise than that the government has not sustained this army. If you do not do so now, the game is lost. If I save this army now, I tell you plainly that I owe no thanks to you, or to any other persons in Washington. You have done your best to sacrifice this army.

Lee ordered a hot pursuit, hoping to smash the entire Federal army before it could retreat to its base on the York River. But McClellan transferred his army and artillery across the Peninsula to a new base on the James River where gunboats could bring up more arms and men. On the way to Harrison's Landing, they paused atop Malvern Hill and lined up their great guns, wheel to wheel, in a defense line under the leadership of their able artillery chieftain Colonel Henry Hunt, and withstood wave upon wave of reckless Rebel attacks, mowing the infantry down with shrapnel, grape, and canister and inflicting horrible wounds and deaths. "It was not war, it was murder," mourned Confederate Gen. Daniel Harvey Hill. Lee had to withdraw his troops to their Richmond defenses as the Seven Days' battles ended.

Shocked by the news of the Federal retreat, the Northern people feared that the Army of the Potomac had been terribly defeated. Lincoln spent sleepless nights worrying that the army had been wiped out. McClellan reassured him that his soldiers, though exhausted, were intact and after rest and reinforcements, would be eager to resume their drive on Richmond. "A thousand thanks for the relief which your two dispatches gave me," the careworn president wired back. "Be assured that the heroism and skill of yourself and officers and men is, and forever will be, appreciated. If you can hold your present position, we shall hive the enemy yet."

"Try just now to save the army ... and I will strengthen it for the offensive again as fast as I can," Lincoln promised. "The governors of eighteen states offer me a levy of three hundred thousand, which I accept." Secretary Stanton, too, assured McClellan that he had ordered Gen. Henry W. Halleck, commanding the large Union forces of the West at Corinth, Mississippi, to forward 25,000 troops immediately to the Richmond front. "Hold your ground and you will be in Richmond before the month is over," Stanton asserted. McClellan believed these assurances for a while, but Lincoln later told Halleck not to "send a man" from the West if that would delay holding the railroad in east Tennessee and capturing Chattanooga. That, he said, was "fully as important as the taking and holding of Richmond." So the 25,000 soldiers never came.

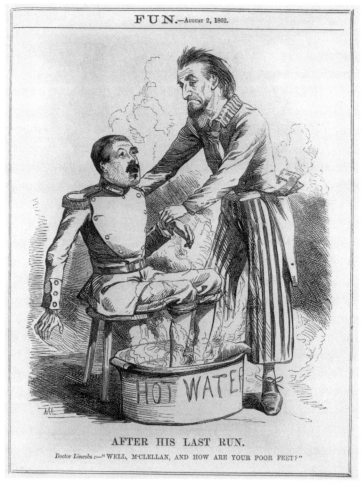

This cartoon shows General McClellan with his feet in "hot water" after his retreat across the Penisula in Virginia in the summer of 1862, the fiasco of his attempt to capture Richmond. "Doctor" Lincoln is asking: "Well, McClellan, and how are your poor feet?" The cartoon appeared in *FUN* magazine August 2, 1862. It is from the collections of the Library of Congress.

Chapter Four
McClellan's Fateful Letter

ON JULY 8, PRESIDENT LINCOLN cruised up the James River aboard the steamer *Ariel* to Harrison's Landing. Lincoln was pleased to find the troops in much better condition than he had imagined. He shocked General McClellan by offering a new idea for the future of his troops: He no longer spoke about his promises to send thousands of reinforcements to resume the siege of Richmond; now, he suggested that the entire Peninsula campaign be given up as a failure. He wanted to break up the Army of the Potomac and feed it in pieces into a new Army of Virginia for the defense of Washington.

The commander of the new force, which would include scattered Federal troops in northern and western Virginia, would not be McClellan. Lincoln's choice was Gen. John Pope, who had recently arrived in Washington, bragging about the victories he had won in the West. A dark and handsome warrior with bright black eyes, a mass of dark hair and a full beard, Pope looked exactly like the bold cavalier that Lincoln and Stanton had been yearning for to replace the slow and cautious engineer, McClellan.

While inspecting the Army of the Potomac, the president questioned the corps commanders, individually, about the idea of merging their troops into Pope's. Only two of five, Generals Franklin and Erasmus D. Keyes, saw any merit in the scheme. Others called it ruinous. Three wanted to stand firm at their new base, and, when reinforced, to drive the last several miles into Richmond.

General McClellan emphatically demanded more soldiers, as he had been promised, and said that, with the aid of gunboats on the James and his massive artillery, he could finally take Richmond. He also volunteered his own ideas about the overall strategy of the war embodied in what came to be known as his Harrison's Landing letter. It would prove to be a decisive factor in eventually ending his military career.

McClellan presented the letter to Lincoln when they were alone on the *Ariel*.

"First of all," he wrote, "the Constitution and the Union must be preserved, whatever the cost in time, treasure, and blood." The war, he insisted, must be conducted upon "the highest principles known to Christian civilization. It must not be a war looking to the subjugation of the people of any state … It should not be at all a war upon population, but against armed forces and political organizations."

In a shaft at General Pope's rough treatment of civilians in Virginia, McClellan continued: "Neither confiscation of property, political executions of persons, territorial organization of states, or forcible abolition of slavery should be considered for a moment," continuing,

> In prosecuting the war, all private property and unarmed persons should be strictly protected. However, slaves seeking military protection should be considered to be contraband of war and military necessity might even require the manumission of all slaves in the state, provided their masters were fully compensated. In Missouri, perhaps in western Virginia, and possibly even in Maryland, the expediency of such a measure is only a question of time.
>
> A system of policy thus constitutional and conservative, and pervaded by the influence of Christianity and freedom, would receive the support of almost all truly loyal men, would deeply impress the rebel masses and all foreign nations, and it might be humbly hoped that it would commend itself to the favor of the Almighty.

Unless such a clear declaration of principles is made, the general warned, it would be "almost hopeless" to recruit enough men for the army. "A declaration of radical views, especially on slavery, will rapidly disintegrate our present armies."

McClellan suggested that a general in chief be appointed "to direct all the military forces of the nation." Although he must have longed to be reinstated in that command, he said: "I do not ask that place for myself. I am willing to serve you in such position as you may assign me and I will do so as faithfully as ever subordinate served superior. I may be on the brink of eternity, and as I hope for forgiveness from my Maker, I have written this letter with sincerity towards you and from love for my country."

The president pocketed the letter without comment, leading the general to wonder what he really thought about it. When Lincoln read the letter to his cabinet a few days later, Stanton and Treasury Secretary Chase demanded McClellan's immediate removal from command. They realized that he was totally opposed to carrying on the war to subjugate the South and destroy slavery. Lincoln wanted a tough new general with a killer instinct who would march on Richmond by the overland route while still protecting Washington. He found his man in John Pope.

Republican politicians also saw a deadly parallel between McClellan's views and the "Address to the Democracy of the United States," recently issued by the Democrats in Congress. Largely drafted by Ohio's Clement L. Vallandigham, who had openly opposed the war from the start, the manifesto denounced Federal interference with slavery and said: "Democrats recognize it as their duty as patriots to support the government in all constitutional, necessary and proper efforts to maintain its safety, integrity and constitutional authority; but at the same time, they are inflexibly opposed to waging war against any of the states or people of the Union for any purpose of conquest or subjugation or of overthrowing or interfering with the rights or established institutions of any state." The phrase "established institutions" amounted to a politicians' euphemism for slavery.

It was easy for the Republicans to believe that McClellan intended to help his fellow Democrats in the fall elections and to become their nominee for the presidency in 1864. When he warned the president against making a radical move for abolition, McClellan may have learned that Lincoln was on the verge of making exactly such a change in his policy of waging the war primarily to restore the Union. Earlier, Lincoln had told Senator Charles Sumner of Massachusetts that an emancipation proclamation would drive three more border slave states into secession and arouse so much hostility in the army that "half the officers would fling down their arms." McClellan knew about the officers' attitude when he warned that forced abolition would make it "almost hopeless" to recruit and keep enough soldiers in the army.

But on July 10, two days after receiving McClellan's letter, the president indicated that he would yield to the demands of the anti-slavery men who controlled the Republican majority in Congress. He told Seward and Welles that he had decided to issue an emancipation proclamation. Twelve days later, he showed the cabinet the first draft of the document in which he proposed to declare that in the sections of the South still continuing the "rebellion" by January 1, 1863, the slaves would be forever free.

On July 11, Lincoln named a new general in chief—Gen. Henry W. Halleck, who claimed credit for most of the Union victories in the West. Stanton contrived this move and rejoiced that it "substantially degrades McClellan into a mere subordinate." Secretary Welles wrote in his diary: "The introduction of Pope here, followed by Halleck, is an intrigue of Stanton's and Chase's to get rid of McClellan."

At last, McClellan realized that Stanton's recent professions of eternal loyalty and friendship were merely gushings of hypocrisy by a man whom no one could trust—a strange mixture of sycophant and bully. McClellan compared Stanton now to Judas Iscariot. On July 13, he wrote to his wife: "Had he lived in the time of the Saviour, Judas Iscariot would have remained a respected member of the fraternity of the apostles and that magnificent treachery and rascality of E. M. Stanton would have caused Judas to have raised his arms in holy horror and unaffected wonder—he would certainly have claimed and exercised the right to have been the betrayer of his Lord and Master."

Writing to Barlow July 15, McClellan expressed sadness that so many brave men "have fallen victims to the stupidity and wickedness at Washington which have done their best to sacrifice as noble an army as ever marched. I do not care if they remove me from this army—except on account of the army itself. I have lost all regard and respect for the majority of the administration and doubt the propriety of my brave men's blood being spilled to further the designs of such a set of heartless villains."

General Halleck arrived in Washington July 22, and the next day he and the president met with Stanton and Generals Pope and Ambrose Burnside. Lincoln offered command of the Army of the Potomac to Burnside, a tall and affable officer best known for his bushy side whiskers. Burnside refused to supersede his personal friend McClellan.

Lincoln did not dare fire McClellan outright for fear of the political storm that would ensue from sacking the general, who still retained the love and respect of his men. If Lincoln performed the deed personally, he would stir up anger in the army and turn some Union Democrats against the war. So Halleck was tapped as the man to deliver the news.

Senator Browning wrote in his diary July 25 after another visit to the White House:

> The President told me that General Halleck had gone to the army at James River and was to have supreme command of the entire army—that he was satisfied McClellan would not fight and that he had told Halleck so; and that he could keep him in command or not as he pleased. That if by magic he could reinforce McClellan with a hundred thousand men today he would be in an ecstasy over it, thank him for it, and tell him that he would go to Richmond tomorrow, but when tomorrow came he would telegraph that he had certain information that the enemy had four hundred thousand men, and that he could not advance without reinforcements.

Visiting McClellan at Harrison's Landing, July 25, Halleck gave him a choice between trying to take Richmond with 20,000 additional troops or giving up the whole idea and moving all his men over to join General Pope. McClellan replied that there was "a chance" of taking Richmond, and he was willing to try. He proposed to cross to the south side of the James River and go through Petersburg to the capital. But Halleck vetoed that.

On August 3, the axe fell. Halleck ordered McClellan to move all his troops off the Peninsula to support Pope, whose army was near Culpeper, facing Confederate forces under Thomas Jonathan "Stonewall" Jackson. Shocked by the order, McClellan protested passionately against it, warning that the move would demoralize his men and prove "disastrous." He also argued that the move made no practical sense. "We are twenty-five miles from Richmond," he said, "and with the aid of the gunboats, we can supply the army by water during its advance, certainly within twelve miles from Richmond." If they joined Pope, he noted, they would be "seventy-five miles from Richmond with land transportation all the way." McClellan could see no logical reason to march his men down the Peninsula and then back up again on another route, "a march of one hundred and forty-five miles to reach a point now only twenty-five miles distant, and to deprive ourselves of the powerful aid of the gunboats."

McClellan contended: "Here, directly in front of the army, is the heart of the rebellion ... A decided victory here and the military strength of the rebellion is crushed ... Here is the true defense of Washington." He begged that the order be rescinded and that his army be reinforced "to resume the offensive," as Lincoln had previously promised to do. It was a logical argument, but logic could not prevail over the determination of Lincoln and Stanton to get rid of McClellan even if it meant breaking up his army. The order "will not be rescinded," Halleck replied, "and you will be expected to execute it with all possible promptness."

The withdrawal order greatly embittered McClellan's soldiers, who had endured months of struggling in the swamps and muddy roads of the Peninsula, battling wave after wave of Rebel attacks in the virtual outskirts of Richmond, suffering wounds, disease, and death, yet retaining their esprit de corps and eager to make one more attempt to capture the Confederate capital, only to find that the politicians in Washington thought nothing of their heroism and sacrifices, considered their campaign a failure, and proposed to throw away all that they had gained.

Gen. Samuel Heintzelman wrote in his diary: "They need to get rid of McClellan and don't dare to go at it openly. This splendid little army has to be broken up to get rid of him." Brevet Maj. Gen. William W. Averell lamented: "All the successes and sacrifices of the army were now to be worse than lost, they were to be thrown away."

Joel Tyler Headley in *The Great Rebellion* terms the withdrawal "a huge blunder" which directly benefited the Confederates; for, as soon as General Lee found out that he no longer had to worry about 80,000 Federal soldiers in the Richmond area, the city seemed safe; so he decided to throw most of his army northward, overwhelm Pope, and advance toward Washington.

Learning that Lee had left no more than 30,000 men as a token force to guard Richmond, McClellan saw a sudden opportunity to dash against the Confederates and seize their capital "while they are lamming away at Pope." Frantically, he tried to telegraph Halleck for permission to throw his troops upon the smaller Rebel army. But he could not change Halleck's almost frantic demand that all possible troops from the Army of the Potomac be rushed to help Pope.

Reluctantly, McClellan gave up his dream and continued moving his troops, with their immense supplies of arms and equipment and his heavy artillery, down the Peninsula to be funneled, piece by piece, into Pope's Army of Virginia. Lincoln and Stanton hoped that the combined Federal armies could conquer Lee and Jackson and march triumphantly toward Richmond. McClellan was left at Alexandria, Virginia, in command of nothing.

Chapter Five

"Little Mac Is Back!"

IN A DARING MANEUVER, GENERAL LEE divided his army and sent Stonewall Jackson with 20,000 "foot soldiers" on a secret flank attack on Pope's rear. They swooped down on the Orange and Alexandria Railroad and captured Manassas Junction, the main Federal supply base. All day August 27, the hungry, ragged Rebels gorged themselves on Yankee food and wine, set fire to all the supplies they could not carry away, and disappeared. Pope mistakenly believed they were fleeing to the Shenandoah Valley so he set out "to bag the whole crowd."

Finding the Rebels dug in on the old Bull Run battlefield, Pope assailed them August 29 in a series of fierce attacks, which forced them back. Pope boasted to Washington: "We fought a terrific battle here yesterday with the combined forces of the enemy which lasted with continuous fury from daylight until after dark, by which time the enemy was driven from the field. ... The enemy is retreating towards the mountains. I go forward at once ... "

Pope, who had a bad reputation for lying, had once more excelled as a fiction writer. He had not driven back "the combined forces of the enemy" but only those fighting under Jackson's command. Soon, Gen. James Longstreet brought up five more divisions and attacked the

Federal left flank while Jackson struck on the right, forcing Pope's forces to withdraw to Centreville. The second battle of Bull Run ended, like the first, in a Federal defeat.

Lincoln, Halleck, and Stanton had been delighted by Pope's victory dispatch and went to bed Saturday night expecting more "glad tidings at sunrise," as John Hay, Lincoln's private secretary, recalled. But early Sunday morning, Lincoln came to Hay and sighed: "Well, John, we are whipped again."

Pope's defeat broke up Stanton's latest intrigue—an effort to have the cabinet members sign a round-robin letter to Lincoln demanding that he fire McClellan. Stanton claimed that McClellan had dilly-dallied in feeding his troops into Pope's army and Pope blamed McClellan's men for his own failure. But official records show that Pope had about 75,000 men to Lee's 50,000 but frittered his advantage away. McClellan could hardly be blamed for the mistakes in tactics; he had been barred from the battlefield so that he could not share in Pope's anticipated triumph.

By September 1, thousands of miserable, rain-soaked stragglers in blue uniforms were stumbling along the muddy roads of Northern Virginia, causing Lincoln to fear that the Rebels would soon capture Washington. Terrified and confused, Halleck appealed to McClellan: "I beg of you to assist me in this crisis with your ability and experience. ... I am entirely tired out."

"Mad as a March hare," McClellan rode to the War Department to see Halleck and "had a pretty plain talk with him and Abe." At breakfast time, September 2, the president and Halleck called upon McClellan at his Washington home and asked him to take command of the troops defending the capital. Lincoln feared that the city was lost but McClellan vowed to hold it.

When the cabinet met the same day, Stanton stalked in, trembling with rage. He had just learned that McClellan had been given command of all the forces defending Washington. Other members expressed their anger, too, but Lincoln explained that no other general could pull the demoralized troops together, for they refused to serve any longer under the blundering braggart, Pope.

Stanton and Chase, according to Blair, said they would rather lose the capital than see McClellan restored to command. Chase said McClellan ought to be shot.

On the afternoon of September 2, McClellan rode out with a few of his aides to meet the first of the bedraggled soldiers limping in from the battlefield. They were a sorry sight. Captain William H. Powell recalled that they were "gloomy, despondent, and almost tired out; had no change in clothing from August 14 to 31, living on 'salt horse,' 'hard tack,' and 'chicory juice,' and all about them was the wreckage of a shattered army."

McClellan found Pope with some staff officers and relieved him of his command by presenting the official orders from Halleck. Then Brig. Gen. John Hatch shouted: "Boys, McClellan is in command again! Three cheers!" As the good news spread, the cry "Little Mac is back!" echoed down the line. George Kimball of the Twelfth Massachusetts Volunteers remembered: "From extreme sadness, we passed in a twinkling to a delirium of delight. A deliverer had come."

Pope was sent out to quell rebellious Sioux Indians, who had massacred several hundred settlers in Minnesota. Before leaving Washington, he sought his revenge upon McClellan's "pet" officers, whom he blamed for his own mistakes. Pope had Gen. Fitz-John Porter court-martialed and kicked out of the army in disgrace on charges of disobeying orders on the battlefield. Not until 1886, by an act of Congress, did the gallant Porter win his long battle for complete vindication, and he was restored to his permanent rank of colonel in the regular army.

Meanwhile, on September 5, 1862, General Lee, with about 50,000 of his victorious Rebels, crossed the Potomac, marching northward toward Pennsylvania. This time, Lincoln and Halleck gave McClellan command of "the forces in the field," with instructions to find Lee and to stop him.

"Again, I have been called upon to save the country," McClellan wrote to Ellen. "The case is desperate, but with God's help, I will try unselfishly to do my best and if He wills it, accomplish the salvation of the country. ... I have now the entire confidence of the government and the love of the army—my enemies are crushed, silent, and disarmed—if I defeat the Rebels, I shall be master of the situation."

When George Templeton Strong, in New York, learned that the Confederates had crossed the Potomac, heading for Pennsylvania, he despaired of any attempts to stop the gray tide. "I feel that our army is in no condition to cope with Lee's barefooted, lousy, disciplined, desperate ruffians," the diarist lamented. "They may get to Philadelphia or New York or Boston, for fortune is apt to smile on audacity and resolution."

As an example of his audacity, Lee divided his army, and the Union garrison at Harpers Ferry quickly fell to only a portion of the invaders. A captured surgeon could not understand how this band of "rag-pickers" could achieve such a quick success. "Both officers and men were extremely lousy, and the stench from the passing columns was almost unbearable," he reported. The Rebels' trousers, he noted, "were generally in tatters up to the knees. The coats … were dirty and ragged and often well greased by the piece of bacon, which each man carried on his bayonet. The shirts were black with long use. … Their blankets were … often bits of carpeting and old bed comforters, nearly half of the men were barefooted."

The Rebels' feet were sore and bleeding from the impact of the hard Maryland roads, so many stragglers fell behind, reducing Lee's actual fighting force from 55,000 to about 40,000. But the survivors were battle-hardened fighting men, determined to whip the Yankees again.

Lee believed his veterans could cut key railroads in Pennsylvania and then move on to Philadelphia, Baltimore, or Washington, before McClellan could catch them. "McClellan is an able general but a very cautious one," Lee told a fellow officer. "His army is in a very demoralized condition and will not be prepared for offensive operations—or he will think it so—for three or four weeks."

Little Mac responded to the challenge with surprising speed. He pulled together about 67,000 soldiers and led them up the road to Frederick, Maryland, arriving a few days after the Rebels had left. On the Confederates' abandoned campground, a Union soldier found an envelope containing three cigars wrapped in a sheet of paper. The paper was a copy of Lee's Special Order No. 191, detailing the locations of all his divided forces.

Moving much faster than Lee had expected, McClellan's troops drove the Confederates through three key gaps in South Mountain, September 14. This Union victory completely upset Lee's timetable for invading Pennsylvania. The next day, Stonewall Jackson hurried from Harpers Ferry to join Lee's main force seventeen miles away at

Sharpsburg. Then both armies camped at nearby Antietam Creek. They collided September 17 in savage fighting that marked the bloodiest single day in the entire Civil War.

With a booming artillery barrage at dawn, Gen. Joseph "Fighting Joe" Hooker and his legions rushed down the Hagerstown pike and struck Stonewall Jackson on the Confederate left. The Federals' superior cannon mowed men down in rows like stalks of corn. The Corn Field, the East Woods, the West Woods, and many other scenes of battle would become famous in the history of this terrible day.

The Union assaults endangered the center of the Confederate line, where Gen. D. H. Hill's men occupied an old farm lane, the Sunken Road, later renamed "Bloody Lane." "This was a fearful situation for the Confederate center," General Longstreet recalled. "If the Federals broke through our lines there, the Confederate army would be cut in two and probably destroyed."

McClellan had an opportunity to break the line by hurling his reserves into the weak spot. But he and his staff believed they were battling 100,000 troops; they could not imagine that Lee, with half that number or less, was moving men up and down the line and giving the impression of a superior force. His desperate bluff barely succeeded.

McClellan became greatly concerned over a long delay in the attack he had ordered General Burnside to make against the Confederate right by crossing a stone bridge over Antietam Creek, known ever since as "Burnside Bridge." Burnside had been expected to move in the morning but did not advance until early afternoon. Then his men stormed across the bridge and began driving the Rebels back toward Sharpsburg.

Burnside's delay proved "the greatest mistake of the day," one officer commented, for it enabled Lee to move forces from his right to his embattled center and save it from collapse. Brevet Brig. Gen. Francis Winthrop Palfrey, in a first-hand account by an officer actually in the fighting, concluded that, if Burnside had attacked early as ordered, "Lee's army must have been shattered, if not destroyed."

In the nick of time, red-shirted Gen. A. P. Hill brought in a few thousand bone-tired Rebels, who had hot-footed it from Harpers Ferry; they drove Burnside's men back to the heights above the creek and saved the day for Lee.

When the blazing sun went down at last on that awful day, more then 23,000 soldiers had fallen. Some units were entirely wiped out. About a third of Lee's troops were either dead or wounded. Federal losses were equally severe. James A. Godfrey, a Union soldier, wrote to his parents from the blood-soaked battlefield: "We went into the battle with six hundred men, and at the roll call there was only three hundred answered to their names. ... The dead are laying around us now in thousands, together with hundreds of unburied horses. The ground is covered with broken arms and cannon." Yet, the soldier marveled, he and his brother, George, had come through the battle "without a scratch." "Thank God I escaped," he went on. "I may get killed in the next battle. ... Oh, if only I was home again, how happy I would feel!"

The armies braced for a furious new clash at daybreak but both were too exhausted for another round of carnage. So, the following night, Lee and his ragged, weary soldiers slipped quietly across the Potomac into Virginia, leaving McClellan and his men in command of the field.

Joyfully, McClellan telegraphed Washington: "Our victory is complete. The enemy is driven back into Virginia. Maryland and Pennsylvania are safe."

"God in his mercy a second time made me the instrument for saving the nation," he wrote Ellen. "I feel some little pride in having with a beaten and demoralized army defeated Lee so utterly and saved the North so completely. ... I have shown that I can fight battles and win them."

At first, Lincoln greeted the Antietam victory with great relief. He need no longer fear that the Rebels would soon seize Washington and the White House, and for that he expressed his gratitude to McClellan. Soon, however, the general's enemies persuaded the president that McClellan had failed to demolish Lee's army and therefore the triumph was not really complete.

But most historians agree that Antietam was an important victory—the first time any Union army had forced the invincible Lee to retreat in defeat. A Confederate triumph in Maryland could have opened the way to an invasion of Pennsylvania, as Lee had planned, and it could have caused the British to intervene in the war for a compromise peace.

Confederate General Longstreet considered it a "miracle" that "the conquering army of the South," fresh from its triumph in the second battle of Bull Run, had been transformed into "a horde of disordered fugitives before an army that two weeks earlier was flying to cover under its homeward ramparts." The question must follow: Who made the difference between the beaten, demoralized Union army under Pope and the victorious army at Antietam? The answer, though his enemies hated to admit it, had to be McClellan, who had picked up the pieces of that broken army, pulled them together, and defeated Lee.

If a grateful people should reward McClellan with the presidency in 1864, his advocates believed that that would be his just recompense for saving the nation. His enemies, however, feared that he could, indeed, reach the White House so they must destroy him politically, and they lost no time in their campaign against him.

Chapter Six
"Plenty of Rotten Old Democrats"

IT IS ONE OF THE IRONIES of the Civil War that McClellan's victory at Antietam led directly to the Emancipation Proclamation, which he bitterly opposed. On September 22, President Lincoln told his cabinet that when the Confederate army marched into Frederick, he had made a vow to himself—and to his Maker—that when the enemy had been driven out of Maryland, he would consider it "an indication of Divine Will," that God had "decided the question in favor of the slaves" and it was his duty to move forward in the course of emancipation. Taking a paper from his pocket, he read the text. It declared that in the states still in rebellion January 1, 1863, all slaves would be declared forever free.

Heretofore, Lincoln had maintained that although he loathed slavery, he had no authority to end it in the states where it was legal. Now, however, he discovered that as commander in chief of the armed forces he had "war powers" enabling him to end slavery as a measure to weaken the Confederacy and thus help win the war.

Most Republicans welcomed the Preliminary Emancipation Proclamation of September 22, but Democrats roared their opposition, refusing to take part in a struggle to free the slaves. Lincoln's historic act confirmed the Democrats' suspicion that Republicans had been plotting, all along, for abolition and this act proved their perfidy.

McClellan vowed that he would never fight for abolition; he would quit first. He wrote to William Henry Aspinwall, a railroad and steamship millionaire, September 25, saying he was very anxious to know "how you and men like you regard this recent proclamation by the President inaugurating servile war, emancipation of slaves, and, at one stroke of the pen, changing our free institutions into a despotism—for such I regard the natural effect of the last proclamation suspending the Habeas Corpus throughout the land." Aspinwall, an influential Democrat, came down from New York to the general's camp in Maryland and told him he must submit to Lincoln's orders, whether he liked them or not—and quietly continue doing his duty as a soldier. "I guess he is right," McClellan told Ellen, "and at least he is honest in his opinion."

Montgomery Blair, McClellan's only friend left in the cabinet, wrote him September 27 that he must explain his views about slavery, especially because of the abrupt dismissal of Maj. John J. Key, a brother of Col. Thomas M. Key, a close adviser on McClellan's own staff. Lincoln had been told of Major Key's remarks, Blair wrote, "that the reason why the Rebel army had not been destroyed at Sharpsburg was that the plan was to exhaust our resources so that a compromise might be made, which would preserve slavery and the Union at the same time."

Calling the major before him, the president sternly demanded to know if Key had said that destroying the Rebel army was "not the game" but that, after both armies were tired out, "we must come together fraternally, and slavery be saved." Key did not deny having said this, but argued in favor of a compromise and insisted that he had loyally fought for the Union. Lincoln abruptly dismissed him from the service as an example and as a warning to a class of officers, who, he said, "were playing a game not to beat the enemy when they could."

Blair said he knew that McClellan had gone to war only to preserve the Union, but that he must realize now that slavery must go. McClellan must declare himself to that effect, "particularly if you had ... ambitions to the presidency ... for I can assure you no appreciable portion of the nation will favor the long continuation of slavery once this war is over."

Blair's father, canny old Francis Preston Blair, wrote to McClellan September 30 that the proclamation was a war measure intended to destroy one of the foundations of the Confederacy; that the slaves formed the South's "sinews of war, whether in the trenches or in the cornfield." So McClellan must manifest a fixed purpose to give full effect to the decree, and thus "baffle those who follow you with 'fire in the rear' while you advance on that of the enemy."

Finally, McClellan issued a general order to the army, saying "discussions by officers and soldiers concerning public measures" substituted "the spirit of political faction" for the higher duty of respect and support for the civil authority; that the only remedy for political error was at the ballot box.

Still, ugly rumors about a "McClellan conspiracy," as John Hay called it, persisted among the general's many enemies in Washington. Henry Wilson, the Senate Military Affairs Committee chairman, told Secretary Welles that he had learned from an unnamed McClellan staff officer that some officers were plotting a revolution and a "provisional government," which sounded like a bid for a military dictatorship.

George Templeton Strong recorded in his diary "the most alarming kind of talk" among old Breckinridge Democrats claiming that McClellan and his henchmen would strike a deal with their prewar friends in the Confederacy's high command "to agree on some compromise or adjustments, turn out Lincoln and his 'Black Republicans' and use their respective armies to enforce their decisions North and South and re-establish the Union and the Constitution."

"We have among us plenty of rotten old Democrats ... traders and money lenders like Belmont and political schemers ... who would sing a Te Deum over pacification, however infamous, and would rejoice to see Jefferson Davis our next president," Strong charged.

Strong recorded reports that "Abe Lincoln is far from easy in his mind" over the Major Key affair, that "he wanders about wringing his hands and wondering whom he can trust in what he had better do." In the diarist's opinion, the president "has fallen. Nobody believes in him any more. ... His only special gift is fertility of smutty stories."

Strong had suspicions about August Belmont, because the New York financier had been pleading with Lincoln to accept a peace without total victory. Writing to Thurlow Weed, Belmont thought the

South would accept "an amnesty for all political offenses during the war," and a national convention to revise the Constitution. He suggested that "the war debts of the North and South might ... be funded and assumed by the general government." This idea of Federal funding, some critics noted, would assure that the holders of Confederate bonds would see their paper, now sadly depreciated, soar up to par. Belmont would later deny persistent rumors that the Rothschilds had invested in Confederate bonds.

It is interesting to note how Belmont's letter ties in neatly with General McClellan's Harrison's Landing letter. Some of the same ideas about a convention and revision of the Constitution were advocated by S. L. M. Barlow, McClellan's close friend and self-appointed manager of the presidential boom being carefully nurtured by New York financiers.

In early October, Lincoln paid a surprise visit to the Army of the Potomac, inspecting its Maryland camp and the battlefields of South Mountain and Antietam. "I incline to think that the real purpose of the visit is to push me into a premature advance into Virginia," McClellan told his wife. Unimpressed by the general's pleas that his men were "completely tired out" and needed more rest and supplies, Lincoln wanted him to move against Lee immediately. The president voiced his frustration to his friend, Ozias M. Hatch, as they looked at the vast array of soldiers' tents on the campground. Lincoln asked if Hatch knew what they were seeing. It was the Army of the Potomac, Hatch answered. No, the president said, "it is only McClellan's bodyguard."

"The President was very affable, and I really think he does feel very kindly toward me personally ... told me he was convinced that I was the best general in the country," McClellan told Ellen. Later, he quoted Lincoln as saying to him: "General, you have saved the country. You must remain in command and carry us through to the end. General, I pledge myself to stand between you and harm."

Two days later, Lincoln was back in Washington and under the spell of Secretary Stanton and the radicals dominating Congress. Halleck telegraphed McClellan: "The President directs that you cross the Potomac and give battle to the enemy or drive him south. Your army must move now while the roads are good."

McClellan delayed, demanding more horses, more mules, more guns, more of almost everything. Secretary Welles noted "sinister rumors of peace and intrigue" and said many believed McClellan was acting on Major Key's policy, and that was why he moved so slowly in October despite Lincoln's urgent demands for an attack on Lee. John Hay, one of the busiest little bees spreading rumors about army officers' plots for coups, wrote that Lincoln began to suspect that McClellan was "playing false—that he did not want to hurt the enemy."

Lincoln, who desperately needed a decisive Union victory somewhere to improve his party's prospects in the fall elections, was driven almost frantic by McClellan's delays. In addition, the president received a series of bad news dispatches from Kentucky, where the Southerners had taken over the state capital, Frankfort, installed a Rebel governor, and proclaimed Kentucky a new state in their Confederacy.

Gen. Don Carlos Buell, commander of Union troops pursuing the Rebels, came under fire from Washington; first, for allowing Gen. Braxton Bragg to lead his troops from Tennessee to Kentucky and second, for failing to crush them. The Kentucky campaign came to a climax in October.

Chapter Seven

Separate Peace Urged on the Northwest

LINCOLN HAD GOOD REASON to worry about the Confederates' drive to extend their domain to the Ohio River and even beyond. The Rebels, in the words of General Halleck, "boldly determined to re-occupy Arkansas, and Missouri, Tennessee and Kentucky and, if possible, to invade the states of Ohio, Indiana, and Illinois, while our attention was distracted by the invasion of Maryland and Pennsylvania, and an extended Indian insurrection in the western frontier."

It was in hopes of stirring up an uprising by Kentuckians against iron-fisted Federal military rule that two Confederate armies began marching northward from Tennessee in August 1862. Gen. Braxton Bragg led about 40,000 men from Chattanooga while Gen. Edmund Kirby-Smith led about 20,000 out of Knoxville. The two armies moved in parallel lines, Bragg heading for Louisville and Kirby-Smith toward Cincinnati.

Both commanders relied upon solemn promises by pro-Southern Kentuckians that their people would rise en masse and throngs of young men would join the Confederate Army. Bragg brought along wagonloads of guns, enough to arm 20,000 men. But he was sadly disappointed. Only about 2,000 volunteers came forward and half of those later deserted.

By hard marches from Tennessee, Buell's troops won the race for Louisville, and volunteers pouring in from the Northern states protected Cincinnati from an expected attack.

When his total force swelled to nearly 100,000 men through reinforcements from Ohio, Indiana, and elsewhere, Buell finally obeyed orders from Washington to move out of Louisville, find Bragg, and beat him. On October 8, portions of the Union and Rebel armies collided at Perryville, Kentucky, and a savage, all-day battle ensued with heavy casualties. The Confederates claimed a victory because they held the field at the close of the bloody day.

Well aware that his forces were outnumbered by two or three to one, Bragg moved back to eastern Tennessee. Buell made only a half-hearted attempt to intercept him on his way back to the mountains.

Early in the campaign, when he still had hopes of reaching the Ohio River, General Bragg issued an extraordinary proclamation directed to the people of the Northwest—Ohio, Indiana, Illinois, Michigan, Wisconsin, and Minnesota. He called upon individual states to make a separate peace with the Confederacy—an unprecedented idea—and thus end "this useless and cruel effusion of blood."

"If the war must go on, the future scenes of desolation must be in the North," not the South, Bragg warned. He said the state governments could "secure immunity from the desolating effects of warfare on their own soil by a separate treaty of peace."

Actually, the *New York Herald* said, the general was "dispatched" by Jefferson Davis to make this direct appeal as a political power move to separate the West from the East. It clearly foreshadowed an attempt to arouse such a cry for peace that Indiana, Ohio, and Illinois would stop fighting and perhaps even join the Confederacy.

Indiana's Governor Oliver P. Morton, who feared that his state could go over to the Confederacy, warned Lincoln: "The fate of the North West is trembling in the balance." Morton wrote: "The Democratic politicians of Ohio, Indiana and Illinois, assume that the rebellion will not be crushed and that the independence of the Rebel Confederacy will, before many months, be practically or expressly acknowledged. Starting upon this hypothesis, they ask the question:

What shall be the destiny of Ohio, Indiana and Illinois? Shall they remain attached to the Old Government, or shall they secede and form a new one—a North West Confederacy—as a preparatory step to their annexation to the Government of the South? This latter project is the programme and has been for the last twelve months."

Morton cited the Democrats' campaign appeal that the people of the Northwest were natural allies with those of the South and "could never consent to be separated politically from the people who control the mouth of the Mississippi River, "the great artery and outlet of all Western commerce."

"If we have to abandon the war and concede the independence of the Southern states," Morton prophesied, "Ohio, Indiana and Illinois can only be prevented, if at all, from a new act of secession and annexation to those states by a bloody and desolating civil war."

Morton correctly foresaw Republican defeats in the 1862 elections, chiefly resulting from citizen dissatisfaction with the high death toll of the war and a war without any end in sight. Many Democrats also denounced the Emancipation Proclamation scheduled for January 1, 1863, and the mass arrests of civilians suspected of disloyalty. The arrests deserve special attention in the following chapter.

Chapter Eight

Arbitrary Arrests

PRESIDENT LINCOLN AUTHORIZED an unprecedented crackdown on the civil liberties of Americans in the fall of 1862. He suspended the writ of habeas corpus and required military trials for civilians accused of interfering with the war. His orders of September 24 arose from the Militia Act, enacted by Congress, which really amounted to a draft. It empowered the secretary of war to draft for nine months' service the militiamen of states that had not upgraded their militias.

Secretary Stanton had earlier ordered the arrest of any man of draft age who tried to leave the country, or even to leave his home county. One purpose of the order was to check a wave of draft dodging. Hundreds of young men were fleeing to Canada or to the Far West to evade serving in the war. With Lincoln's approval, Stanton also ordered all police officers "to arrest and imprison any person or persons who may be engaged by act, speech, or writing, in discouraging volunteer enlistments, or in any way giving aid and comfort to the enemy, or in any other disloyal practice against the United States."

In plain English, this meant that a U.S. citizen could be thrown into jail on the whim of anyone who might accuse him of any "disloyal practice." Government officials would decide what "act, speech, or writing" could be branded "disloyal." The offender might be no more than a drunken man shouting, "Hurrah for Jeff Davis!"

Ohio Congressman Samuel S. "Sunset" Cox accused the administration of deceiving the people by "incessantly charging that those who favored a speedy termination" of the war were traitors. Thousands of loyal citizens, the Democratic congressman said, "were arrested in the most brutal manner, without charge or specification of offense. All the national fortresses and military prisons were ... crowded with citizens who were denied any appeal to the courts of justice or even the tender mercies of a military commission."

John A. Marshall's *American Bastile*, a voluminous narrative of the Lincoln era's arbitrary arrests, first published in 1869, said the military prisons contained, in four years, "from ten to twenty thousand men, besides women and children—free citizens of free states." The 1885 edition of this popular book raised the victims total to "from twenty to thirty thousand." Nearly all were antiwar Democrats, some of them prominent politicians in their communities. Often, they were taken from their homes and jailed far away in Fort Lafayette, New York; Fort Delaware; Fort Warren in Boston harbor; or the Old Capitol Prison in Washington, D.C.

Not only Democrats, but leading Republicans, deplored the obvious violations of the citizens' constitutional right to have fair trials before juries, to face their accusers, to present defense evidence, and to have counsel. New York lawyer George Templeton Strong, although a strong advocate of the war, denounced the arbitrary arrests in these words: "They have been utterly arbitrary. ... Not one of the many hundreds illegally arrested and locked up for months had been publicly charged with any crime or brought to the notice of the grand jury. They have all been capriciously arrested ... and some have been capriciously discharged; locked up for months without legal authority and let out without legal acquittal. All this is very bad—imbecile, dangerous, unjustifiable."

The Democrats assailed the widespread arrests as a major theme in their election campaign in the fall of 1862, while also voicing rage over the Preliminary Emancipation Proclamation issued September 22. They charged that freed slaves would come North and compete with white workers for their jobs and their women.

Above all, the Northern people felt despair and disillusionment with the Lincoln administration for its failure to win the war after nearly two years of bloodshed. The voters had poured out blood and treasure to equip the finest armies to restore the Union, but these sacrifices had been in vain because of incompetence and imbecility at high levels of government. The people yearned to send a message to Washington to stop bungling and win the war. The people generally had not turned against the war itself, but they were tired of losing it and beginning to wonder if there could be any peace ahead, or only more years of carnage. Arrests, plus the Emancipation Proclamation, gave substance to the Democrats' charge that the war for the Union had turned into a crusade to end slavery.

John Slidell, the wily former senator from Louisiana seeking French recognition of the South's independence in his new role as the Confederacy's minister to Paris, assured Emperor Napoleon III: "There is a large majority in the Northern states in favor of a peaceful separation, but they dare not express the sentiment save in New York, where there has lately been a great peace meeting."

New York, the heavily Democratic city with old commercial ties to the South, harbored the largest number of pro-Confederates anywhere in the entire North. George Templeton Strong lamented in his diary, October 23: "The whole community is honeycombed by secret sympathizers with treason, who will poke out their heads and flaunt their 'red, white and red' tentacles the moment the loud division of Northern sentiment enables them to do so safely."

Red, white, and red was the combination of colors displayed in shirts and neckties and other clothing and other articles by those favoring peace with the South. Southern sympathizers were often branded as "Copperheads" while country people who wore simple handmade clothing were ridiculed as "Butternuts." Some Republicans branded all Democrats as "Copperheads" or worse. Clearly, rifts along class and social lines were growing across the North because people no longer felt united in a common cause to restore the old Union.

In New York State, the Democrats united their warring factions in support of a nominee for governor, Horatio Seymour. Citing fears of a slave revolt, Seymour assailed emancipation as "a proposal for the butchery of women and children, for scenes of lust and rapine, and of arson and murder." He denounced arbitrary arrests and insisted upon freedom of speech and of the press.

The Republicans chose Gen. James Wadsworth, a Union army officer who was also an abolitionist and a foe of General McClellan. *New York Herald* editor James Gordon Bennett assailed Wadsworth as "one of those abolition intriguers, who, intermeddling with our plans and generals, have cost the country much unnecessary blood, much squandered money and an indefinite prolongation of the war." Horace Greeley in the *New York Tribune* and Henry J. Raymond in *The New York Times* called Democrats traitors and threatened them with Fort Lafayette. Greeley denounced Seymour as a dishonest demagogue and predicted that "Jeff Davis will regard his success as a triumph." Cassius M. Clay, a Kentucky abolitionist, political major general, declared that Seymour should be hanged.

At the end of the bitter campaign, Seymour won back the governorship by a margin of 11,000 votes. The fall elections resulted in a Republican rout in the key states of New York, Pennsylvania, Illinois, Ohio, and Indiana, all of which had given their electoral votes to Lincoln two years before. In Illinois, the Democrats elected nine of fourteen congressmen; in Indiana, seven of eleven; in Ohio, fourteen of nineteen. The Republicans kept control of the United States Senate, but their margin in the House of Representatives was sharply reduced. Antiwar Democrats seized control of the legislatures of Illinois and Indiana and prepared to use their newfound power to push for peace, and they threatened even to take their states out of the war.

In despair, George Templeton Strong lamented: "It looks like general abandonment of the loyal, generous spirit of patriotism that broke out so nobly and unexpectedly in April, 1861. Was that after all nothing but a temporary hysteric spasm? I think not."

"Seymour is governor. God help us!" Strong exclaimed. He also deplored the victories of the Wood brothers: both New York City ex-mayor Fernando Wood and his brother, Ben, editor of the pro-Southern *Daily News*, won seats in Congress. Worst of all, in the diarist's view, the Democrats' resurgence caused "the resurrection to political life and power of the Woods," S. L. M Barlow, and August Belmont. These worthies "had been dead and buried and working only underground, if at all, for eighteen months," he mourned, and every one of them "deserves hanging as an ally of the rebellion."

↦ • ↤

On November 5, the day after New York voted in the last of the fall elections, Lincoln fired General McClellan.

The *New York Herald* flashed this bulletin:

> HIGHLY IMPORTANT
> Removal of General McClellan
> Washington—General McClellan has been superseded and General Burnside appointed in his place. ... Great excitement prevailed in the city tonight. ... It was known here that the radicals had boasted that McClellan was to be removed immediately after the New York elections.

The official reason for McClellan's dismissal was that he was moving too slowly in Virginia and had allowed General Lee to place his army between the Federal forces and Richmond. But there were deeper reasons than that, and some of them were political. Lincoln had been trying for months to get rid of the arrogant little Democrat. Twice he had offered the command of the Army of the Potomac to General Burnside and each time "Burn" pleaded that his good friend "Mac" was the only man who could command the loyalty of the Army.

McClellan himself believed that Burnside was unfit to command anything larger than a regiment, as shown by his costly delay in moving his troops across Antietam Creek. When finally ordered to take over the command, Burnside wept, and, McClellan said, seemed almost "crazy." Why Lincoln insisted upon promoting such an incompetent bungler remains a great mystery.

Some of McClellan's enemies had spread rumors that he might lead his idolatrous troops in a march on Washington and seize control of the government. Rejecting this slander, McClellan commented in his memoirs: "The order depriving me of the command created an immense deal of deep feeling in the army, so much that many were in favor of my refusing to obey the order and of marching on

Washington and taking possession of the government." But, as a professional soldier, keenly sensitive to points of honor, McClellan resisted their pleas and marched obediently into exile.

Naturally, the Democrats deplored his ouster and called it the political sacrifice of a brave and loyal soldier to the radicals who demanded a commander devoted to the cause of crushing the South and freeing the slaves. Congressman Cox said McClellan was sacrificed "to appease the ebony fetish" and that Burnside could be the next victim of "the mumbo-jumbo of abolition."

Amos Kendall, a veteran of Andrew Jackson's "Kitchen Cabinet," backed McClellan for the presidency and asserted in a pamphlet, "the men who forced the President upon the abolition platform required him to dismiss General McClellan. The truth is that his removal was contemplated before he left the peninsula, and that it was only a matter of necessity that he was allowed to command during the Maryland campaign."

Now, with Burnside heading the Army of the Potomac despite his tears and his fears, Lincoln had a commander who would follow orders and go straight down the road to Richmond and make a direct assault upon the entrenched Confederates, just as Lincoln had always wanted to do. The results of this presidential strategy would become clear the following month at Fredericksburg, Virginia.

Chapter Nine

Democrats' Intrigue with British for Peace

WHEN LORD LYONS, THE BRITISH ambassador to the United States, arrived in New York City one day in early November 1862, he found Democrats exulting in their "crowning success" in the fall elections and predicting that, as a result, President Lincoln "would increase the moderate and conservative element in the cabinet; that he would seek to terminate the war, not push it to extremity; that he would endeavor to effect a reconciliation with the people of the South; and renounce the idea of subjugating or exterminating them."

These rosy dreams, all reflecting the ideas of General McClellan and advocates of a limited war, died the following morning with the startling news from Washington that McClellan had been fired. "His dismissal was taken as a sign that the President had thrown himself entirely into the arms of the extreme radical party; and that the attempt to carry out the policy would be persisted in," Lord Lyons reported to his Foreign Minister, Lord John Russell.

Several Democratic Party leaders met with the envoy at his hotel in New York. They discussed foreign mediation between the North and the South, and the diplomat found that, "Many of them seemed to think that this mediation must come at last, but they appeared to be very much afraid of its coming too soon. It was evident that they apprehended that a premature proposal of foreign intervention would afford the Radical party a means of reviving the violent war spirit, and of thus defeating the peaceful plans of the conservatives." Lyons reported further:

> I thought I perceived a desire to put an end to the war, even at the risk of losing the Southern states altogether; but it was plain that it was not thought prudent to avow this desire at the present moment; therefore, the chiefs of the Conservative party call loudly for a more vigorous prosecution of the war and reproach the government with slackness as well as with the want of success in military measures.
>
> But they repudiate all ideas of interfering with the institutions of the Southern people, or of waging a war of subjugation or extermination. They maintain that the object of the military operations should be to place the North in position to demand an armistice with honor and effect. The armistice should (they hold) be followed by a convention in which such changes in the Constitution should be proposed as would give the South ample security on the subject of the security of slave property, and would enable the North and the South to reunite and live together in peace and harmony. ...
>
> They are no doubt well aware that the more probable consequence of an armistice would be the establishment of Southern Independence, but ... it is wiser to agree to separation, than to prosecute a cruel and hopeless war.

The names of prominent Democrats involved in the secret chats with the British ambassador never came out. However, on April 3, 1863, the *New York Herald* printed a list of likely conferees, including S. L. M. Barlow, August Belmont, and James Brooks, an antiwar congressman and editor. "We would not be surprised," the *Herald* said, "if it would turn out that Brooks, Barlow and Belmont ... had all the fingers of both hands in the pie."

The hand of the master craftsman, Barlow, could be detected in the proposals for an armistice to be followed by a convention, which would produce constitutional amendments giving the Southern states assurances about the security of their slave property. Barlow had proposed these notions a year earlier, and Belmont had echoed them in his pleas to Lincoln for peace. Also, McClellan's trusted aide, Col. Thomas Key, had talked peace with Confederate Brig. Gen. Howell Cobb during a lull in the Peninsula campaign, without success.

Conservative Democrats such as McClellan, whom Barlow was steadily promoting for the presidency, persisted in their dream that war carried on under "Christian" principles, such as sparing Southern civilians' lives and property, could lead eventually to the reunion of the two sections in a fraternal embrace. Maj. John Key, Col. Thomas Key's brother, had suggested this in remarks that caused Lincoln to sack him. Lincoln was no longer interested in protecting Southern civilians and their slave property; he proposed to free their slaves in his Emancipation Proclamation if they didn't stop their "rebellion" by January 1, 1863.

In his December 1 message to Congress, the president recommended that the Constitution be amended to provide that any state abolishing slavery at any time before January 1, 1863, should be paid for its freed slaves in Federal bonds with interest. This was primarily a bid for the border states to free their slaves and to remain loyal to the Union. He sought to calm Northerners' fears that emancipation would cause a mass migration of blacks to the North, a favorite bugaboo raised by Democrats. Free blacks could stay at home and "work for wages until new homes can be found for them in congenial climes and a people of their own blood and race," he said. "I strongly favor their colonization," Lincoln said, although the first small attempts to settle freed blacks overseas had failed; furthermore, most blacks wanted to stay at home.

Most of the president's message lacked literary style. But some of the closing sentences deserve to be remembered as examples of his overpowering logic and his demand that the members of Congress face up to the crisis and try new solutions to the problem of slavery:

> The dogmas of the quiet past are inadequate to the stormy present. The occasion is piled high with difficulty, and we must rise with the occasion. As our case is new, so we must think

anew, and act anew. We must disenthrall ourselves, and then we shall save our country.

Fellow citizens, we cannot escape history. We of this Congress and this administration will be remembered in spite of ourselves. No personal significance, or insignificance, can spare one or another of us. The fiery trial through which we pass will light us down, in honor or dishonor, to the latest generation.

We *say* we are for the Union. The world knows, we do know how to save it. We—even *we here*—hold the power and bear the responsibility. In *giving* freedom to the slave, we *assure* freedom to the *free*—honorable alike in what we give, and what we preserve. We shall nobly save, or meanly lose, the last best hope of earth.

Lincoln's appeal did not receive the attention it deserved. The members of Congress, back in Washington after the fall elections, were more concerned about the political consequences of the Republicans' defeats—and especially their prospects in the next presidential election.

Some laid the blame on Lincoln because of the Emancipation Proclamation and the order authorizing military trials for persons accused of disloyalty that resulted in a wave of arbitrary arrests. Former Senator Thomas Ewing said the two proclamations had ruined the Republicans in Ohio. Senator Orville Browning of Illinois quoted Senator William Pitt Fessenden of Maine as saying the suspension of the writ of habeas corpus in the loyal states, where no insurrection existed, "was an exercise of despotic power ... and very dangerous."

Browning said the two proclamations had been "disastrous to us" in Illinois. Before they came out, he told Lincoln, "the masses of the Democratic Party were satisfied with him and warmly supporting him, and that their disloyal leaders could not rally them in opposition. But the proclamations had revived old party issues, giving them a rallying cry," and the result was the Republican disaster.

Now that he had finally gotten rid of General McClellan and replaced him with the obedient General Burnside, Lincoln pressed his new commander of the Army of the Potomac to make a direct frontal attack and destroy General Lee's army before the end of the year. So Burnside led his force of more than 100,000 men across the Rappahannock River at Fredericksburg, and on December 13, he threw them in one futile charge after another against the Confederates, who were entrenched behind a fortified, stone wall on the heights above the town. Cannon and musket fire mowed down the brave bluecoats with terrible slaughter. The carnage cost the Union troops a toll of 12,000 men, twice as high as the Confederates' losses. The shattered army fell back across the Rappahannock.

Lincoln, who had expected a great victory, received news of the disaster as a terrible shock, which plunged him into a deep depression. Several visitors in the dark days thereafter feared that he might lose his mind or even commit suicide. Governor Andrew G. Curtin of Pennsylvania, coming in directly from the battlefield, said: "Mr. President it was not a battle, it was a butchery." Curtin said later: "Lincoln was heartbroken at the recital, and soon reached a state of nervous excitement bordering on insanity."

Illinois Congressman Elihu B. Washburne received this letter from a constituent who had talked with the president: "He is, I have no doubt, perplexed to death with the present unsettled matters of the nation. It certainly is enough to drive a man crazy."

Benjamin R. Curtis, a former supreme court justice, after conversing with "a good many prominent men" in Washington, commented: "I have not seen one who does not say that the country is ruined, and that its ruin is attributable largely to the President. He is shattered, dazed, and utterly foolish. It would not surprise me if he were to destroy himself."

In his agony, Lincoln knew that he must bear much of the blame for the Fredericksburg debacle because he was the man who had chosen Burnside, a weak and admittedly incompetent general, and ordered him to make the frontal attack. George Templeton Strong accused Secretary Stanton of forcing Burnside's attack contrary to the advice of his senior officers and of thus causing so many brave men to be "uselessly sacrificed to the vanity … the political schemes of this meddling, murderous quack."

Many Republican senators blamed Lincoln for the nation's woes and some, in caucus, demanded that he resign. Others called for the removal of Secretary Seward. Senator Morton Smith Wilkinson of Minnesota said Seward "had never believed in the war—had been averse to it from the beginning, and so long as he remained in the cabinet nothing but defeat and disaster could be expected."

Bemoaning the senators' criticisms, Lincoln told Senator Browning: "They wish to get rid of me and I am sometimes half disposed to gratify them."

"Some of them do wish to get rid of you, but the fortunes of the country are bound up with your fortunes," Browning replied. "You stand firmly at your post and hold the helm with a steady hand. To relinquish it now would bring upon us certain and inevitable ruin."

"We are now on the brink of destruction," Lincoln sighed. "It appears to me the Almighty is against us, and I can hardly see a ray of hope."

Browning told his old friend that Secretary Chase and some of his "partisans" had hatched a plot, first to oust Seward on charges that he was a malignant "backstairs influence" holding Lincoln back from vigorous measures to win the war, and then to drive out all the cabinet and form a new cabinet of "ultra men" led by Chase.

Lincoln, his temper up, declared that "he was master, and they should not do that."

So, after a showdown meeting with the senators and the cabinet at the White House, the president rejected the resignations of both Seward and Chase and did, indeed, remain master of his own house.

On New Year's Day, 1863, despite the earnest pleas of conservative friends, the president kept his promise and signed the Emancipation Proclamation. His right hand felt nearly paralyzed because he had shaken the hands of so many visitors who had trooped into the White House for the annual New Year's Day reception. Nevertheless, he signed the proclamation with a firm, clear hand, and the historic deed was done.

To Browning, his trusted confidante, who had warned him against it, Lincoln explained that he had to issue the final proclamation. If he had refused, he said, "there would be a rebellion in the North, that a dictator would be placed over his head within the week."

Chapter Ten

"Treason Is Everywhere"

AS THE CIVIL WAR DRAGGED INTO its third year, with no sign of victory in sight, Northerners felt despondent over the heavy losses of brave young soldiers in futile battles, and some voters were almost ready to give up the fight and let the South have its independence.

General Burnside's Army of the Potomac remained stuck in the mud at Falmouth, Virginia, the soldiers demoralized and deserting by the hundreds, some even on the verge of mutiny. In Tennessee, the armies of General Bragg and Union Gen. William S. Rosecrans had fought the fierce but indecisive battle of Stones River, near Murfreesboro, Tennessee, at the dawn of the new year. This was a costly clash, which ended with Union forces holding the field but unable to pursue the Rebels. Gen. U. S. Grant had failed to take Vicksburg, the Rebel fortress on the Mississippi River, and the 109th Illinois had so many desertions that the entire regiment was arrested at Holly Springs, Mississippi.

A Confederate officer, Wirt Adams, after the Union reverse at Vicksburg, reported some "strange utterances" by Union Gen. Joseph J. Reynolds: "He states that the people of the West had engaged in this contest, solely for the preservation of the Union and the unrestricted navigation of the Mississippi." Adams wrote to Brigadier General Hébert, adding that Reynolds said the Emancipation Proclamation had "converted the war into an abolition crusade, which would not be approved by the people of the West and would entirely estrange them from the Lincoln government."

Democratic newspapers demanded that General McClellan be called back once more to save his army from falling apart. "The soldiers would be excited to the highest pitch of enthusiasm at the return of their favorite leader," the *New York Herald* said. The president turned a deaf ear to the clamor for McClellan's return. He would never give another command to the author of the Harrison's Landing letter, which had aroused his suspicions that McClellan would not wage an all-out war and end slavery.

Lincoln's suspicions about McClellan's presidential aspirations increased when the general became a resident of New York City and appeared at dinners, concerts, and balls as a guest of the Democratic Party's most prominent men—S. L. M. Barlow, August Belmont, William Aspinwall, Dean Richmond, and Governor Horatio Seymour. The wealthiest of these men installed Little Mac and his family in a four-story brick mansion on a fashionable street in Manhattan, a handsome gift that demonstrated their devotion and their faith in his future.

In January 1863, the general made a triumphal tour of New England, ostensibly a pleasure trip, but depicted by Democratic journals as a series of warm receptions, even in supposedly rock-ribbed Republican territory. Conservative Democrats and Old Line Whigs in Boston joined in welcoming him as a military hero, the victor at Antietam, and the victim of administration incompetence and jealousy.

One February night, two dozen of New York's powerful conservative Democrats, dined at Delmonico's, a fashionable restaurant, in a private conclave depicted in the press as a sinister cabal of rich men plotting opposition to the government. There, on "the luxurious seats of Parlor number 14," said the *New York Evening Post*, were August Belmont, "a Hebrew from Germany," and Samuel F. B. Morse, noted artist and wealthy inventor of the telegraph. Among the other guests at the exclusive feast were S. L. M. Barlow, Samuel J. Tilden, and Governor Seymour. "The rich men of New York are to supply the money ... for an active and unscrupulous campaign against the government of the

Union and in the behalf of a body of rebels now in arms," the *Post* charged. Actually, the alleged conspirators were not engaged in treason; they formed the New York Society for the Diffusion of Political Knowledge, organized to finance a widespread propaganda campaign urging revocation of the Emancipation Proclamation.

They deplored Lincoln's epochal decree as an unconstitutional edict, which would keep the South from returning to the Union. Morse, who became the society's president, passionately opposed the war as a tragic fratricidal bloodbath. In the ensuing months, the society published twenty pamphlets, claiming that Federal authorities were illegally interfering with civil liberties, states' rights, and slavery.

While Barlow and his allies promoted McClellan for the presidency, Seymour also cherished yearnings to reside in the White House, and Lincoln began a campaign to enlist him as an ally in the war. As his first move, the president conversed with Thurlow Weed, the longtime boss of Whig and Republican politics in New York State. Weed's grandson, Thurlow Weed Barnes, in his biography of the Albany editor, tells the story of Lincoln's unusual proposition to Weed one wintry night at the White House: "Governor Seymour has greater power just now for good than any other men in the country," Lincoln said. "He can wheel the Democratic Party into line, put down rebellion, and preserve the government. Tell him for me that, if he will render this service to his country, I shall cheerfully make way for him as my successor."

Historians have interpreted this as an astonishing bid by the Republican president to give up his desire for a second term and to throw his prestige behind a move to draft a Democrat as his successor. If true, the offer meant: Seymour, help me win the war, and I will help you become the next president.

However, in his inaugural message to the New York Legislature in January, the governor plainly aligned himself with the anti-Lincoln camp, saying: "This war should have been averted, but its floodgates were opened and the administration could not grasp its dimensions nor control its sweep. The arbitrary arrests, the suppression of journals and imprisonment of persons has been glaringly partisan."

Shortly after the overtures from Lincoln to Seymour, Weed abruptly sold his Albany newspaper, the *Evening Journal,* which he had built into a profitable powerhouse through a lifetime of labor, and withdrew from journalism. "I differ widely with my party about the best means of crushing the Rebellion," he explained. "The difference is radical and irreconcilable." Like Seymour and McClellan, the editor urged that the Northern people be united to fight solely for the Union and not for abolition.

The Democrats, in the opinion of Republican Congressman James G. Blaine of Maine, had this plan in early 1863 for regaining national power in the following year: "The opponents of the administration intended to press the attack, to destroy the prestige of Mr. Lincoln, to bring hostilities in the field to an end, to force a compromise which should give humiliating guarantees for the protection of slavery, to bring the South back in triumph, and to reinstate the Democratic Party in the Presidential election of the ensuing year for a long and peaceful rule over a union in which radicalism had been stamped out and abolitionists placed under the ban." Clearly, these were the aims, which the New York Democratic leaders outlined to the British minister as a plan to end the war, not to win it.

In Blaine's view, the first shots of the Democrats' campaign were fired by Clement L. Vallandigham, who delivered a passionate antiwar speech in the House of Representatives January 14. It was a farewell address, because the Dayton congressman had lost his seat in the fall election after the Republican legislature had gerrymandered his district by adding a heavily Republican county. One eyewitness to the drama in the House chamber described the orator as being "as cold as ice, and as hard as iron."

Proudly, Vallandigham recalled that he had been against the war from its very first day; he had opposed the horrible spectacle of Americans butchering each other over a political issue, "and today I bless God that not one drop of its blood is upon my garments." "The war for the Union is … a bloody and costly failure," he shouted. "Sir, some twenty months have elapsed, but the rebellion is not crushed out. … A thousand millions have been expended, and three hundred thousand lives lost or bodies mangled; and today the Confederate flag is still near the Potomac and the Ohio, and the Confederate government is stronger, many times, than at the beginning."

The president confessed the failure on September 22 when "the war for the Union was abandoned and war for the Negro openly begun with stronger battalions than before," Vallandigham thundered. "With what success? Let the dead at Fredericksburg and Vicksburg answer.

"Ought this war to continue? I answer, no, not a day, not an hour. What then? Shall we separate? Again, I answer, no, no, no! ... Stop fighting. Make an armistice—no formal treaty. Withdraw your army from the seceded states. Declare absolute free trade between the North and South. ... Recall your fleets. Break up your blockade. Restore travel. Open up railroads. Re-establish the telegraph. ... Visit the North and West. Visit the South. ... Let slavery alone. Let us choose a new president in '64."

As for foreign mediation of the war, offered by Emperor Napoleon III of France but rejected by Lincoln, the Ohio Democrat declared: "I would accept it at once."

Vallandigham's sensational speech enraged the Republicans. They denounced it as demagoguery certain to increase the war weariness and defeatism already running rampant in the North, especially in the states of the old Northwest, where some Democrats were openly talking about forming their own Confederacy and allying it with the South. For example, former Illinois Governor John Reynolds declared in a December 17, 1862, letter to the *Crisis*, a Columbus, Ohio, newspaper that loudly opposed the war: "I am for peace under any plan or able readjustment the people will make. I think a reunion is the plan of adjustment; but, in the name of God, no more bloodshed to gratify a religious fanaticism. ... I think the people have decided that the war must cease and peace be restored."

Residents of Illinois, Indiana, Ohio, and neighboring states poured letters into Washington, expressing their fears and despair. Typical were messages received by Republican Congressman Elihu B. Washburne of Galena, Illinois: "The minds of all our friends are filled with forebodings and gloomy apprehensions," wrote J. F. Ankeny of Freeport. "All confidence is lost in the administration and a disaster to our armies now at Vicksburg, in Tennessee, or on the Potomac will disintegrate this whole country. Treason is everywhere, bold, defiant, and active, *with impunity*."

"For God's sake, give us decided military success or we perish," wrote George Hamilton also of Galena. "Must the Great Northwest be plunged into anarchy and ruin? ... Are we to be forced to defend our hearths and homes? Are the streets of dear old Galena to be the scenes of blood and those we love to be at the mercy of an ignorant and infuriated mob led by ... miserable demagogues?"

"Rebel Democrats are doing all in their power to produce a panic in the North," Amos Miller of Rockford warned Washburne. "They threaten a *revolution* against the administration, evidently acting in concert with the Southern traitors. ... Many expect the rebel Democrats will resort to arms ... assassinate President Lincoln and inaugurate Jeff Davis President at Washington."

Even Joseph Medill, editor of the fiercely Republican *Chicago Tribune*, sent Washburne a defeatist letter advocating that the North accept an armistice and a divided Union, leaving the Confederacy in command of the Southeastern states. First, he wrote, the Federal army must take Vicksburg and complete its possession of the Mississippi River for, if the South should control the lower part of the great waterway, "there is no certainty that the Northwest will stay in the Union."

There is no way to avoid a divided Union, the editor lamented. "The Democratic Party is so hostile and threatening that complete success has become a moral impossibility. ... The war has been conducted so long by 'central imbecility,' Seward intrigue, and McClellan, Buell, Halleck, Steele, Franklin, Nelson, McCook, and other pro-slavery, half-secesh generals, that the day of grace is past. ... Halleck and his gang are still being retained. Lincoln is half-awake and never will do much better than he has done. He will do the right thing always too late, and just when it does no good."

Chapter Eleven
"Don't Care a Damn"

AMID ALL HIS TROUBLES in the depressing days of early 1863, President Lincoln most dreaded "the fire in the rear." Senator Charles Sumner of Massachusetts, after a visit with him, wrote to Professor Francis Lieber: "These are dark hours. ... The President tells me he now fears 'the fire in the rear'—meaning the Democracy, especially at the Northwest—more than our military chances."

By "the Democracy," the president meant the Democratic Party, which often called itself by that name. He told two other senators, John P. Hale of New Hampshire and Orville Browning of Illinois, that the Democratic legislatures of Illinois and Indiana "seemed bent upon mischief, and the party in those states was talking of a union with the lower Mississippi States." If Illinois and Indiana should actually break away and join the Southern Confederacy, there was good reason to fear that Kentucky and Missouri would go, too, and the prospects of restoring the Union would seem hopeless.

Horrified Republicans feared that the hot-blooded antiwar Democrats were arrogant enough to make such an attempt unless they could be blocked by force, and the result could be a new civil war on Northern soil. Serious men really feared this awful possibility when they heard Democrats in the legislatures shouting tirades against the Federal government and the president and calling for an end to the war. The nearly hysterical letters to Congressman Washburne from his Illinois constituents referred to the prospect of such a conflict.

"The Illinois legislature has been in session, one week, during which the Copperheads have not uttered one loyal word, but have belched treason, day and night," the *Chicago Tribune* declared in disgust January 15. "Not a word of condemnation has been spoken against Jeff Davis and his armed bands of regicides. ... Their purpose is manifest. It is nothing less than to produce civil war in our own state, and to drench its soil with the blood of its own sons. They desire to reenact the scenes that have been witnessed in Missouri, and turn the state a prey to rapine, fire, and assassination. They wish to make common cause with the rebels, and drag Illinois out of the Union."

From Springfield, the state capital, a correspondent reported: "The feeling in the city since the Democratic secession meeting ... is getting exceedingly warm and a number of collisions have occurred in bar rooms, hotels, and in the streets. ... There were shouts for Jeff Davis, and shouts for a Northwestern Confederacy.

"The Democrats are crazy for an armistice. An armistice, they know, means acknowledgment of the Southern Confederacy ... and this is to be followed by an attempt to unite the Northwest with its destinies."

"The main topic of conversation" in the Illinois legislature, the *Chicago Tribune* reported, "was the Negro—how to keep free Negroes out and to get slave Negroes into the state."

"If this country does not go to the devil, it will be for no want of folly on the part of our fellows in the Illinois legislature," Republican editor C. H. Ray asserted in a gloomy letter to Washburne. "Such ignorance, such folly, such 'don't care a damn' ... never disgraced a party before."

Republican governors Richard Yates of Illinois and Oliver P. Morton of Indiana both resisted Democrats' efforts to take away many of their powers, especially their control of the militia. The Illinois legislature, Yates told Morton, "is a wild, rampant, revolutionary body."

"What is to be done?" he asked. "Have you made any preparations for an emergency?"

Dashing the governor's hopes of becoming a member of the United States Senate, the Democrats chose Congressman W. A. Richardson by a vote of sixty-five to thirty-eight to complete the term of his friend, the late Senator Stephen A. Douglas. Richardson, a fervent antiwar Democrat, replaced Senator Browning, who was serving temporarily by appointment.

In the Illinois House, the Democrats easily approved a resolution calling for an armistice in the war and "the cessation of hostilities," and authorizing commissioners to attend a national convention at Louisville in April to settle all issues of the war. The speaker named the commissioners, but the measure stalled in the Senate, where the Democrats had only a thirteen to twelve margin, and one Democrat died, causing a deadlock.

In Indianapolis, the Democrats demonstrated their new control of the legislature by electing Thomas A. Hendricks and David Turpie to the United States Senate, despite fierce opposition by the Republicans, who accused Hendricks of having advocated that the Northwest pull out of the Union and form its own Confederacy. It was true that while presiding over the state Democratic convention, on January 8, 1862, Hendricks had said: "The first and highest interest of the Northwest is in the restoration and preservation of the Union upon the basis of the Constitution and the deep devotion of her Democracy to the cause of the Union is shown by its fidelity in the past; but if the failure and folly and wickedness of the party in power render a Union impossible, then the mighty Northwest must take care of herself and her own interests."

Hendricks insisted that the great Northwest would "look to her own interests," especially its richest commerce with its best customers in the South, if the Eastern Yankees continued to profiteer from the war while the men of other states did most of the fighting.

In sending Hendricks and Turpie as senators to Washington, Indiana Democrats savored sweet revenge. Their pro-slavery senator Jesse Bright had been kicked out for having written a friendly letter to Jefferson Davis. Republicans charged that Bright, Hendricks, and Turpie really ran the Indiana legislature and were involved in nefarious schemes to take the state out of the Union.

Thus, the *Cincinnati Commercial* reported:

> The Northwestern scheme is boldly advocated. ... Hendricks,
> Bright, Turpie, and others have been preaching for months that
> they want to restore the Union of the South with the North. ...
> The policy of the present legislature of Indiana, which is
> nothing but a tool in the hands of Bright and Hendricks, will
> be to paralyze the general government, as far as possible, by
> refusing to appropriate money for the maintenance and equip-
> ment of Indiana troops in the field, and thus to render as much
> assistance as possible to the Confederate arms, knowing that
> upon the success of Jeff Davis' revolution depend the chances
> for the establishment of their utopia.

Republican Governor Morton warned the Lincoln administration, in a frantic letter to Secretary Stanton, February 9: "The
Democratic scheme may be briefly stated thus: End the war by any
means whatever at the earliest possible moment. This, of course, lets
the Rebel states go, and acknowledges the Southern Confederacy.
They will then propose to the Rebels a reunion and reconstruction,
upon condition of leaving out the New England states. This they
believe the Southern states will accept, and so do I. It would withdraw
twelve votes from the Senate, and leave the slave states in a permanent
majority. ... Seymour and the leading Democratic politicians of New
York and Pennsylvania are in the scheme."

The high-flying Indiana Democrats encountered a formidable
foe in the person of the fiercely partisan, pro-Union governor, first
christened "Oliver Hazard Perry Throckmorton" but now calling
himself simply "Morton." A massive man with a high forehead, dark
eyes, and black hair, and a voice unusually strong and deep, Morton
became the dominant figure in the stormy Indiana political scene in
1861, when he took the reins of power at age thirty-eight. Originally
a Democrat, he broke with his party by opposing the Kansas-
Nebraska Act* and made himself one of the most powerful advocates
of Lincoln and the Republican Party in the crucible of the Civil War.

* The Kansas-Nebraska Act of 1854 opened those free territories possibly to become
slave states if their settlers voted for it. Rammed through Congress by Democratic
Senator Stephen A. Douglas, it caused such an uproar that it led to creation of the
modern Republican party.

Morton boasted that, under his leadership, Indiana raised and equipped far more volunteers for the army than its quota, and he constantly prodded Washington to get rid of easy-going generals such as McClellan and Buell and replace them with commanders who would wage a ruthless, all-out war to conquer the South and free the slaves.

At a packed Union rally in Indianapolis in January 1863, the governor denounced "the scheme of the Northwestern secession, now the rallying cry and animating purpose of the Democratic party." He said: "Indiana won't go into any Northwestern Confederacy nor out of the Union without such a fight as will make it a wreck of no value to the Rebels."

Morton charged that many Democrats were forming secret lodges of the subversive Knights of the Golden Circle, although the party denied any links to such an antiwar group. Boldly, the governor defied threats of his enemies to kill him. According to one newspaper, "the assassination of Governor Morton has been frequently talked of … A few days ago … one of the K. G. C. said: 'We can easily dispose of him, when the time comes. It will be an irrepressible assassination, that's all.'"

The same paper reported: "The southern part of Illinois contains a number of these 'whang doodles,' or K. G. C.'s and they are all … in communication with the Southern Confederacy."

In their most daring move, the Democrats bossing the Indiana legislature advanced a bill to take control of Indiana troops away from the governor. They intended to reorganize the state militia under a four-man board, which would raise troops, commission officers, and have custody of all the militia's weapons. They would then be able to keep Indiana troops out of the Union war effort.

Introduced in the House, February 17, the bill "was intended to strip me as governor of all military power in the state," Morton later recalled. "It was revolutionary and unconstitutional in every feature, and intended for disloyal purposes. … The Democratic members of the Legislature were determined to pass the bill at all hazards, which would unquestionably have resulted in civil war. … The purpose of the proceeding was to neutralize the position of Indiana in the war and to take her out of the line of loyal states northwest of the Ohio River."

Morton saw only one way to avert this calamity: The Republicans had barely enough members in the House to prevent a quorum and thus to break up the legislature. They took this desperate step and caused the legislature to adjourn. Thus, they blocked the Democrats' bid to seize control of the state militia. But all financial bills also died, so Morton faced the dilemma of trying to run the state on his own for the next two years without any money.

He scraped up some cash by appeals to patriotic businessmen to advance funds to the state. He calculated that he would need a quarter of a million dollars more to carry him through to January 1865 when, he hoped, the Republicans would once more control the legislature. In desperation, he went to Washington and appealed to President Lincoln and Secretary Stanton for Federal cash. They gave him the quarter of a million dollars out of War Department funds. Did they act illegally? Perhaps. But they rationalized that it was a military necessity to keep Indiana in the Union.

"They both agreed that Indiana was threatened with rebellion and that the condition of the state came directly within the letter and spirit of the act of Congress approved July 31, 1861," the governor explained. "Mr. Stanton declared to the President, with great emphasis, that if Indiana lost her position as a loyal state the final success of the government in suppressing the rebellion would be endangered, and that the government must be sustained at whatever cost or hazard."

Morton ruled Indiana as a dictator for the remainder of the war and later was elected to the United States Senate. On May 3, 1876, when he told the Senate about his wartime vicissitudes, Senator Simon Cameron of Pennsylvania gave him credit for saving Indiana from being lost to the Union.

"No other man, but that young governor of Indiana could have saved that state from being carried out of the Union," said Lincoln's former secretary of war. Without Morton's "wonderful energy" and courageous devotion to the Union, Cameron said, "Indiana would have fallen and would have been a part of the Southern Confederacy."

Governor Richard Yates, to a lesser degree, also stood up to the "don't care a damn" politicians in the Illinois legislature and succeeded in stemming the tide of their antiwar follies. When everything else failed, he finally prorogued the legislature and sent it home. As the members departed, without adopting the extreme pro-Confederate measures advocated by their loudest members, Republican newspapers heaved a great sigh of relief.

"When the Legislature first met, the prospect of a revolt against the authority of the President was imminent," the *Chicago Tribune* commented. "Threats to take Illinois out of the Union were freely uttered. Now, however, those threats have not been carried out and a great danger has been escaped."

Chapter Twelve

Lincoln Exiles Vallandigham

FACING A NEAR MUTINY among his officers, Gen. Ambrose Burnside gave up the command of the demoralized Army of the Potomac. President Lincoln replaced him with Gen. Joseph Hooker, even though "Fighting Joe" had been conspiring to oust Burnside and was calling for a dictator. "Of course, it was not for this, but in spite of it, that I have given you the command," Lincoln told Hooker. "What I now ask of you is military success, and I will risk the dictatorship."

The president sent Burnside out to take charge of the Department of the Ohio with orders to crack down on the disaffection there, typified by the seething unrest among Democrats and their radical moves in the Illinois and Indiana legislatures to seek an armistice and even to take those states out of the war. Lincoln chose Burnside as his "fire chief" in an effort to extinguish that dreaded "fire in the rear." Presumably, the intrepid warrior who had failed to defeat the armed Rebels at Fredericksburg could be more successful in quelling the unarmed civilians of the Northwest.

The general found far too many citizens, mostly Democrats, expressing sympathy with the South. For months, loyal citizens of Columbus had been complaining about the kind treatment accorded to Confederate officers in prison at nearby Camp Chase when they came into the capital city on parole.

"They are permitted to visit the town and swell up about the hotels," one newspaper protested. "They prowl about the barrooms, drink the mean whiskey for which Columbus is famous, and condescend to make acquaintance with the poor white trash of the North, who fawn upon them. ... Foolish women, crack-brained on the subject of the South, are permitted to minister to them ... to encourage them to persevere and 'whip the Yanks.' These female Copperheads are naturally found crawling about the prisons where the aristocracy of niggerdom can be seen in the enjoyment of the rights they have acquired by secession."

"Columbus turned over to Secesh," headlined another newspaper story, which said: "Our city is turned over to the 'Secesh' to such a degree to make our streets and hotels more resemble Richmond, than a loyal city of the Northwest. A stranger happening in at our hotels in view of the swarms of rebel uniforms and fierce utterances of rebel oaths and threats might fancy himself set down at the capital of Jeff Davis' dominions instead of at the capital of Ohio. ... Our whole community feel the constant insults to which as loyal people they are subjected by these flaunting popinjays in rebel uniforms" who "preach treason in our midst under the protection of a parole."

Under the headline, "Treason in Ohio," the *Chicago Tribune* lamented: "Cheers for Jeff Davis ... are heard every day on the streets. Copperheads and butternut badges and emblems are openly and boastingly worn; news of Federal reverses is received with extravagant manifestations of joy; and intelligence of Rebel victories with corresponding exultation; threats of resistance to the tax law and conscription—resistance with arms—are loudly proclaimed; deserters are defiantly protected."

Determined to shut the mouths of people prattling sympathy for the South, Burnside on April 13 issued his notorious Order Number 38, in which he announced that "all persons within our lines who commit acts for the benefit of the enemies of our country will be tried as spies or traitors and, if convicted, will suffer death." The same order declared: "It must be distinctly understood that treason, express or implied, will not be tolerated in this department."

Clement Vallandigham seized upon Order Number 38 and openly defied its threat of jail or even death for those opposing the war or committing any other vaguely defined forms of "treason." Before a cheering crowd of Democrats at Mount Vernon, Ohio, on May 1, he shouted that he despised the order, he spat upon it, he trampled it under his feet. Hundreds of his followers, who wore butternut badges and Copperhead emblems cut from copper pennies, roared their applause when he virtually dared the authorities to arrest him. He charged that President Lincoln had "plunged the country into cruel, bloody, and unnecessary war." He called the president "King Lincoln" and appealed to the people to come together at the ballot box and "hurl the tyrant from his throne." He closed by warning the people not to be deceived, that an attempt would soon be made to enforce the conscription act; that, if those in authority were allowed to accomplish their purposes, the people would be deprived of their liberties and a monarchy established.

Three army captains in civilian clothes stood close to the platform and took notes of the speech, then reported to Burnside in Cincinnati. Three nights later, at 3:00 A.M., a company of soldiers appeared at Vallandigham's Dayton home. They broke down the doors with axes, seized Vallandigham, and took him by train to Cincinnati. When word of his arrest raced through Dayton, an angry mob burned down the office of the *Dayton Journal*, a Republican newspaper, and the fire spread to several other buildings in the block.

On May 1, the same day of Vallandigham's speech, General Hooker led the Army of the Potomac on its long-awaited spring offensive to encircle General Lee's army and drive on to Richmond. With his usual audacity, Lee divided his force and sent Stonewall Jackson and a band of "foot soldiers" around the invaders and made a successful flank attack upon their rear, shrieking the ear-splitting Rebel yell that panicked some of the bluecoats into retreat. In the confusion and the darkness, one of Jackson's own men shot and wounded him by mistake, and he died a few days later. The battle at the little hamlet of Chancellorsville ended in a Confederate victory but at a great cost, the life of the incomparable Stonewall.

Northern newspapers had hailed Hooker's advance as a glorious victory for the first few days of May but on May 6 the *National*

Intelligencer, a Washington newspaper, announced "a reverse to the Union arms," and it admitted that Hooker's troops had fallen back across the Rappahannock. When news of the defeat reached the White House, Lincoln groaned: "My God, my God, what will the country say?"

It was while he was stunned by the Chancellorsville debacle that the president grappled with repercussions of Vallandigham's arrest. A military commission in Cincinnati tried the former congressman for "publicly expressing, in violation of General Order Number 38 … sympathy for those in arms against the Government of the United States and declaring disloyal sentiments and opinions with the object and purpose of weakening the power of the Government in its efforts to suppress an unlawful rebellion."

Former Ohio congressman Clement Laird Vallandigham, a Democrat, exiled to the Southern Confederacy as punishment for making speeches against the Civil War, is depicted in this cartoon as the "shuttlecock" being batted back and forth by President Lincoln and Confederate President Jefferson Davis. "No good sending him here," Davis says. "I'll have to send him back." Lincoln replies: "He's none of mine, anyhow." Published in Frank Leslie's *Illustrated Newspaper* in 1863, the cartoon is from the collections of the Library of Congress.

Specifically, the prosecution alleged that Vallandigham had made remarks that would "aid and comfort" the rebellion and had declared the war "a wicked, cruel, and unnecessary war;" "a war for the purpose of crushing out liberty and erecting a despotism;" and "a war for the freedom of the blacks and the enslavement of the whites."

Vallandigham protested: "The alleged 'offense' is not known to the Constitution of the United States nor to any law. It is words spoken to the people of Ohio, in an open and public political meeting. … It was an appeal to the people to change that policy, not by force, but by free elections."

The military commission found Vallandigham guilty as charged and sentenced him to confinement at Fort Warren, Boston, for the duration of the war. Democrats across the country thundered protests, praising Vallandigham as a martyr to the cause of free speech. Newspaper editors, realizing that this gag on free speech also threatened their own freedom of the press, demanded that Lincoln restore the citizens' constitutional rights of trial in the civil courts of the North; otherwise, they warned, civil war could break out in the very region where he had sent his bumbling general to stamp out the fires of dissent.

A throng of New York Democrats, at a mass protest meeting in Albany, sent a set of strong resolutions to the president, insisting that he free Vallandigham and stop arbitrary arrests. In reply, Lincoln said Vallandigham was arrested "because he was laboring, with some success, to prevent the raising of troops, to encourage desertions from the army, and to leave the rebellion without an adequate military force to suppress it." He asked: "Must I shoot a simple-minded soldier boy who deserts, while I must not touch a hair of a wily agitator who induces him to desert?"

Vallandigham's friend, Congressman Samuel S. Cox, also a harsh antiwar critic of the administration, expected to become the next victim of Burnside's men who broke down citizens' doors with axes in the middle of the night and hauled them off to prison. For protection, "Sunset" rigged up, at his bedside in Columbus, a rope connected to a bell to warn his Democratic friends to come quickly and rescue him. He survived.

Lincoln soon realized that the nationwide storm of protest threatened further damage to his administration, already weakened in public esteem because of its military defeats. He solved his political problem by an astute move: He suspended Vallandigham's prison sentence and banished him to the Confederacy.

Escorted by Federal cavalry under a flag of truce, Vallandigham arrived safely inside Confederate lines south of Murfreesboro, Tennessee. General Bragg received him there as an unwelcome guest. In conversations with Confederate officials, the "martyr" showed no interest in helping the South achieve its independence. But he wanted the struggle to go on at least for another year to help the Democrats beat Lincoln and regain the White House.

John Beauchamp Jones, in *A Rebel War Clerk's Diary*, recalled having seen a memorandum of a conversation between Vallandigham and Robert Ould, Confederate commissioner for prison exchanges:

> He says if we can only hold out this year that the peace party of the North would sweep the Lincoln dynasty out of political existence. He seems to have thought that our cause was sinking and feared we would submit which would, of course, be ruinous to his party. ...
>
> Mr. V. said nothing to indicate that either he or the party had any other idea than that the Union would be reconstructed under Democratic rule. ... Mr. V. is for restoring the Union, amicably, of course, and if it cannot be done, then possibly he is in favor of recognizing our independence.

On June 1, General Burnside made another gallant charge against the enemy on the home front—this time, a pro-Southern newspaper. He ordered the *Chicago Times* suppressed and sent soldiers to occupy its printing plant. A wave of outrage immediately arose from Chicago citizens, especially the Democrats who liked the *Times*. They had only recently reelected Mayor F. C. Sherman, a notorious Copperhead. Lincoln revoked Burnside's order and the *Times* continued on its merry way, daily attacking the president and the war.

Chapter Thirteen

"The Great Dead Rabbit"

ON JUNE 3, 1863, ABOUT 20,000 Democrats packed the Cooper Institute hall in New York City, shouting for the release of Vallandigham and demanding an end to the "illegal" Civil War through negotiations with the Confederacy. The maestro orchestrating this symphony of antiwar protests was Fernando Wood, the former New York City mayor now using his power as a member of Congress to seize the leadership of the peace movement in the East just as Vallandigham had become its champion in the Northwest.

Tall, dark, and rather handsome in a sinister way, with keen blue eyes and the air of a scholarly philosopher, Wood looked like a statesman, "dressed in gentlemanly black" who "twirls his eyeglass … speaking with great ease and grace," like a combination of "Talleyrand and Mephistopheles." Newspaper accounts captured the drama of the mob scene.

Inspired by the howling crowd of Democrats, Wood shouted his defiance of the Lincoln regime, daring it to send General Burnside to New York to arrest him for opposing the war. Amid groans for Burnside and cries of "Hang him! Hang him!" Wood roared: "Fellow citizens, I may have uttered the language of treason. ("No, no!") I have certainly said more than the language uttered by our lamented friend Vallandigham, who was struck down by the administration, and I may be the next glorious martyr upon the altar of my country's liberty." ("No, you'll be the next President!")

"God did not intend that we should succeed in this war," Wood contended. "Had He intended it, He would not have placed in command a Lincoln (great groans and cries of "Say that again!") with such coadjutors as Burnside and Butler [Gen. Benjamin F.]. We will not compare these with Davis, Lee, or Stonewall Jackson." Tremendous applause greeted the names of these Confederate chieftains. When the crowd was asked to "Proclaim for peace," said the *New York Times*, "the hall presented the wildest confusion, men rising in their seats and waving their hats and handkerchiefs with cries of 'Peace, peace!'"

Speaking after Wood, A. G. Niven, a Democratic candidate for the State Senate, called for an immediate end to "this war for the purpose of political demagogues." "What is this war for?" he demanded.

"Nigger, nigger, nigger!" the crowd roared back.

"Yes," he said, "this is a war for him and we have had enough of it!"

To attain his high place in the cutthroat world of New York politics, Fernando Wood had risen from poverty through a series of maneuvers that earned for him a reputation as a slick manipulator of both business and political deals. He became notorious for showing how to make politics pay. As one sarcastic critic said, "[I]t is impossible to accuse the man of principle."

Born in Philadelphia in 1812, Wood moved with his parents to New York at age nine. At twenty-four, he began his rise to fortune by running a grocery and grog shop a block from the Manhattan waterfront, selling bad liquor to stevedore gangs at three cents a glass. From the profits of this enterprise, he invested in several sailing ships, which brought him fantastic prosperity during the California gold rush. Next, Wood amassed a fortune in real estate as the metropolis soared in population during the boom years of the 1850s. He also plunged into the city's rough-and-tumble politics at a time when gangs boasting such names as "Blood Tubs," "Dead Rabbits," and "Bowery Boys" waged bloody wars in the Five Points district, infamous for its crime.

When Southern states began seceding, Mayor Wood proposed that New York City should also secede and set itself up as a free city to carry on its lucrative trade with the South. His "free city" idea went nowhere.

When New York Democrats patched up their feuds in 1862 and placed Horatio Seymour once more in the governor's chair, both Fernando Wood and his younger brother, Benjamin, were elected to Congress. One critic described Ben as "tall, well shaped, slightly stooping, has a gray-blue eye, overhanging light, long hair, a doughy face, lightly-colored large mustache, and has a vulgar, dishonest look."

Fernando aspired to become the next Speaker of the House but a hostile commentator wrote: "The Great Dead Rabbit, it is pretty certain, will fail in the object of his ambition." Assuming that Fernando could count on his brother's vote, the reporter wrote that the other New York City congressmen "will not touch him with a forty-foot pole."

In a typical display of audacity, Fernando wrote to President Lincoln December 8, 1862, claiming to have "reliable and truthful" information that the Southern states would send representatives to the next Congress if granted "a full and general amnesty." He suggested that some gentleman having "former political and social relations with the leaders of the Southern revolt" be allowed to hold unofficial correspondence with them to find out "whether a peaceful solution of the present struggle may be obtainable."

Well aware that he was dealing with a slippery individual, the president replied: "I strongly suspect that your information will prove groundless." If the Southerners really were willing to send representatives to the next Congress, he reasoned that they were ready to submit to the national authority and, in that case, "a full and general amnesty would not be withheld." However, Lincoln did not "think it proper now to suspend military operations to try any experiment of negotiations."

Fernando Wood's demands for peace at almost any price, plus his denunciation of War Democrats as no better than abolitionists, widened a split in the Democratic Party over the future of George McClellan. The general had already been chosen by the leaders of the old Albany Regency in New York as their candidate for the presidency. Soon after his dismissal as commander of the Army of the Potomac, McClellan was virtually adopted by prominent New York Democrats following the lead of S. L. M. Barlow, who had been personally promoting his presidential boom since 1861. Among his admirers were Democratic national chairman August Belmont, John Van Buren, son of former President Martin Van Buren, and such rich entrepreneurs as William Aspinwall and John Jacob Astor.

In a sense, also, McClellan "came home" to the railroad executives who had first appreciated his charm and efficiency as an army engineer in the 1850s when he became president of the Ohio and Mississippi Railroad Company. Dean Richmond, who had consolidated several railroads into the New York Central system, was the Democratic state chairman. Likewise, McClellan had strong support in New Jersey, where executives of the Camden and Amboy rail system dominated Democratic state politics.

The *New York Herald* noted editorially that the Mozart and Tammany factions of the New York Democrats "are both placing their houses in order for the 1864 campaign," while there was a "Wall Street clique," under the lead of "Baron Belmont & Co. with the *World* as its organ."

S. L. M. Barlow owned the largest share of stock in the pro-Democratic *New York World,* having saved it from financial failure by generous loans to its editor, Manton Marble, who became McClellan's most ardent advocate. Because Marble and the Regency both favored winning the war and opposed ending it with some kind of peace deal pushed by Fernando Wood and Vallandigham, the War Democrats aroused the Copperheads' jealousy and placed McClellan in the middle of a dilemma.

He could not come out against the war outright, since he had led the Army of the Potomac in an effort to win it; on the other hand, he strongly opposed Lincoln's policy of transforming the war into a remorseless struggle to subjugate the South and free the slaves. His enemies spread the word that McClellan really did not have his heart in the war, so they questioned his loyalty. Their charges would intensify as he moved closer to becoming Lincoln's challenger in the next election.

Thurlow Weed tried to woo McClellan away from the Democrats and make him the champion of a new "Union" coalition devoted to winning the war. Weed's biographers write that in 1863, "the President, after the series of defeats which our armies had suffered, felt that the nation could not be saved if the Democrats, as a peace party, carried the Northern states." So Weed, acting as a mediator, arranged for a great war meeting in New York City June 15, with McClellan presiding. As Weed wrote: "This demonstration was intended to give him an opportunity to take unqualified ground in support of the government and to be the first step in an organized movement to secure his candidacy on a Union ticket. Everything was satisfactorily arranged, when General McClellan suddenly evinced inability to rise above political associations and surroundings."

McClellan would not give up his "political associations" with the Democrats, nor would he "take unqualified ground" in support of the Lincoln administration's war policies. In a June 13 letter to Weed, he declined to preside over the war rally, writing: "The war must be prosecuted to save the Union and the government at whatever cost of time, treasure and blood." But he insisted that the war policy must look to "ultimate reunion" and should preserve the rights of the union-loving citizens wherever they may be."

The author of the Harrison's Landing letter still stuck fast to his opposition to forced abolition and subjugation of the South. So he could not preside over a rally promoting anything except a war for the Union. That left him firmly in the embraces of the New York Democrats, notably Barlow, Belmont, Dean Richmond, Manton Marble, and Samuel J. Tilden.

The Republican aristocrat, George Templeton Strong, noted in his diary:

> S. L. M. Barlow & Co … are making a cat's paw of poor, confiding McClellan and using his unaccountable popularity to stir up disaffection … George B. is brave, honest, and true, but he has no eye for men, no insight into human character. So he has subconsciously allowed his old friends from days before the war … to use him for their own ends.
>
> And as they happen to be Breckinridge Democrats— Constitutional Conservatives—sympathizers and Dirt-Eaters— they have so played him off against the government that he has been for six months past well worth any two rebel generals to the rebel cause.

Across the North, war weariness increased after Hooker's fiasco at Chancellorsville, and Fernando Wood made the most of it in his harangue to his New York audience. His faction also made great progress in the Northwest. On June 11, the Ohio Democrats convened at Columbus to select a candidate for governor, and the clear favorite was Vallandigham. S. S. Cox feared that "Val" had stirred up so much hatred that he would lead the party to defeat in the fall election. So Cox tried to nominate General McClellan who had resided in Cincinnati during his prewar career as a railroad executive.

But McClellan refused to let his name be presented. He did not "harmonize" with the Peace Democrats, the *Chicago Tribune* said. It was just as well that he stayed out of the race for governor the paper added, "for he would have no chance in this convention." The delegates chose "Val" with a whoop and a holler and approved Wood's "peace platform" seeking a negotiated end to the war.

A few days later, the Ohio Republicans chose John "Johnny" Brough, a War Democrat, as their nominee for governor in a shrewd move to attract the votes of Ohio Democrats who disliked Vallandigham.

Illinois Democrats, convening in Springfield later in June, were so hotly antiwar that one reporter commented: "I believe if Jeff Davis had been proclaimed President of the nation, the nomination would have been endorsed by the crowd. ... The populace shouted for Vallandigham and a few cheers were given for Jeff." The delegates adopted the Wood faction's resolutions for peace.

"The Democracy of Illinois has thus placed itself upon the peace and recognition platform of the Fernando Wood faction of New York and the Vallandigham faction of Ohio Democracy," the *Chicago Tribune* charged. "Thus, in three of the leading states of the Union, the Democracy has declared against coercion and in favor of secession."

The peace tide even surged into New England, the fortress of antislavery Republicanism. Former president Franklin Pierce emerged as the leader of Democrats in New Hampshire opposing Lincoln's war. Connecticut Democrats nominated Thomas Seymour, cousin of the New York governor, as their candidate for governor in a platform calling for "honorable" parleys "to stop the ravages of war."

The Northern Democrats' calls for peace and reconciliation and the return of the seceded states drew a cold response from Jefferson Davis and the Confederate hierarchy and from some Southern newspaper editors who denounced any peace deal that would not guarantee the complete independence of the Confederacy. But Gen. Robert E. Lee warned Davis that this hostile attitude was discouraging Northerners who wanted peace at almost any price.

Lee, in a June 10 letter to Davis, wrote that Southerners should "give all the encouragement we can, consistent with truth, to the rising peace party at the North. Nor do I think we should ... make nice distinctions between those who declare for peace unconditionally and those who advocate it as a means of restoring the Union, however much we may prefer the former. ...

"Should belief that peace will bring back the Union become general, the war would no longer be supported and that after all is what we are interested in bringing about. When peace is proposed to us, it will be time enough to discuss its terms."

In one supreme effort to achieve independence by force of arms, Lee and Davis decided to send the Army of Northern Virginia into Pennsylvania once more, with the goal of defeating the Army of the Potomac, threatening Philadelphia and other Eastern cities, perhaps even winning satisfactory terms for peace. This would prove to be the worst gamble of the general's career.

The Southerners' hopes of winning their independence on the battlefield suffered a double setback in early July 1863, when General Lee's invasion of Pennsylvania ended with a retreat to Virginia after a three-day bloodbath at Gettysburg, and the Confederates yielded their Vicksburg stronghold on the Mississippi after a long siege by the army of General Grant.

The glorious news of the double victory gave the North its happiest Fourth of July. It revived the drooping spirits of the people and sent them into transports of delight. In cities and towns all over the North, church bells pealed, parade guns boomed, bands played patriotic airs, and politicians pleased cheering crowds with rosy predictions of an early triumph, ending the war at last.

After the two devastating blows, the Confederates could never count on staging another invasion in hopes of imposing terms of peace. The fall of Vicksburg sliced the South in two. Federal control of the entire Mississippi River meant that Texas, Arkansas, and western Louisiana would be cut off from the rest of the region. Still, despite their despair, most of the Southern people grimly settled down to continue fighting for their homeland and to hope that the Yankees might become so sick of bloodshed that they would eventually agree to a compromise peace.

Chapter Fourteen

Bloody Chaos in New York

AS THE WAR GROUND ON, THE NORTH needed thousands of fresh troops to make up for those killed and wounded and others who had deserted. So the draft law enacted by Congress had to be enforced. The first names were drawn from a huge drum in a New York City office on Saturday, July 11, 1863.

A blindfolded man chose 1,200 names at random from the lottery wheel. The names were published over the weekend, so 1,200 men had good reason to believe that they would be shipped south to be possibly wounded, sickened, or killed. Politicians preaching for peace told them they would be mere cannon fodder in a war aimed at freeing slaves. Furthermore, the draft was illegal, according to such orators as Governor Seymour and Fernando Wood and the editors of the *World*, the *Daily News* and the *Journal of Commerce*. Because any man with $300 could buy his way out of the draft by providing a substitute, it really was "a rich man's war and a poor man's fight."

So draftees and their families had a strong incentive to gather with their friends and neighbors, as did the tough guys from the Bowery and Five Points, to march against the draft. Over the weekend, agitators cruised through the city's five hundred bars and saloons, haranguing ironworkers, stevedores, firemen, and criminal gangs, telling them that the draft was an unfair, illegitimate burden imposed upon poor workers and that it forced them to risk their lives in a war they despised; a war that would free slaves down south and let them come north to take the white men's jobs and perhaps their women, too.

The agitators especially appealed to the Irish, who numbered about half of the foreign-born residents of New York, a city of about 800,000. The Irish already felt themselves a downtrodden minority imposed upon by the upper classes in their fine mansions uptown, who looked down upon the poor immigrants with fear and loathing, which inspired equal hatred in return.

Early Monday, July 13, a hot, sunny day, thousands of working men and women came out of the slums at the lower end of Manhattan Island and marched northward demanding an end to the draft. They were soon joined by gangsters from the criminal wards of the Bowery and Five Points, armed with rocks, clubs, knives, and guns. Sweeping out of their rendezvous place, a vacant lot opposite Central Park, the marchers overwhelmed the thin line of policemen and attacked the draft office on Third Avenue at Forty-sixth Street, knocking over the draft wheel and destroying books and papers and lists of draftees. Draft officials fled for their lives, and the rioters set the building on fire. When firemen arrived, the mob would not let them put out the blaze.

Because nearly all the militia had been sent to the battle of Gettysburg, the city police force of about 1,500 men bore the burden of battling the mob, and they were badly outnumbered. Dozens of policemen fell, killed or wounded, during four days of strife that brought the nation's chief commercial city to the brink of anarchy.

After venting their wrath on the draft offices, the rioters seized hundreds of guns from the State Armory on Second Avenue, an old wooden building. It was soon burned to the ground with a heavy loss of life among the thieves who were trapped inside.

At nightfall Monday, while fires from a score of burning buildings sent a pall of black smoke over the city, a mob marched downtown to Park Row with the aim of burning the *Tribune* office and seizing its abolitionist editor, Horace Greeley. Thousands chanted: "We'll hang old Greeley to a sour apple tree/And send him straight to Hell!"

Greeley escaped by running down the back stairway and hiding under a table in a nearby restaurant, while about a hundred policemen chased the mob away and put out the fires that had been set in several places on *Tribune* property.

By now, the rioters had stopped protesting against the draft and turned to burning and looting homes of the rich of all the valuables they could steal and carry away. Gazing with horror as they sacked and burned houses on Lexington Avenue, George Templeton Strong declared: "The fury of the low Irish women was noteworthy. Stalwart young vixens and withered old hags were swarming everywhere, all cursing 'the bloody draft' and egging on their men to mischief." Strong believed "this is an organized insurrection in the interest of the rebellion, and Jefferson Davis rules New York today."

Francis Lieber, huddling in fear in his house which was barely saved from thieves, wrote to Adjutant General Joseph Holt in Washington: "You can have no idea of the satanic fiendishness and depravity of the women of the lowest class and the love of plunder which this riot has laid bare. The draft has nothing to do with it except that it was made a handle. It is an Irish revolution in favor of the South, led by Democratic Catilines."

Most outrageous of all were the maniacal attacks upon Negroes. At least thirty blacks were lynched, shot, or beaten to death; some bodies were slashed and burned; some clubbed like rats for no offense whatever. One published account blamed a Southern sympathizer named John Andrews for instigating the fiendish assaults by stirring up a mob of fanatics with a call for them to vent their fury on the blacks, whom he called the basic cause of the trouble. Amid wild applause, this lawyer shouted: "Lincoln, this Nero, this Caligula, this despot means by this conscription bill to let the rich man go and earn more money by shoddy contracts and have the poor man dragged from his family and sent to war to fight for the nigger!"

Armed with guns stolen from the armory, about 10,000 rioters marched to the Colored Orphan Asylum on Fifth Avenue between Forty-third and Forty-fourth Streets, intending to burn it and kill the children inside. Fortunately, nearly all of the 237 boys and girls escaped through the back door and ran to a nearby police station.

About twenty little ones lagged behind and they "would have been murdered in cold blood," a reporter wrote, but a giant Irishman named Paddy McCaffrey, aided by some bus drivers and firemen, saved them by battling the mob. Swinging a huge pole studded with spikes, McCaffrey shouted: "Before I die, I'll kill a hundred!" The crowd retreated but not before it had burned the asylum to the ground.

Terrified for their lives, hundreds of black residents fled to upstate New York or to New Jersey along with many white citizens. The death and destruction in Negro neighborhoods continued on the second day, Tuesday, while city officials pleaded with state and Federal governments to send troops to help the outnumbered police who were valiantly resisting the mob at a heavy cost in injuries. Police Superintendent John Kennedy was clubbed to the ground and beaten nearly to death but saved his life by running into a large, deep pond. Policeman John M. Bennett was knocked unconscious, stripped naked, and left for dead, but recovered.

Col. Henry O'Brien of the Eleventh New York Infantry, home on leave from the war front, "was captured by the fiends and beaten into jelly, [and] hung from a lamp post," one newspaper reported. Another version of this atrocity related: "For more than three hours they tortured him, slashing his flesh with knives and daggers, dropping stones upon his head and body, and hauling him up and down the street with fierce howls of victory. ... A gang of Five Point harpies squatted about him and, after mutilating him with knives, flung stones at his head until he was dead."

On the second day of rioting, Tuesday, July 14, Governor Seymour addressed an immense crowd in front of City Hall that included many listeners who were bloody and bandaged. Greeting them as "my friends," he pleaded with them to stop the disorders. He said he had just received a telegram from Washington stating that "the draft is suspended."

The Board of Aldermen, in special session, voted $2.5 million to pay the $300 exemption fee for each poor man called up in the draft who did not want to fight. Nevertheless, the killing, burning, and looting raged on throughout the city, for the riot was no longer a protest against the draft; it was a grand opportunity to kill and to steal.

At last, battle-hardened soldiers of the Seventh Regiment landed at dawn on Thursday and marched into the city and quelled the drunken, last-ditch rioters with blasts of canister and grapeshot, which left many corpses littering the streets. Estimates of deaths ranged from 2,000 to 5,000. No one could tell exactly how many people had died in the dozens of burned-out houses, factories, and stores, or how many bodies were secretly buried. The army refused to confirm reports that about 50 soldiers had been killed and 300 wounded in battles with the mob. Property loss totaled at least $5 million, plus the losses from normal business, which had to be suspended during the four-day carnival of death and destruction.

John Andrews, the instigator of the purge of the blacks, was one of the few men imprisoned for their part in the violence that disgraced New York City. He drew three years in jail. Many believed that he and others were Confederate agents, but there was never any positive proof that the government at Richmond had instigated the riots although the South certainly welcomed them.

Rebel War Department clerk John Beauchamp Jones rejoiced in his diary July 18: "We have *awful* good news from New York: An INSURRECTION, the loss of many lives, extensive pillage and burning, with a suspension of the conscription."

The *New York Herald* ridiculed the Southerners' belief that the riots in New York, and similar ones in several other cities, heralded a general insurrection against the United States government.

Naturally, a lot of finger-pointing raged as Republicans stressed that the rioters had come from the section of New York City where Democrats had stirred up their faithful Irish voters to resist the draft.

The *New York Post* claimed that followers of the Wood brothers were "the ring-leaders in the dastardly and bloody riot." Fernando Wood, who was out of the city during the violence, blamed Republicans for enforcing an unfair draft law against the poor. He said: "The poor man's sons, who voted the Democratic ticket," found their names enrolled to be conscripted while the rich escaped military service and "stayed home making more money."

The *New York Times* blamed the disorders on Democratic politicians and editors who stirred up class hatreds of the poor against the rich. "Cunning and dangerous men ... in bar rooms, caucuses, political meetings, and newspapers," the *Times* asserted, "busied themselves in doing the devil's work of firing the masses of 'the people' against the better classes."

The Northern people, who had cheered so happily about the prospects of final victory after the great achievements of Gettysburg and Vicksburg, now had to face the cold reality that the war was far from over and that many of their fellow countrymen opposed it so bitterly that they would resort to murder to resist the draft. The pretty picture of a united people fighting for freedom proved to be only a mirage.

Chapter Fifteen

Antiwar Feeling Rises

HORATIO KING, THE LAST postmaster general in the Buchanan administration, now in retirement in Maine, spent half an hour in the Portland *Argus* newspaper office August 17, 1863, and listened to a shocking conversation between Fernando Wood and several prominent local Democrats. This was only a few weeks after the Union victories at Gettysburg and Vicksburg were supposed to have aroused a united Northern people to renewed enthusiasm for the war. Instead, Maine Democrats denounced President Lincoln and the draft and gave King the impression that they would "be willing to have Lee in possession of Washington."

Two of the Democrats frankly declared that "they would prefer to be under the rule of Jeff Davis" rather than the "abolitionists" Wendell Phillips and William Lloyd Garrison and Senators Sumner, Benjamin T. Wade of Ohio, and Zachariah Chandler of Michigan, who, in their view, were controlling the Lincoln government.

"The state of feeling here in regard to the war is deplorable," King lamented in a letter to Joseph Holt, Buchanan's former secretary of war now Lincoln's judge advocate general. The Democrats, he found, "are united and bitterly opposed to the administration."

"Many who, one year ago, were earnest in support of the administration and in the raising of volunteers, are now hostile and unsparing in their denunciations," King wrote. He listed four main causes of the Democrats' complaints:

1. The Emancipation Proclamation
2. The arbitrary arrests
3. The removal of General McClellan
4. The Confiscation Act

Also, King found, the Democrats were sure that Lincoln's party would "insist upon the continuance of the war until slavery is entirely abolished throughout the South."

In September, Noah Brooks, the Washington correspondent of the *Sacramento Union*, made an equally shocking discovery of antiwar feeling. "If we travel through the towns and villages of Maine, New Hampshire, Indiana, Illinois, and western New York, we find disloyalty under the guise of Copperheadism of the most malignant and rampant kind," he recorded, continuing: "There seems to be neither shame nor patriotism left in these mean creatures, who make no bones of openly expressing their sympathy with the rebels and avowing their belief in the ultimate triumph of the cause which they espouse. … During a late tour of New England I heard sentiments freely expressed by the natives in the interior which, if uttered in this city, would consign the caitiffs to the Old Capitol Prison in a trice.

"Copperhead farmers along the road would ask if 'Jeff Davis hadn't sent Abe Lincoln to hell yet.'"

Fernando Wood's travels to New England were part of a campaign by Peace Democrats to control their party and move it in the direction of ending the war—not winning it. The *Chicago Tribune* charged that the delegates of the various lodges of the Knights of the Golden Circle in Illinois were plotting "a great rebellion of the North," but their plans were frustrated by the Rebels' defeats at Gettysburg and Vicksburg.

"Alliances were formed with the would-be revolutionaries in various other states; delegations were sent to their lodges, and wherever a Democratic governor reigned, ambassadors were appointed to sound them," the *Tribune* claimed. New York's Governor Seymour was, naturally, the foremost target of visiting politicians demanding "open and armed opposition to the government," the Republican paper said, "but Seymour was too timid" to act.

The *Tribune's* s tales of conspiracies are subject to considerable discount because of its fanatical support of the war and its contempt for "peace sneaks." Nevertheless, evidence of the pressure on Seymour can be found in the *The War of the Rebellion: A Compilation of the Official Records of the Union and Confederate Armies* in the form of a letter that Christian Kribben, a Missouri "peace" champion, sent from New York City August 15, 1863, to Col. Robert M. Renick in St. Louis, after a frustrating meeting with Seymour in Albany.

Writing from the New York Hotel, the favorite gathering place of the pro-Confederates on Manhattan, Kribben expressed keen disappointment over his conference with the New York governor. "I sincerely believe that Seymour is infinitely more radical at heart than he can be permitted to express for he is a public officer, under responsibilities appalling to weak and ordinary men," Kribben wrote. "He and his advisers … have set up a species of counterfeit Machiavellian wisdom, what we at home in plain English would term 'cowardice.'" The New Yorkers, he mourned, were content to go along with the "corrupt and imbecile" Lincoln regime and think themselves "lucky if they can prevent a civil war at the North."

Seymour, Kribben continued, "is of the opinion that the Abolitionists only labor to bring about a conflict in New York City in order to a justify the proclamation of martial law by the General Government, in which case … the elective franchise would be destroyed or at least cramped." The key to the New Yorkers' timid policy, he found, was "the great bugaboo," next year's presidential election: "To hear them speak, the results of the elections in New York, Pennsylvania, Maine, and California are foregone conclusions in favor of the Democracy."

Meanwhile, Clement Vallandigham had ended his sojourn in the South as a guest of the Confederates, boarded a blockade runner at Wilmington, North Carolina, and sailed to Canada, where he lived like a banished prince in exile awaiting his call to power. Kribben met him at the Clifton House in Niagara Falls and concluded, "Vallandigham is the representative man for the great West." If elected governor of Ohio in the fall, Vallandigham could become a powerful ally of those who schemed to pull the state's troops out of the war and create a Northwest Confederacy, although he insisted that he sought only to end the war and bring the Southern states back into the Union. As governor, he could also become a prospect for the presidency, challenging the Eastern politicians and money men who had their hearts set on electing General McClellan.

"The convicted traitor, Vallandigham, has arrived at the Clifton House, Niagara Falls," the *Chicago Tribune* reported. "A band of pilgrims came down from Buffalo ... to see the Great Martyr and Prophet. ... All they wanted was to hang Abe Lincoln, Bill Seward, and the abolitionists. ... If Vallandigham was elected president, which they fondly hoped would be the case, Jeff Davis should have the best place in the cabinet."

Vallandigham did not dare to campaign in person in Ohio, for fear of being arrested and thrown into prison for the remainder of the war. So, many prominent Democrats, led by the candidate for lieutenant governor, former Senator George Pugh, stumped the state for him amid a wave of rallies, bonfires, parades, and oratory. Running under the "Union" label, the Republicans promoted their candidate for governor, "Honest Johnny" Brough, as a War Democrat favoring bipartisan national unity. They quietly eased out General Burnside, author of the despised Order No. 38, the cause of Val's arrest.

Brough charged that Vallandigham's election would be an invitation to Rebels to come into Ohio and "inaugurate civil war" in that loyal state. Brough played upon Republicans' fears that Vallandigham, as governor, would use control of the militia to reduce Ohio's part in the war and encourage those advocating that the state should join a Northwest Confederacy.

Campaigning for Brough, Indiana's powerful governor Oliver P. Morton said the Democrats were wrong in demanding the restoration of "the Union as it was." It was impossible to turn back the clock, he said. "You may as well attempt to raise the dead. Slavery has cut its own throat and there is no surgery in the reach of Providence to close the wound."

Both parties in the fierce Ohio battle sang campaign songs designed to cheer their troops and to ridicule their foes. The Republicans sang: "Hurrah for Brough and Abraham, and a rope to hang Vallandigham." The Democrats sang, to the tune of "Wait for the Wagons": "O, won't Old Abe be furious and won't Burnside look blue when they find out we've elected Vallandigham and Pugh. They call us 'traitors,' 'Copperheads,' we care not though they do, but they'd best not tread on Copperheads, or they will surely rue."

The Lincoln administration used its control of the army and the distribution of war contracts in its all-out efforts to achieve the total, political ruin of Vallandigham. In one propaganda move, a dead Confederate colonel was quoted as saying that Vallandigham, when he entered the Confederate lines in Middle Tennessee, had advised the Southerners to "transfer the battlefields to Ohio and Indiana" and thus win their independence.

J. R. Wright, a Union army surgeon who had attended the Rebel Col. Webb of Alabama who was dying of his battle wounds, made the charge in a published letter.

> Knowing that he was the officer who had received Vallandigham when he entered the Confederate lines, I made some inquiries about the great Copperhead. The colonel told me Vallandigham had said that the South did not pursue the right policy; that, instead of allowing the North to invade Kentucky and Tennessee, and making the battlefields in said states, they should transfer the battlefields to Ohio and Indiana; and, if they did so, a strong party would declare in their favor, that the administration would be compelled to recognize the independence of the South.

Much to the surprise of both sides, Vallandigham lost the election by 100,000 votes. His followers could not explain it. Their hero had actually polled more votes than any other Democrat had ever received in any previous statewide election in Ohio. Yet he fell victim to a steamroller.

Some Democrats cried "fraud," claiming that Union soldiers by the thousands had been brought in to vote for Brough and nobody could tell how many of them were from out of state. The soldiers could account for some of the unusually high total vote for the Republican ticket. But Brough's majority was far too large to be interpreted as anything but a repudiation of Vallandigham and his demand for peace.

Under the headline, "Victory of Gigantic Proportions!" the *Chicago Tribune* exulted:

"Union men are in the wildest ecstasies and Copperheads are as glum as the Dismal Swamp.

"Ohio is saved, glory to God!"

"The streets are vocal with the shouts of the rejoicing loyal hearts," said a dispatch from Cincinnati. "The legislature will be four to one for the Union."

The Republicans' victory wave also engulfed Pennsylvania, where Governor Andrew G. Curtin narrowly won reelection over Judge George W. Woodward, who had received a last-minute endorsement from General McClellan.

McClellan, who had tried to avoid participation in party politics, felt impelled to align himself openly with the Democrats when the Republicans falsely claimed that he was backing their candidate, Governor Curtin. Woodward, chief justice of the Pennsylvania Supreme Court and a strict conservative, had favored allowing the Southern states to secede in 1860 without war, and he had ruled the draft law unconstitutional, so the Republicans branded him a Copperhead and a Peace Democrat.

On Election Day, October 14, the *Philadelphia Press* printed a letter from McClellan denying that he had ever promised to support the Republican governor for reelection. "I desire to state clearly and distinctly that, having some days ago had a full conversation with Judge Woodward, I find that our views agree, and I regard his election as Governor of Pennsylvania called for by the interests of the nation," he declared. McClellan's letter continued,

> I understand Judge Woodward to be in favor of the prosecution of the war with all the means at the command of the loyal states, until the military power of the rebellion is destroyed. I understand him to be of the opinion that, while the war is being urged with all possible decision and energy, the policy directing it should be in consonance with the principles of humanity and civilization, working no injury to private rights and property not demanded by military necessity and recognized by military law among civilized nations.

> And, finally, I found him to agree with me in the opinion that the whole great objects of this war are the restoration of the unity of the nation, the preservation of the Constitution, and the supremacy of the laws of the country.
>
> Believing our opinions entirely agree upon these points, I would, were it in my power, give to Judge Woodward my voice and my vote.

Written October 12, the letter was timed as a last-minute boost for Judge Woodward, especially among soldiers, without allowing the Republicans time to refute it. Some critics called the letter a mistake—especially because Judge Woodward lost the election anyway—but Democratic leaders in Pennsylvania had insisted upon it as essential to their cause. McClellan understood that, if he did not help them in their hour of need, they would not feel obliged to support him for the presidency. He had to show his good faith by endorsing Woodward.

The October triumphs followed the pattern set in April in Connecticut, where Governor Buckingham with direct help from Lincoln in the form of Federal patronage and war contracts, turned back a strong challenge by Democrat Thomas Seymour, who denounced the war and called for peace. In the border states, the iron fist of the Lincoln administration made sure that none but loyal Union men would win political office. In Kentucky, the Union Democrats backed Thomas L. Bramlette, who had recently resigned from the Union army, as the candidate for governor blessed by Lincoln, opposing the conservative Charles A. Wickliffe. General Burnside declared martial law and Union soldiers stood guard at the polls to keep "disloyal" persons from voting. Those who had the temerity to vote for Wickliffe were threatened with arrest and confiscation and some were thrown into prison. So only 85,000 of the 140,000 eligible voters dared to show up, and Bramlette won by 50,000 votes.

Similar tactics achieved success in Maryland, where Baltimore and the entire Western Shore were placed under martial law and several newspapers were suppressed. Maj. Gen. Robert C. Schenck required all voters to take a loyalty oath and ordered the arrest of Southern sympathizers who tried to vote. Troops patrolled the polling places and, to no one's surprise, the total vote fell far below the 1861 figure.

Maryland Governor Augustus W. Bradford complained that the soldiers were "engaged in stifling the freedom of election in a faithful state," but his predecessor, Thomas H. Hicks, now a United States senator, approved the crackdown. "Every rebel, North or South," he declared, "should be put to death."

If the Democrats' failure to elect Vallandigham and Woodward in the Ohio and Pennsylvania governors' races made General McClellan worry about his own prospects of winning the presidency, he gave no sign of it. His mother told him, in a letter, "The Democrats say, the *War Democrats*, that George B. McClellan is to be the next President." The general replied December 6, 1863: "I feel very indifferent about the White House—for very many reasons. I do not wish it—I shall do nothing to get it & trust that Providence will decide the matter as is best for the country."

Chapter Sixteen

Dahlgren's Fatal Raid

IN LATE FEBRUARY 1864, 4,000 Union cavalrymen rode forth on a secret mission personally approved by President Lincoln. Their mission was to free thousands of Union soldiers confined in prisons at Richmond. A secondary objective may or may not have been to destroy the Confederate capital and to kill or capture Jefferson Davis and his cabinet. This possibility remains a hot topic to this day. The *Official Records* show that Lincoln had previously pointed out to his commanders that they had missed a chance to burn Richmond and capture Davis, and his comments can be interpreted as indicating he regretted their failure.

The president's interest in the idea of burning Richmond and seizing Davis was expressed in a May 8, 1863, letter to Gen. Joseph Hooker, whose Army of the Potomac was struggling to recover from its defeat at Chancellorsville, which ended May 4. Lincoln reported receiving some "very important" news on the eighth from an exchanged Federal prisoner, who had just come in from Richmond. "He was there when our cavalry cut the roads in that vicinity," Lincoln wrote. "He says there was not a sound pair of legs in Richmond and that our men, had they known it, could have safely gone in and burned everything and brought out Jeff. Davis."

Brig. Gen. Judson Kilpatrick certainly shared Lincoln's regret that the Yankees had not "burned everything" in Richmond and captured the Rebel president, and he welcomed a new opportunity to stage a successful raid there. In approving the plan for the February 1864 raid, Lincoln specified that Kilpatrick must share the anticipated glory with Col. Ulrich Dahlgren, the handsome son of the president's friend, Admiral John A. Dahlgren. Promoted to the rank of colonel when only twenty-one, the daring soldier had lost a leg in a cavalry skirmish during the Gettysburg campaign. Upon his recovery, Dahlgren eagerly asked the president for this chance for new heroic action on behalf of the prisoners suffering at Richmond.

The 4,000 Yankee horsemen crossed the swollen Rapidan River without being seen by General Lee's troops who were in winter quarters there. Kilpatrick led the main force and swooped down upon the capital from the north, intending to free the captives at Libby Prison. Meanwhile, Dahlgren's command of about 500 men was to come in from the south side of the James River, free the captives at Belle Isle, and arm them for an incendiary attack upon the city.

But the plans went awry. Kilpatrick ran into stiff resistance from Gen. Wade Hampton's cavalry and began retreating toward the safety of Fortress Monroe. Dahlgren found the James River higher than expected, and a slave guiding him could not find either a ford or a bridge for a crossing. Furious, the young colonel thought he had been betrayed by the slave. So, "in his indignation he hung him," reported Captain John F. B. Mitchell of the Second New York Cavalry, who came along a little later and found the poor black man's body "hanging from a tree on the roadside."

Dahlgren led his men around toward Richmond by another way, but he never found Kilpatrick and never freed any prisoners. A band of home-guard warriors and local cavalrymen harassed the invaders and ambushed them in King and Queen County March 2. Dahlgren, leading a charge against the Virginians, died instantly with five bullets in his body.

William Littlepage, a thirteen-year-old in the home guard, searched the crippled colonel's body and found in his pockets a cigar case, special orders for various units of his command, a memorandum book, and an address from Dahlgren to his men. Relayed by a courier, the papers went up the chain of command to Jefferson Davis, who read them with amazement—and rising fury. These were the most shocking lines of Dahlgren's proposed address to his troops: "We hope to release the prisoners from Belle Island first, and, having seen them fairly started, we will cross the James River into Richmond, destroying the bridges after us and exhorting the released prisoners to destroy and burn the hateful city and do not allow the rebel leader Davis and his traitorous crew to escape."

The address was written in ink on two sheets of official stationery from Headquarters Third Division Cavalry Corps, and signed "U. Dahlgren, colonel commanding." A second paper, in the same handwriting, was special orders detailing exactly how his troops were to carry out their missions: "The men must keep together and well in hand, and once in the city it must be destroyed and Jeff Davis and Cabinet killed."

Richmond newspapers quickly published complete copies of Dahlgren's papers with many fierce demands for revenge. The *Examiner*, a critic of Davis, thundered: "If the Confederate capital has been in the closest danger of massacre and conflagrations, if the President and the Cabinet have run a serious risk of being hanged at their own doors, do we not owe it chiefly to the milk-and-water spirit in which this war has hitherto been conducted?"

Gen. Braxton Bragg said Yankee prisoners captured in the raid should be executed. But General Lee saved their lives by arguing that, even though Dahlgren himself had planned such a "barbarous and inhuman plot," it was not carried out, and it would not be right "to visit upon the captives the guilt of his intentions."

The Confederate government photographed the most incriminating documents in the Dahlgren file, circulated them among foreign governments, and made them available to the press. Copied in Northern newspapers, the accounts in the Richmond press created a sensation. So the administration in Washington faced a sticky public relations problem. Something had to be done—fast—to protect Lincoln, who had personally approved the expedition and—as his May 8 letter to Hooker revealed—rather liked the idea of seeing "everything" burned in Richmond and Davis "brought out."

General Kilpatrick admitted having seen an advance copy of Dahlgren's address to the troops and had approved it in red ink.

Kilpatrick said the text was indeed the same as published, but he could not remember any threats to burn Richmond and kill Davis and his cabinet. That part, he insisted, was a Rebel "fabrication."

The Northern press took up the claim that the papers must have been forged. But Confederate Secretary of State Judah P. Benjamin avowed that the courier had brought them directly from the battle-field. "I happened to be in conference with the President," he said, "and read with him the papers, of which copies were furnished to the Richmond journals for publication. I am therefore able to vouch personally for the fact that the passage as to the killing of the President and Cabinet existed in the original, and the photographic copy leaves no room for doubt upon the point."

Maj. Gen. Fitzhugh "Fitz" Lee, who had handed the papers to Davis, asserted: "The original papers bore no marks of alteration, nor could they have possibly been changed except by the courier who brought them to me which is in the highest degree improbable, and the publication of them in the Richmond papers were exact copies in every respect of the original."

Gen. Robert E. Lee sent a stiff note to Union Gen. George G. Meade April 1, enclosing photographic copies of the damning quotations and demanding to know whether or not Dahlgren's "designs and intentions" had the approval of the United States government. General Meade replied April 17: "Neither the United States Government, myself, nor General Kilpatrick authorized, sanctioned, or approved the burning of the city of Richmond and the killing of Mr. Davis and cabinet."

So the official line blamed everything on Dahlgren, who was dead and could not implicate anyone else. "This is a pretty ugly business," General Meade wrote to his wife April 18, "for in denying having authorized or approved the burning of Richmond or killing Mr. Davis and cabinet, I necessarily threw odium on Dahlgren. ... However, I was determined that my skirts should be clear."

The Virginia Historical Society has an anonymous "Memoranda of the War," which quotes Gen. George Armstrong Custer as saying that Dahlgren told him "that he would not take Pres. Davis & his cabinet, but would put them to death and that he would himself set fire to the first house in Richmond and burn the city." Custer "did not think this purpose right."

Despite all the unproved claims of "forgeries," the Southern people believed that the Dahlgren papers were authentic and that they proved the Lincoln administration had begun a new and more barbaric form of warfare. It was true that Lincoln had sent the young colonel on the ill-fated adventure, and it was not Dahlgren alone who had the idea of burning Richmond and either seizing or killing Jefferson Davis and his cabinet.

The Dahlgren documents provided startling new evidence that Southerners had no choice but to fight on despite their war weariness, for defeat would mean their total ruin. These dire prospects affected the Confederate chieftains' strategy when they met in Richmond in March 1864 to plan their last desperate moves—which would include subversion, espionage, sabotage, and even an attempt to create a Northwest Confederacy. They also intended to lure certain Northern Democratic politicians into their dark intrigue by insinuating that an armistice, halting the war for only a few months, might lead to the restoration of the old Union.

Chapter Seventeen

Confederates' Intrigue in Canada

IN EARLY MARCH 1864, soon after the Dahlgren raid, the Confederate high command determined upon a daring new strategy to win the war. Despite their losses at Gettysburg and Vicksburg, President Davis and his chief counsellors refused to admit that defeat was inevitable. In effect, they planned to open a second front in the North. Their plans involved stirring up a revolution among the peace advocates, mostly Democrats, in such key states as Illinois, Indiana, and Ohio; and freeing thousands of Confederate soldiers from Northern prisons to fill the thinning ranks of the armies that would soon face the Federals' massive new offensives in the spring.

The Confederates had to devise some revolutionary plans because they faced the spectre of exhaustion. Large parts of their territory had been overrun by invading armies; the naval blockade was causing shortages of essential supplies; the value of Rebel paper money—which earlier had been almost at par with Yankee greenbacks—now had sunk to only a few cents against the gold dollar and many previously prosperous people were reduced to poverty.

It was against this background of severe shortages in men, materiel, and money that the Confederates determined upon their desperate gamble of the new strategy, which involved sending a special mission to Canada. Herschel V. Johnson, who had run for vice president on Stephen A. Douglas's Democratic ticket in 1860 and who now was a Confederate senator from Georgia, first proposed a secret mission to Canada in a letter to President Davis January 4, 1864: "If Lincoln could be defeated ... in the next presidential election, it would end the war and lead to peace," Johnson wrote. "Would it not be wise to have a secret agent in Canada who, by seeking interviews with the right men of the North and N. West ... might aid in stimulating & organizing more efficiently the opposition and securing influences that would result in the withdrawal of the N. Western states from the Union?"

Behind closed doors, the Confederate Congress exceeded Senator Johnson's hopes. On February 15, the congress voted $5 million to finance secret missions of subversion and sabotage that were to be directed by a commission sent to neutral Canada.

The first man chosen to carry out the daring scheme was Capt. Thomas Henry Hines of the Ninth Kentucky Cavalry, C. S. A. He came to Richmond in March to confer with President Davis, Secretary of State Benjamin, and Secretary of War James A. Seddon. Although only twenty-seven, Hines had been selected because of his reputation as one of the coolest cavaliers in the ranks of Gen. John Hunt Morgan's Rebel raiders, who raised havoc with Union control of Kentucky and Tennessee. When Hines and Morgan had been captured in an Ohio raid in 1863 and thrown into the state penitentiary at Columbus, it was Hines who had masterminded their successful escape and return to the South.

Hines cut a romantic figure: He was about five feet nine inches tall, slim, sinewy and tough, with cold blue eyes beneath a heavy brow, curly black hair and a mustache. John Breckinridge Castleman, the young Kentuckian who became his chief lieutenant, admired him without reserve as an "intimate friend and comrade" who was not only a courageous cavalryman but also modest, courteous, and imperturbable, with a voice "as soft as that of a refined woman." "With the exception of Gen. Basil W. Duke," Castleman declared, "I knew in my army life no man so resourceful and so composed in all difficulties."

General Duke, Morgan's right-hand man, said the "Northwest Conspiracy" led by Hines was an audacious enterprise that could have changed the course of the war and had to be kept so secret that the public never knew the full extent of the plot. The danger involved in the scheme compelled "an unusual degree of secrecy," Duke wrote. "Every one in any manner connected with it took his life in his hand."

The Northwest Conspiracy was the effort of "the peace party at the North to compel a discontinuance of the war and policy of coercion," the general added. Attempts to free Confederate prisoners were to be concentrated in "the states where the political discontent was most general and acute." So the Confederates tied in their scheme with the campaign of the Peace Democrats who followed Vallandigham and Fernando Wood.

Hines had glorious visions of success. "If forty or fifty thousand trained and hardy soldiers could be restored to the skeleton Confederate regiments" by their release from Northern prisons, and if they could be joined by many volunteers recruited in Kentucky and Tennessee, he reasoned, they could open a second front in the North.

On March 16, Hines received his orders "for special service, to proceed to Canada, passing through the United States under such character and such mode as you may seem most safe." He was also ordered to "confer with the leading persons friendly or attached to the cause of the Confederacy, or who may be advocates of peace," and to encourage them to strive for peace terms to achieve "the independence of the Confederate States."

Hines, who claimed the temporary rank of major general, also received authority to lead his soldiers in "any fair and appropriate enterprises of war against our enemies," consistent with Canada's neutrality. To finance his operations, he was given a letter to Gen. Leonidas Polk transferring two hundred bales of cotton in north Mississippi to him, which he sold for $70,000. Much more cash would flow later from the Confederate treasury.

Clad in civilian clothes, the captain posed successfully as a businessman, wending his way through enemy territory to Canada with cool bravado. Federal agents along the way never suspected that they were allowing a Confederate cavalryman—an escaped convict—to slip through their fingers. If they had caught him, he could have been executed as a spy. Hines traveled northward to Cincinnati, then rode by train to Detroit, and by ferry to Windsor, in Canada. In late April, he arrived in Toronto, where he found the Queen's Hotel to be the center of Confederate activity.

In Richmond, meanwhile, President Davis chose three commissioners to supervise Hines and to carry on many more missions, such as sabotaging U. S. ships and military installations, influencing political maneuvers, and paying subsidies to sympathetic Northerners to help Democrats win the presidential election.

The first candidate approached to head the Canadian mission was a Virginia gentleman named Alexander Hugh Holmes Stuart. A Whig and a former secretary of the interior, Stuart found that he would have "a diplomatic family or court, the mission of which by means of a secret service would be to foster and give direct aid to a peace sentiment ... along the border states and particularly to give aid to a peace organization known as the Knights of the Golden Circle, which flourished in the Northwestern states." Stuart was told that he could draw on "a deposit of three million pounds in London" to pay for his clandestine activities. But the cautious conservative shrank from the responsibility and refused the offer, pleading family obligations.

Davis then persuaded Jacob Thompson, a fellow Mississippian, to become chief of the Canadian mission. The other commissioners were former U.S. Senator Clement C. Clay, Jr., of Alabama, and J. P. Holcombe, a scholar from Virginia who was already in Canada on a mission to repatriate some escaped Confederate prisoners. Thompson was a strong-minded, resourceful man who had grown up in poverty in North Carolina and made a fortune in a Mississippi cotton boom. As interior secretary under President Buchanan, Thompson had not been a "fire-eating" secessionist until he found out in January 1861 that Buchanan had secretly ordered the steamer *Star of the West* to reinforce Fort Sumter at Charleston. Charging that Buchanan and Secretary of War Joseph Holt had "played the meanest trick in the world on me," Thompson resigned.

Clay, an intimate friend of Davis's when both were Democrats in the U. S. Senate, readily agreed to take part in the Canadian mission, although he suffered severely from asthma, which would trouble him throughout his stay in the bitterly cold winter climate of the North.

Davis gave Thompson his orders verbally, in strict secrecy, telling him to carry out enterprises which had better not become known to the Canadian government if they violated the technical neutrality of the British province.

On April 25, Davis drew a warrant for a million dollars in treasury funds and Benjamin transferred $900,000 in bills of exchange to Thompson. Secretary of State Benjamin wrote to John Slidell in Paris that Thompson and Clay were going to Canada "on secret service in the hope of aiding the disruption between the eastern and western states in the approaching election in the North." This letter clearly shows the Confederates' intention of influencing the election so as to beat Lincoln and elect a new Democratic president who would negotiate an end to the war on terms satisfactory to the South.

From Wilmington, North Carolina, where he and Thompson were waiting to board a blockade-running ship, Clay wrote an emotional letter to Davis, whose adored little son, Joe, had died in a fall from a porch at the Confederate White House in Richmond April 30: "Be assured, my dear friend, it has stirred the affections of my heart for you more than all the many favors you have shown me and that I will forever cherish a sacred memory of that pledge of yr. affection on wh. God has set the solemn seal of death."

With William V. Cleary, a Kentuckian, as secretary, Thompson and Clay sailed from Wilmington May 6 aboard the *Thistle*, a swift, sleek, sidewheel steamer. It ran the blockade successfully, although it was closely pursued by a U.S. warship on the way to Bermuda. There they switched to the British mail steamer *Alpha*, which carried them to Halifax, Nova Scotia, and they arrived by rail in Montreal May 29. The next day Thompson opened an account at the Ontario Bank.

In true cloak-and-dagger fashion, the principal Confederate agents in Canada all had aliases. Thompson posed as "Colonel W. P. Carson" while Hines passed as "Dr. T. H. Hunter," and Castleman as "H. Clay Wilson."

In early June, Thompson and Hines met with Vallandigham, now residing in Windsor and feverishly preparing for his return to Ohio to play an influential role in his party's campaign to force

Lincoln out of the White House. Still ambitious despite his defeat in his bid for the governorship of Ohio, the "martyr" had a new title. He had been recently elected Grand Commander of the Sons of Liberty. He told his visitors all about the order, formerly known as the Knights of the Golden Circle or Order of American Knights, which claimed 300,000 members, all Democrats. He indicated that they were mobilizing to make sure Lincoln could not win reelection by "force or fraud." Vallandigham painted a glowing picture of an army of peace-loving patriots, 85,000 in Illinois, 50,000 in Indiana, and 40,000 in Ohio, plus smaller contingents in Missouri, Kentucky, and New York. These figures later proved to be ridiculously inflated. But they sounded impressive to Thompson.

Thompson offered to provide money and weapons freely to promote a Northwestern Confederacy. Vallandigham declined to receive any money personally—he would not soil his hands with filthy lucre from the Confederacy—but he arranged for cash to be distributed through James A. Barrett of St. Louis, whom he introduced as the "grand lecturer" of the Sons of Liberty.

Vallandigham not only favored a Northwestern Confederacy, "but was confident in belief of the power of the organized 'Sons of Liberty' to displace the governing officials in Illinois, Indiana, Ohio, and Kentucky," Captain Castleman recalled. Castleman said Thompson supplied Barrett with "ample funds to purchase arms and perfect organization wherever required by the Sons of Liberty. For the same purpose funds were liberally supplied by Commissioner Thompson to General John C. Walker of Indiana. The demand for arms came from Illinois, Indiana, Ohio, and Kentucky, Amos Green commanding in Illinois, H. H. Dodd in Indiana, T.C. Massie in Ohio and Joshua F. Bullitt in Kentucky. At the same time arms purchased by W. W. Cleary in New York were shipped direct to Canada."

Thus, Castleman confirmed that weapons provided to the Sons of Liberty in those states were financed by gold from the Confederacy—despite the protests of innocence voiced by leaders of the order when their grand plans for revolution went astray. Vallandigham later admitted having talked with Thompson but said he merely explained about the order and did not become entangled with Confederate agents promoting subversive activity.

His professions of innocence, however, clash with the recollections of the Confederates.

Thompson was so favorably impressed by Vallandigham's account of the Sons of Liberty's eagerness to rise in revolt, that he informed Secretary Benjamin, "The belief was entertained and freely expressed that by a bold, vigorous, and concerted movement, the three great Northwestern states of Illinois, Indiana, and Ohio could be seized and held. This being done, the states of Kentucky and Missouri could easily be lifted from their prostrate condition and placed on their feet, and this in sixty days would end the war." The usually hard-headed Mississippian was carried away by his dreams of ending the war "in sixty days." Captain Hines expressed equal optimism in his first report from Toronto to Secretary Seddon. It is noteworthy that Hines refers to the Sons of Liberty more than once as "Democrats," indicating that they were generally considered one and the same.

"The Confederates in Canada, together with two regiments in process of formation at Chicago," Hines wrote,

> will be placed under my command to move upon that place for the release of the prisoners confined at Camp Douglas. Simultaneous with that movement, the Democrats in every county of Ill. and portions of Ind. and Ohio will rally to arms. A force of three thousand Democrats under a competent leader will march upon Rock Island for the release of the seven thousand prisoners at that point. Five thousand will move upon Indianapolis, where there are six thousand prisoners.
>
> The remainder will concentrate upon Chicago and Springfield. The state governments of Ind., Ohio and Ill. will be seized and their executive heads disposed of. By this means we hope to have, in ten days after the movement has begun, a force of fifty thousand men. We hope to make a certainty of releasing the prisoners.

If this dream could actually become a reality, temporary "Major General" Hines could lead a potential army almost as large as the one commanded by General Lee. At the time, Lee was resisting General Grant's great offensive begun in early May in the tangled Wilderness campaign before Richmond. In theory, the new Rebel force could provide "a fire in the rear" of Gen. William T. Sherman, who was pressing Gen. Joseph Johnston's army in the hills of north Georgia. There was no limit to the dreams of the bold cavalier—except the harsh reality that the Sons of Liberty were not an army, but basically an untrained band of civilian Democrats no better than militia and quite unaware of the plans to make them volunteers to help the Confederacy. No one could know how well they would fight—or if, indeed, they would fight at all.

Chapter Eighteen

Federal Spies Find Disloyalty in the North

WHILE THE CONFEDERATES IN CANADA were planning sabotage and revolution, their friends in Washington kept busy stirring up defeatism among the Northern people. Congressman Alexander Long, an Ohio Peace Democrat, touched off an uproar on the House floor April 8 with a sensational speech calling upon the United States to recognize the Southern Confederacy as an independent nation. "A tall, well-formed man, with a small head and a noticeably red face and fiery hair," the Cincinnati Democrat asserted that, after three long years of bloody warfare, there were only two alternatives left—either recognition of the Confederacy or its "complete subjugation and extermination."

Long infuriated Republicans by charging that the war was "wrong" and "illegal" and ought to cease immediately. He said the conflict had resulted from President Lincoln's "scheme" in April 1861 to reinforce Fort Sumter "under pretense of furnishing provisions for the troops" there. When the telegraph brought news that the Southerners had bombarded the Charleston fort, Long said, Lincoln exclaimed, "I knew they would do it!" That remark convinced Long that the naval expedition, which had included troops and weapons as

well as food, "was intended for that purpose." Lincoln's "purpose,"
Long implied, was to cause a conflict.

"The rebellion was to be crushed inside of sixty days," Long
recalled, but after three years of slaughter, the Southern people are
fighting on because the North offers them only "outlawry, disfran-
chisement, social, moral, and political degradation, penury for
themselves and their children." Although Lincoln's administration at
first proclaimed that the war was only to preserve the Union, he went
on, "it is not now even pretended" that this is the current policy.
According to Long, "Subjugation is the watchword. Liberty and
freedom for the slave and subjugation or extermination for the master
is the public cry." Long warned his own party against choosing a War
Democrat for the presidency. He favored a "peace" man on a "peace"
platform because "the masses of the Democratic party are for peace."
This shaft evidently was aimed at the Eastern power brokers busily
promoting General McClellan.

Long's tirade evoked a blistering reply from James A. Garfield,
an Ohio Republican who, at thirty-three, had resigned his commission as a major general in the Union army and left the battlefield to
take his seat in Congress. "While hundreds of thousands of brave
souls have gone up to God ... and thousands more, maimed and shattered in the contest, are awaiting the deliverance of death ... there
rises a Benedict Arnold and proposes to surrender us all up ... to the
accursed traitors to our country," the future president declared.
Garfield charged that Long had lifted up "the banner of revolt" by
such secret orders as the Knights of the Golden Circle, which he
accused of trying to corrupt the Federal army by insidious antiwar
appeals to the troops and by inciting "riots and murders throughout
the loyal North."

"So help me God," Long retorted, "I have never had and with
God's help never will have, never!" any ties to a secret political organization. Garfield said he did not accuse Long of being a "knight" but
still regarded the order as "under the protection and direction of the
Democratic party."

Benjamin Gwinn Harris, a Maryland Democrat, also made a
fiery speech demanding recognition of the Confederacy as a nation.
"Harris is a small, nervous man, has been sick almost all of the session,

and is notorious for his outspoken secessionism," a reporter observed. "He said he is a radical peace man, a believer in the peace that could only be obtained by the recognition of the Southern Confederacy."

"You've got to come to it!" Harris shouted. He had stood alone in this Congress calling for peace but now, he added, pointing to Long, "there's another soul saved and I am alone no longer." Harris had been a slaveholder "before the Abolitionists stole all his slaves away from him," he said, but he insisted, "I'm a better man than any of you," a claim that evoked great laughter.

Amid cries of "Order! Order!" Republican Congressman Elihu Washburne of Illinois branded Long's speech as "the keynote of the Democratic party in the coming election."

Republican motions to kick Long and Harris out of the House won a majority but fell short of the two-thirds required for expulsion. So foes of the two Peace Democrats had to content themselves with motions of censure and these carried easily.

The alarming increase in opposition to the war, extending throughout the Northwest and the border states, became clear in June 1864 in an exhaustive report by Federal agents who had infiltrated secret societies accused of plotting revolution under the various names of "Knights," or "Star," or "Sons of Liberty."

Col. J. P. Sanderson, the St. Louis provost marshal, wrapped up his reports in a thousand pages of foolscap paper and filed the document with Gen. W. S. Rosecrans, now commander of the Department of the Missouri. Rosecrans had lost the battle of Chickamauga in September 1863 and had been accused of fleeing the Georgia battlefield. President Lincoln had sacked him and sent him to St. Louis.

Lincoln received the report without much enthusiasm. He had grave doubts about the accuracy of its charges and the exaggerated claims of large membership totals, and he preferred to keep his hands off this hot potato.

Soon the report was leaked to the St. Louis press, quickly copied by Republican newspapers across the North, and furiously attacked by Democrats, who charged that it was full of lies. Although it was indeed inaccurate, the controversial document threw a bright light upon the actual situation in the "loyal" states, where innumerable people, who had gone along with the war to save the Union, had now turned against it and were longing only for an end to the useless sacrifice of lives.

One of Col. Sanderson's favorite agents, traveling as "Edward F. Hoffman," reported from Louisville that he found the city a hotbed of underground pro-Southern activities. He quoted a "Dr. W. T. Thornton" as estimating that "the population of Kentucky is seven-eighths Confederate."

"I have never seen so much disloyalty manifested, even in the palmiest days of the rebels in Missouri, as I saw manifested in Louisville," Hoffman lamented. "In various saloons in the city I heard Jeff Davis hurrahed for, publicly, daily. Dr. Thornton spoke to me of the devotedness of the rebel women of Kentucky; ... and they secreted upon their persons vast quantities of percussion caps, powder, etc., and carried them to where they were successfully conveyed to the Southern lines." Dr. Thornton told Hoffman that "the peace party to stop the war by recognition—if need be, by blood—is organizing in Missouri and here; that in Illinois it is perfect and he thinks it is in Indiana."

Posing as a "true Southern man," the Yankee spy enlisted in the secret order, known in Louisville as "the Star." He reported: "One of the obligations ... is not to enlist in the Federal army; another is to resist the draft by force of arms; to vote for a candidate for president who is utterly opposed to the present administration ... Each member is required to keep a double-barreled shotgun, a revolver and plenty of ammunition."

Visiting Cincinnati, Hoffman learned that one-third of the voters in that southern Ohio city were members of the secret order, known there as the Organization of American Knights (O.A.K). Many residents openly flaunted their pro-Southern feelings in this way: "The ladies here costume themselves in rebel colors. Hundreds of the red, white and red summer shawls can be seen on the streets any fair evening. They are known to each other by this. Rebel boys and men are known by white shirt and red necktie. Then there is the 'butternut' cassimere, much in vogue among dandy rebels. Besides, they have their own streetcars, saloons, & c." The Copperheads, Hoffman noticed, flocked around the office of the *Cincinnati Enquirer*, the Democratic newspaper, which he called "the great focus of evil." From Cincinnati, Hoffman moved to Butler County, Ohio, which was so full of pro-Southerners that it had earned the nickname of "the South Carolina of the North."

Another Sanderson agent, William Jones, toured northern Illinois. He learned that the Organization of American Knights claimed 80,000 members, who "go invariably armed." Jones quoted editor Wilbur F. Storey of the *Chicago Times* as saying that while his colleagues "professed to be conservative Union men, they would really prefer that Lee should be victorious."

James Forrest, another Federal agent posing as a Rebel sympathizer, found the O. A. K. "flourishing" in Quincy, Illinois, where its leader was former United States senator James S. Green, a Missouri Democrat.

Although officially "loyal," Missouri actually was torn by a bitter guerilla war. Col. Sanders blamed the secret organization for "the recent numerous cold-blooded assassinations of military officers and unconditional Union men throughout the military district of North Missouri."

Brig. Gen. Henry B. Carrington, commanding at Indianapolis, charged in "an important letter to the President," that the secret orders were inciting desertions from the army in a campaign to "stop the war." He said they aimed at the restoration of the Democratic Party and the overthrow of Lincoln. Carrington said Indiana's Sen. Thomas Hendricks, a Democrat, declared: "The majority of the people of Indiana were desperate under the despotism of the government. "Indiana's secretary of state, Dr. James Athon, said a visit to the Southern part of the state convinced him that "every man is armed to the teeth."

Carrington, a close ally of Governor Morton's, published an alarming report in June detailing the activities of the secret orders in Indiana and neighboring states. They are determined that the Lincoln administration "shall never hold power again," he wrote. "They are a dangerous body of men. … They are to take steps looking towards the Chicago convention, claiming that if Richmond falls it may precipitate their action while the rebels still have armies in the field."

Chapter Nineteen

Gold Gamblers and Shoddy Rich

BY EARLY JUNE 1864, WAR-WEARY Northerners began to suspect that they had been betrayed by rosy promises of victory, just as they had been disappointed in every spring since 1861. They had been led to believe that the armies of Generals Grant and Sherman, in their combined offensives aimed at crushing the Confederacy, would finally achieve the triumph that had eluded the Federal armies through three years of slaughter.

This time, Grant hurled about 115,000 men across the Rapidan and attacked General Lee's Army of Northern Virginia, a force only half as large but well entrenched behind elaborate defenses in the thicket of The Wilderness. Sherman led about 100,000 men out of Chattanooga, heading south to capture the railroad center of Atlanta, while Gen. Joseph E. Johnston's smaller Confederate force dug in at Dalton, Georgia, and fought a series of delaying actions amid the hills of northern Georgia.

As usual, the War Department sent forth cheerful bulletins about great "victories" and Northern newspapers blazoned headlines: "Glorious Successes—Lee Terribly Beaten." "Our Army in Full Pursuit of the Enemy Towards Richmond." In fact, Secretary Stanton deliberately withheld the truth that Grant's forces had suffered horrendous losses in the Wilderness, Spotsylvania, and Cold Harbor battles and that they had finally moved across the James River to about the same place where General McClellan had been two years before.

In a few weeks of direct frontal attacks on Richmond's defenses Grant lost more than 50,000 men—killed, wounded, and missing—almost as many men as Lee had in his entire army. Other estimates of Union losses ran much higher. John Tyler, an officer with Lee's staff, claimed the toll was 70,000. "Grant has shown great skill and prudence combined with remorseless persistency and brutality," Tyler commented.

Eventually the enormous casualties could no longer be concealed as the people read the lengthening lists of killed and wounded in their newspapers, and boatloads of maimed soldiers arrived at the Washington waterfront from the killing fields of Virginia. Hidden among the seriously injured were hundreds of men only slightly hurt, along with "shirks, stragglers and bounty-jumpers" who forced their way into the boats, as Noah Brooks recorded this ugly truth in his dispatches to the *Sacramento Union:* "The number of 'dead beats,' as the men call the shirks and stragglers in the army, has been, I am sorry to say, very large."

Thurlow Weed observed a depressing scene in New York State: "Regiments are returning home, worn, weary, maimed, and depleted. Our cities and villages swarm with skulking, demoralized soldiers." He also lamented that "there is a reckless, money-making spirit abroad which, profiting by our disasters, favors a long war."

"The commercial metropolis of the Union is flushed with prosperity and riots in extravagance," one newspaper found. "A war may be a fearful calamity, but the gay denizens of Manhattan don't see it. … There is a wasteful race for display between the gold gamblers, the blockade runners, and the shoddy aristocracy … Broadway presents the gayety of a continued holiday."

Throughout the spring of 1864, the *New York Times* observed that speculation mounted madly, higher and higher. "It was openly proclaimed on the Street that too much could not be paid for railway shares or mining allotments, because the currency was going to the dogs." Gamblers in the "gold rings" the paper said, included "every Southern sympathizer and doubting Thomas."

War profiteers made a vulgar display of their ill-gotten wealth by wearing diamond-studded waistcoats and spending money freely on jewelry for their women, and riding in fancy carriages and entertaining with lavish parties in their expensive homes. As far as wealthy pleasure seekers were concerned, the war was only a dim and distant sound coming out of the South making no difference in their carefree lives, as long as they did not have to share personally in the mud and blood of the battlefield. They would not care if the war would go on for another year or so if they could keep their precious carcasses out of the army. They could hire their substitutes for a few hundred dollars each and let the Irish, the Germans, and the freed slaves fill the ranks and endure the hardships of battle and risk their lives for the Union.

Both North and South had their problems with slackers, malingerers, deserters, and those who held onto soft civilian jobs to avoid combat. Desertions plagued the armies of both sides. Young men from the Old Northwest went absent without leave (AWOL) because, they said, the Lincoln administration had induced them to volunteer for a war to save the Union and then double-crossed them by making it a war to free "the nigger." Some Southerners, pro-Union at heart, who were drafted to fight, also "skedaddled" to the hills and dared the conscript officers to come and get them. Deserters often formed gangs of outlaws who robbed and murdered people for profit.

Some Democrats could barely conceal their glee over the bad news from Grant's battered army. Vallandigham, still in exile in Windsor, Canada, received a letter from a friend in Cincinnati confiding: "Grant has been badly whipped. … The main hope of the Republicans here is centered in Sherman. They seem to regard Grant's expedition a failure and, unless Sherman can take Atlanta, the game is played out, with the South the winner." "The Germans are deserting the Administration by scores," Vallandigham's correspondent continued. "The Ninth Ohio, all Germans, 670 strong, came home Thursday. Their time is out and they refuse to re-enlist. They all damn Lincoln. … The Sixth (Guthrie Grays) and Tenth (Irish) will be home in a few days, having refused to re-enlist." Their chief complaints: Conscription, taxation, and the removal of their favorite German-American general, Franz Sigel, from command.

Republicans had reason to fear that the unhappy Germans and their relatives would desert Lincoln in the election and vote for a third party candidate, Gen. John Charles Frémont, the Republicans' first presidential choice in 1856. The new party's platform, adopted in Cleveland in late May 1864, called Lincoln's administration a failure. If Frémont could siphon off enough Republican voters in key states, he might throw the election to the Democrats.

Styling themselves the Union Party in a move to lure War Democrats, the Republicans convened in Baltimore June 7. "Today, the nation will be degraded by the nomination of Lincoln," a Democrat wrote from Dayton, Ohio, to Vallandigham. "Unless the Fremont party prove strong and stubborn, he will be elected the same way he will be nominated—by fraud and violence, by greenbacks and bayonets."

The Baltimore delegates renominated the president with little opposition except for a few radicals from Missouri holding out for General Grant. The convention dumped Vice President Hannibal Hamlin of Maine and replaced him with Andrew Johnson, the grim, courageous military governor of Tennessee. Johnson, a stubborn Andrew Jackson Democrat, had refused to join the other Southern senators in their march out of the Union during the Secession Winter.

Some defenders of Lincoln shy away from believing that he personally manipulated the choice of Johnson, but the evidence from men directly involved in the maneuver indicates that the master strategist in the White House orchestrated it brilliantly behind the scenes. Lincoln believed that Johnson would pull in some Democrats' votes for the Union ticket. His nomination also showed that, by choosing a vice-presidential nominee from a seceded Southern state, the Republicans were proving themselves a national party. Their platform called for a constitutional amendment forever abolishing slavery everywhere in the United States. The Senate, heavily Republican, had approved the proposed Thirteenth Amendment by more than the required two-thirds majority, but the Democrats continued to block it in the House.

Eight days after the Republican convention, General McClellan, Class of 1846, returned to West Point and dedicated a monument to the men of the regular army who had sacrificed their lives in the war. He made a nonpolitical speech, and yet it enabled him to present himself precisely as his backers for the presidency desired—as the loyal commander who had twice saved the Union, who had been wrongfully sacked after his Antietam victory, and who stood ready, if called again, to restore the Union without further bloodshed. "At such a time as this, and in such a struggle, political partisanship should be merged in a true and brave patriotism, which thinks only for the good of the whole country," he declared. "Shall such devotion, as that of our dead comrades be of no avail? Shall it be said in after ages that we lacked the vigor to complete the work thus begun? That after all these noble lives freely given, we hesitated, and failed to keep straight on until our land was saved? Forbid it, Heaven, and give us firmer, truer hearts than that!"

McClellan said the dead heroes had laid down their lives for a cause that was "just and righteous, as long as its purpose is to crush the rebellion and save our nation from the infinite evils of dismemberment." He clearly meant, without saying so, that he still opposed carrying on a war for the subjugation of the Southern people and forcing the abolition of slavery. He continued to hold that the sacrifices were all for the survival of the Union, nothing more.

By demanding that the war be carried on until victory, the general could not have pleased the many peace advocates of his own party who were demanding an end to the slaughter on almost any terms. Vallandigham and his followers were seeking to nominate a presidential candidate on a platform pledged to a "cessation of hostilities"—that is, an armistice, which the Southerners wanted—and they could not have liked such a militant speech.

The worst fears of McClellan's backers were realized in mid-June when Vallandigham slipped away from his place of exile and headed back to Ohio from Canada to seize an influential role at the Democratic national convention to be held in Chicago.

Chapter Twenty
Vallandigham Returns

CLEMENT L. VALLANDIGHAM mysteriously disappeared from exile in Canada one night in June 1864. He crossed over by ferry from Windsor to Detroit, then boarded a train which took him back to his home state, Ohio. There he suddenly appeared, like an apparition from heaven, at the Third District Democrats' convention in Hamilton, June 15.

The most vivid account of his dramatic return, electrifying his cheering admirers, comes from William Thorpe, a Federal secret agent posing as a reporter for the fiercely Democratic *Chicago Times*. Thorpe had been sent to Ohio by Col. J. P. Sanderson, the provost marshal general of Missouri, as part of his investigation of antiwar agitation in the Northwest. Thorpe slipped into the press box at the county courthouse just in time to hear a loud commotion outside. He reported:

> Many of the members rushed out of the doors and windows … shouting "Vallandigham! Vallandigham!" Others climbed on benches, chairs, and tables, waving their hats and yelling like lunatics. In the midst of the most excited crowd imaginable Vallandigham entered the room and with great difficulty

forced his way to the platform, whither his friends followed, climbing over my table, spilling the ink, and almost spoiling my notebook. Vallandigham shook hands with three to five at a time as long as he could, when the president restored a certain degree of order and the business proceeded. It was finished in a few minutes.

Vallandigham was chosen unanimously as a Third District delegate to the Democratic national convention. This was the chief purpose of his sudden return from Canada; the state convention had refused to name him an at-large delegate because some Ohio Democratic leaders feared his presence in Chicago would cause trouble. They would prove to be accurate prophets.

Amid shouts of "There's not enough room here!" and "Let's go outside!" the Hamilton convention swiftly adjourned to the courthouse yard, and happy Democrats rushed out to hear their golden-throated hero speak. Many were armed and spoiling for a fight with any military authorities who might dare to try rearresting the "martyr." Thorpe was told that, in case of Vallandigham's arrest, the most violent men planned on "laying Dayton in ashes and its conversion into a cornfield."

Agent Hoffman reported to Colonel Sanderson: "If V. had been disturbed, the plan was to kill as many leading Republicans as possible and set fire to the town." Realizing that he was in danger of being exposed as a spy among these "desperate men," Hoffman wrote: "If they ever dreamed for one moment that I was a bogus member, never would I leave Hamilton alive. ... My life would not be worth one fig."

"Men of Ohio," Vallandigham told the cheering throng of pistol-packing partisans, "today I am again in your midst and upon the soil of my native state. If Abraham Lincoln seeks my life, let him so declare; but he shall not again so restrain me of my personal liberty, except upon due process of law," Vallandigham said. "The unconstitutional and monstrous Order 38, under which alone I was arrested thirteen months ago, is dead."

Vallandigham denied that the Democrats had organized any "secret society, treasonable or disloyal in its character, affiliated with the South and for the purpose of armed resistance to the authorities of the Federal and state governments." He insisted that the Democrats had formed only "lawful political associations ... for strengthening the Democratic party and its success in the coming presidential election, and as a counter-movement against the Union Leagues," which he called secret and dangerous.

Amid loud applause, the former congressman said he was involved in only one "conspiracy"—"a conspiracy known as the Democratic party," which intended to overthrow the Lincoln administration "not by force but through the ballot box." But then he made an oblique reference to the "Knights," or the "Sons of Liberty," saying: "But I warn also the men in power that there is a vast multitude—a host whom they cannot number—bound together by the strongest and holiest ties, to defend by whatever means the exigencies of the times shall demand, their natural and constitutional rights as free men at all hazards, and to the last extremity."

Vallandigham did not tell his fellow Democrats that, while in Canada, he had become the grand commander of the Sons of Liberty; that he had met with Jacob Thompson, chief of the Confederate mission in Canada, and others who proposed to use members of the Sons of Liberty to foment a revolution which could attempt to overthrow the governors of Ohio, Indiana, and Illinois. His conversations with the Confederates must have been fresh in his mind because they had happened only a few days before.

Colonel Sanderson in St. Louis, who knew that Vallandigham was the grand commander of the Sons of Liberty, said the martyr's defense of the order as merely a peaceful political outfit "proves him to be not only a consummate demagogue but also a terrible falsifier of the truth."General Carrington, at Indianapolis, reported to Secretary Stanton on June 17 that Vallandigham had made a fiery speech at Dayton the night before and had declared that if any military commander tried arresting him again, "the persons and property of those instigating" the arrest would be held as hostage and he would urge "an eye for an eye, and a tooth for a tooth, so help him, ever living Jehovah!"

Agent Hoffman caroused with a gang of Copperheads who met above a Dayton saloon. One man boasted that "they have more arms and ammunition than they know what to do with." "Their object was to resist the draft and rescue ... deserters," Hoffman reported, and their ultimate goal, he was told, was to create a Northwest Confederacy.

Hoffman audaciously requested an interview with Vallandigham and, to his surprise, he was welcomed into the martyr's house in Dayton. The front door, he noted, was still "much hacked and battered ... much shivered and cracked!" The family had left it in that state of disrepair to show how soldiers had broken into the house in the middle of the night and seized Vallandigham.

Not realizing that he was welcoming a federal agent, Vallandigham cordially received Hoffman, who was disguised as a peace advocate from Missouri. "He spoke in bitter yet cautious terms of the administration and preferred Fremont to Lincoln as a choice of evils," Hoffman reported.

Governors Brough of Ohio and Morton of Indiana, learning of Vallandigham's fervent antiwar activity, demanded that he be locked up again—at once. But the new commander of the department, Maj. Gen. Samuel P. Heintzelman, who had replaced Burnside, stalled until he could get orders from Washington. Lincoln decided to pretend that he had no official word of Vallandigham's return and, therefore, did nothing to bother him. Horace Greeley quickly saw the political wisdom of the president's decision, which left Vallandigham free to stir up division among the Democrats. Vallandigham "will do good here," the editor told the president. "Can't we get him on the Copperhead ticket as vice president?"

House Speaker Schuyler Colfax of Indiana explained the president's decision: "Mr. Lincoln knew that there was a secret organization in the Northwest, and its intention was to make Vallandigham's arrest the pretext for lighting the torch of civil war all over the Northwest." So, to keep the peace in that region, Colfax said, Lincoln left Vallandigham alone.

Indeed, the original plans of some Copperhead militants called for Vallandigham to be arrested upon his arrival at the Democratic national convention in Chicago July 4. But that plan had to be scrapped when party leaders delayed the opening date to August 29. Their theory was that, by late summer, people would realize that Grant was bogged down in front of Richmond and that his campaign was a failure, so they would be more eager for peace than ever.

But S. L. M. Barlow, McClellan's chief advocate, sensed that the convention's delay was aimed at his candidate and that the delay would enable Vallandigham to cause serious trouble in Chicago.

McClellan wrote to Barlow from West Point, June 17: "I wish they had kept Vallandigham down South when they had him there!"

General Carrington, briskly digging up evidence to link Vallandigham to the Sons of Liberty, warned McClellan in a June 18 letter that they were "preparing for an open rupture with the government." He added: "I know they have repudiated you and dare not trust your high-toned honor with their plans." McClellan replied from Orange, New Jersey, July 2: "You may be sure that there never can be anything common between myself and the men you allude to."

McClellan suspected that the politicians were about to sell him out to the peace men. When he found out about the convention delay, he smelled a rat and was so angry that he thought of pulling out of the race. "I feel now perfectly free from any obligation to allow myself to be used as a candidate." he commented. "It is very doubtful whether anything could now induce me to consent to have my name used."

Chapter Twenty-One

Jubal Early's Raid Spurs Calls for "Mac"

IN EARLY JULY, THE NORTHERN PEOPLE, who had been anxiously waiting for news that General Grant had stormed into Richmond, suddenly awakened to the danger that their own capital might be captured first. General Lee, whose army had stalled the invading Yankees at Petersburg, secretly dispatched 10,000 of his toughest soldiers under the cantankerous Gen. Jubal "Ol' Jube" Early to make a daring raid down the Shenandoah Valley into Maryland.

Crossing the Potomac July 6, the Rebels levied tribute from frightened residents of Hagerstown, collecting $20,000. Then they extorted $200,000 from banks in Frederick by threatening to destroy the town; finally, they turned southward, aiming for Washington.

At the Monocacy River, three miles beyond Frederick, they clashed with a hastily patched-up Union army under Gen. Lew Wallace, an Indiana soldier-politician destined to win fame later by writing the popular novel *Ben Hur*. Wallace's outnumbered band battled the Rebels nearly all day Saturday, July 9, before retreating to Baltimore. But the battle delayed Early's march down the turnpike to Washington and gave Grant time enough to send troops from Virginia to protect the capital. At first, Grant could not believe that

Lee had detached Early's soldiers but, in response to urgent pleas from Washington, he sent his veteran Sixth Corps steaming up from City Point on the James River. Grant's veterans arrived in time to make Early realize that it would be foolhardy for his little force to make a frontal attack and try to capture the capital.

Curious to see some skirmishing first hand, Lincoln came to Fort Stevens and looked over the parapets while snipers' bullets flew over his head. It is here that, according to a popular story, an army captain cried, "Get down, you damn fool!" and the president obeyed. At least, that is the tale told by Capt. Oliver Wendell Holmes Jr. who, many years later, became a supreme court justice.

Lee's master plan for Early's raid included a separate surprise assault by a combined land and sea force at Point Lookout, Maryland, where several thousand Confederate prisoners were confined on a promontory overlooking the Chesapeake Bay. In theory, the captives were to be freed and then join Ol' Jube in driving into Washington, perhaps even trying to capture Lincoln.

A Confederate named "Darst" had tipped off the Confederate chieftains in Richmond June 9: "We think it all important that a diversion should be made, either to capture or release our prisoners at Point Lookout or a raid upon Washington, with a view to the destruction of the military supplies and public property, or both at the same time would be better. There is not a troop stationed in our county or Prince George at this time. We therefore infer that the garrison at Point Lookout must be weak. ... Grant is supposed to be thrashed to death, but has not sense enough to know it."

Just as Lee was preparing the amphibious enterprise, the Federals somehow found out about it and moved the prisoners out of Point Lookout. So Early did not have nearly enough troops to defeat the Sixth Corps veterans and then seize and hold the capital. "I had, therefore, reluctantly, to give up all hopes of capturing Washington," Early wrote. "I had arrived in sight of the dome of the Capitol, and given the authorities a terrible fright."

Early and his raiders moved safely back across the Potomac into Virginia, taking along a herd of beef cattle, many horses, and sundry supplies plus the money they had extorted from Hagerstown and Frederick. The Federals made only a half-hearted attempt to catch them. Lincoln, who had hoped to "bag" all the Rebels, was disgusted. "They might have captured Washington," Gideon Welles wrote, because of the "neglect, ignorance, folly and imbecility" shown by the "dunder heads in the War Department."

Montgomery Blair agreed with the navy secretary's indictment. When a friend expressed sympathy over Early's burning of Blair's home, the postmaster general replied tartly that nothing better could be expected while "poltroons and cowards" were running the War Department. General Halleck took the remark personally and complained about it to Stanton, who then protested to Lincoln and demanded Blair's head on a platter. Lincoln replied to Stanton: "I do not consider what may have been hastily said in a moment of vexation at so severe a loss as sufficient ground for so grave a step."

The pro-Union *Indianapolis Daily Journal* had a little fun with the story of Early's raid by paraphrasing the pro-Southern battle song, "Maryland, My Maryland." This parody is its revised version:

> The rebel force are on our shore
> Maryland! My Maryland!
> I smell 'em half a mile or more
> Maryland! My Maryland!
>
> These shoeless hordes are at my door
> Their drunken generals on my floor
> What now can sweeten Baltimore?
> Maryland! My Maryland!

Early's raid, and the resulting panic in Washington and the entire Eastern seaboard, touched off another chorus of demands that General McClellan be called back to active duty for a third time to save the capital. Obviously, nobody had been in charge there to keep the Rebel ragamuffins from escaping back to Virginia with the booty of their successful foray into Maryland.

Montgomery Blair had sent overtures to S. L. M. Barlow in May to restore McClellan to command somewhere and thus remove the dire prospect that, as the Democratic Party's nominee, he might defeat Lincoln for reelection. Blair argued that McClellan, not quite thirty-eight, was young enough to wait for the presidency and it would not look good for him to run now as the candidate of an antiwar party in the midst of civil war.

"I believe if he would unbosom himself unreservedly & in confidence directly with the President that he would give him a military place in which he could be most useful," the postmaster general wrote. Barlow relayed the letter to McClellan and received this cold reply: "I will not sacrifice my friends, my country & my reputation for a command. I can make no communication to Mr. Lincoln on the subject."

On July 21, Blair's father, Francis Preston Blair, went to New York and met McClellan at the Astor House. Lincoln's biographers, Nicolay and Hay, say that "through the good offices of S. L. M. Barlow, a long and intimate conversation took place."

The elder Blair said he was not an envoy from the president, but he still felt sure that, if McClellan announced that he would refuse the Democratic presidential nomination, he would be rewarded with a command suitable to his rank. Blair urged the general to make himself "the inspiring representative of the loyal Democrats," supporting the war effort and thwarting the Copperheads. McClellan drafted a reply saying that he was not running for the presidency—that no man should seek the office and "no true man should refuse it if it is spontaneously conferred upon him."

McClellan still opposed emancipation, saying it "unnecessarily embitters the inimical feeling between the two sections & much increases the difficulty of attaining the true objects for which we ought to fight." He proposed a bid for peace to the Southerners: "Our antagonists should be made to know that we are ever ready to extend the olive branch & make an honorable peace on the basis of the Union of all the states." This draft statement, which McClellan never sent, pinpointed the main reasons for his reluctance to take any command, which would require him to carry out an aggressive war policy.

Lincoln and General Grant met at Fortress Monroe July 31 and discussed changes in command in the East. Blair Senior understood that they agreed that "General McClellan would be invited to return to the army" if he would give up the idea of running for president as a Democrat. But McClellan refused to make any overture, and on

August 6 Grant placed Gen. Philip Sheridan in command of troops in the Shenandoah Valley.

Even if Blair had had the authority from Lincoln to promise him an army command, McClellan had little interest in enforcing a war policy that he sincerely opposed. His mind was set on reversing that policy by becoming president himself and, therefore, commander in chief. First, he had to win over the Peace Democrats, who barred his way to the Democratic nomination. They were busy with their Confederate friends, drafting a platform calling for an armistice.

Chapter Twenty-Two

Sanders, Rebel Agent, Woos Democrats

INTO A COMMANDING ROLE among the Confederates conducting their dark intrigue in Canada stepped one of the most mysterious actors in the great drama of the Civil War: George Nicholas Sanders. Sanders, a powerful backstairs wire-puller in prewar Democratic Party battles, transferred his talents to the Confederacy after secession. He carried out several missions in Europe, where he had been a major figure in the 1850s, befriending young revolutionaries plotting to over-throw monarchies.

He hurried home from Paris in 1864 to carry out a scheme he had sold to Jefferson Davis—a plan for enlisting many of his old friends among northern Democrats in a movement for a compromise peace. Sanders hoped to bring back the Southern states, which had been a Democratic stronghold in the past, and to help the Democrats regain control of the Federal government. Davis hoped to use the plan to achieve his goal of Southern independence. The Democrats and their Confederate friends differed on these aims, but they agreed upon one: They intended to beat Abraham Lincoln's bid for a second term in the November 1864 election.

Tall, broad-shouldered, bearded, and burly, Sanders had bright blue eyes that glowed with excitement—sometimes over wild ideas for plots of derring-do. He had an unsavory reputation as a political trickster and was once described as a combination of "idealist and charlatan." Born in Kentucky in 1812, he grew up in a household of Democrats, believing in the states-rights doctrine of Thomas Jefferson and opposing an all-powerful national government. He proudly recalled the achievements of his grandfather, George Nicholas, who fought for Virginia's ratification of the Constitution.

George's father, Lewis, a cattle breeder, owned an estate, Grass Hills, in Carroll County, Kentucky, on the Ohio River. Lewis subscribed

George Nicholas Sanders, a behind-the-scenes operator in prewar Democratic politics who became a Confederate agent and tricked President Lincoln and New York editor Horace Greeley with a bid for peace by the Confederate commissioners in Canada. Later, he was falsely accused of having had a hand in the assassination of President Lincoln.

to a political magazine, *The Passion Flower,* published in New York City by Samuel C. Reid, whose daughter, Anna, was its editor. George began a correspondence with the talented young editor, then traveled to New York to meet her. Within a week of their first encounter, they were married. George, then twenty-four, set out to make a career of lobbying for political and profitable business interests in New York.

In the 1850s, as publisher of the *Democratic Review* magazine, he became the outspoken advocate of the Democrats who called themselves "Young America." They were dedicated to the idea of driving out the "old fogies" among the party's presidential aspirants and electing a youthful, vigorous president. Their winner in 1852 turned out to be Franklin Pierce, an amiable senator from New Hampshire with a good record as an officer in the war with Mexico. Pierce rewarded Sanders by appointing him a consul in the embassy in London.

Without waiting for Senate confirmation, Sanders sailed for London in late 1853 and began campaigning in favor of U. S. support for young revolutionaries who had been crushed in their great uprising against European monarchies in 1848. He gave a lavish dinner in February 1854, honoring several revolutionary exiles, including Lajos Kossuth of Hungary, Giuseppi Garibaldi and Giuseppi Mazzini of Italy, Alexandre Herzen of Russia, and Alexandre Auguste Ledru-Roland of France. Among his guests was the U.S. minister to London, James Buchanan, whose presence gave the impression that the United States backed the revolutionaries' activities—much to the outrage of many high figures in the governments of Europe as well as political leaders in the United States.

The Senate refused to confirm the irrepressible Sanders, but, because no successor was named immediately, he stayed on in London, helping his friends in their intrigues and stirring up more trouble. In October 1854, he wrote an open letter to the people of France imploring them to get rid of Louis Napoleon, who had seized power through a coup. His demand that they "strike once more for the republic" was easily interpreted as a call for the monarch's assassination.

When challenged about his "extermination speech," Sanders frankly declared, "Louis Napoleon should be put to death." Rejecting a suggestion that imprisonment would be punishment enough, Sanders asserted, "The only safety would be in his death." Sanders also said he would always be "a state's right Democrat of the Jeffersonian school;" in European politics, "a Red of the most sanguinary hue."

It was Sanders who pushed Buchanan to join Pierre Soulé, the minister to Spain, and John Y. Mason, the minister to France, in the notorious Ostend Manifesto, which advised that the United States should offer to buy Cuba from Spain and, if refused, to take it by force. When the manifesto reached Congress in 1855, it stirred up a storm, but it helped Buchanan to gain Southern votes in his quest for the presidency. He won the White House with considerable help from Sanders, who masterminded his nomination at the 1856 Cincinnati convention, defeating President Pierce and Senator Stephen A. Douglas.

When asked what reward he wanted, a cabinet post or a diplomatic mission, Sanders replied: "Nothing."

"But," said Virginia's Governor John B. Floyd, who became Buchanan's secretary of war, "you must have some object in mind. What do you want?"

"Nothing," said Sanders, "but money. I had an office without political influence and yet the Senate took it from me."

"You have been shamefully treated," Floyd agreed.

Sanders received the reward he desired: Buchanan named him the navy agent in New York City, a job that paid very well indeed. Sanders lost that lucrative position in 1860 because Buchanan became enraged at him for backing Douglas for the presidency. Sanders had pulled wires in an effort to pick up Southern delegates for Douglas by dangling the vice-presidency before the eager eyes of several Dixie politicians, even including the prince of the secessionists, William L. Yancey of Alabama.

Murat Halstead, the sharp-eyed correspondent of the *Cincinnati Commercial,* observed his machinations at the Democrats' convention in Charleston. Halstead noted a South Carolina politico "in a confidential talk with a burly, piratical looking person in a gray business suit, the sack coat making him look even more squatty than he really is."

The correspondent painted this colorful word portrait of Sanders: "The features of this individual are a little on the bulldog order. ... He does not look like a man of much intellect, but is evidently a marked man—a man of energy and perseverance, of strength and strategy. Ponderous as he is, he moves lightly. Fat as he is, he is restless, and as he smokes his cigar, he consumes it with furious, incessant whiffs. The black whiskers are sprinkled lightly with gray. It is Young America, otherwise George Sanders."

After the Southern states seceded, Sanders turned up at their first capital, Montgomery, Alabama, wheeling and dealing in an apparent attempt to patch up the rift and restore the Democratic Party to its accustomed place of power in Washington—but all in vain. The *New York Times* dismissed him as "a played-out political hack." His son, Reid, rushed to his defense in a spirited letter to the *Times*, declaring that its "slanderous" attack impugned the integrity of a patriot. "In Europe or in America, in office or out, whether genuine republicans were high on the wheel of Fortune or crushed beneath its weight, your own columns have borne witness to his courageous constancy," Reid asserted. "The love and enthusiasm with which he is regarded by the leaders of European citizenship, kindled not in the sunshine of their prosperity but in the darkest hours of their national and individual gloom, will ever be a precious memory and incentive to his sons."

When Sanders turned up in Canada in June 1864, as a volunteer to aid the three Confederate commissioners in their schemes of political skullduggery, he did not receive a hero's welcome. Commissioner Thompson was annoyed because this ambitious meddler was sticking his nose into matters Jefferson Davis had entrusted to him and to Clay and Holcombe.

"George Sanders has gone on to see Mr. V.," Thompson commented June 7, evidently referring to Vallandigham, in residence in Windsor. "He came from Europe to do what he says he did not know we were entrusted to do and he has gone on to do it. There is such a thing as spoiling broth by having too many hands in it."

Captain Hines's right-hand man, Captain Castleman, looked askance at this "strong, visionary, persistent" fellow, commenting: "I have known no counterpart of this very unusual man." Castleman lamented that Sanders, with his persuasive manners, quickly "obtained control of Mr. Clay and Mr. Holcombe and might get anyone in trouble by his active brain and tireless scheming."

Sanders naturally clashed with Thompson, Hines, and Castleman. They were pouring all their energies, plus thousands of dollars in Confederate gold, into their own visionary schemes for fomenting a revolution in the Northwest. They wanted no part of the newcomer's intrigues aimed eventually at bringing the Southern states back into the Union.

In a later letter to President Davis, Sanders told how he had pulled Clay and Holcombe away from Thompson's scheme for the revolt, insisting that it could not possibly succeed, whereas "we could control the Chicago convention" of the Democrats and commit them to peace. These are the most significant passages in the letter sent from Montreal March 7, 1865:

> Encouraged by your approval of my suggestion two years since to visit Canada to form an alliance with the Northern Democracy, I returned here on the 1st of June last with my son, Lewis, to place myself again in communication with you, first seeing what alliances could be formed and whether a satisfactory adjustment could not be effected through the Washington government.
>
> Upon my arrival, I met the Hon. Jacob Thompson, to whom I communicated my plan, after knowing that he had been appointed by you to a confidential mission to the Canadas. Mr. Thompson would not enter into my views; he had no confidence in political movements; he believed in nothing but stirring up rebellion and revolution in the Northwest. ...
>
> Upon the arrival of Messrs. Clay and Holcombe, I endeavored to show them the impossibility of the success of any movement not open and general in its character—that the Northern people could not be induced to rise either by states or by sections, but that we could control the Chicago convention and organize a powerful party, from Portland to San Francisco, that would have power to stop the war, even should they fail to get possession of the Federal government; and that, after such organization was perfected and promised success, we would have a good prospect of making terms with President Lincoln previous to the election; certainly should he be defeated.

So Sanders began wooing many of the Democrats who had known him in the old days, either as a friend or a foe in the factional feuds of the Democracy. In either case, they respected his talents for intrigue. Despite their previous disputes, which had led to the fatal split in 1860, the Democrats now were united on one overriding goal: to beat Lincoln. Their basic plan was to present themselves as the only party capable of winning back the South and ending the war. Note that their aim was to end the war, not win it.

The *New York Herald* found out about the master manipulator and his schemes and informed its readers July 18:

> George N. Sanders, with some twenty or thirty rebel politicians and officers, is at Niagara Falls, plotting and scheming in behalf of Jeff Davis and his villainous cause. Remaining as they do on the Canadian side, they are in a favorable position to operate upon the politicians who visit that location during the summer months. …
>
> Rebel agents, rebel blowers, and rebel plotters have been rushing back from Europe and have made Canada their base of operations. The country from Montreal to Niagara Falls and Windsor, opposite Detroit, is filled with them, all directing their efforts upon the Chicago convention. Vallandigham was sent back to Ohio to play his part of the game there.

To gain time for organizing their forces, the *Herald* said, the peace factions came out boldly for postponing the Chicago conclave from July 4 to August 29, and they won. Dean Richmond and the bosses of the New York state Democracy went along with the delay just as "the same class of Northern politicians played into the hands of the Southern conspirators who broke up the Charleston convention in 1860."

When the Democrats met Sanders in the cool resorts on the Canadian side of Niagara Falls, they escaped the midsummer heat and the glare of publicity. They usually met at the Clifton House, one of the most popular hotels. There they could mingle easily with the crowds of other visitors and thus avoid detection by the Federal spies who kept a vigilant eye on the activities of the Confederate commissioners. But some alert agents noticed them, anyway. So the *New York Tribune* reported that the names of some gentlemen at the Clifton House "are known to the government," including those of former Senator George Pugh and Congressman George Pendleton, both of Ohio and both close to Vallandigham.

Although Commissioner Thompson tried to avoid revealing the secrets of his mission, the identities of several other Democrats at the Clifton House have come to light. Commissioner Holcombe, in a report to his Richmond superiors, wrote that he had seen, "in most cases repeatedly," former Governor Washington Hunt of New York; Senator Charles R. Buckalew and former Secretary of State Jeremiah Black, both of Pennsylvania; former Governor and Senator John B. Weller of California; congressman and former mayor Fernando Wood of New York; Washington McLean, publisher of the *Cincinnati Enquirer;* Judge Joshua Bullitt of Kentucky and Col. John G. Walker of Indiana, both leaders of the Democrats' secret order, the Sons of Liberty.

Some Northern newspapers found out that the Confederate agents were conferring not only with Democrats of the peace faction but also with mainline politicians, notably New York State Democratic Chairman Dean Richmond and Governor Horatio Seymour. Richmond was quoted by one paper as saying, "The fighting must be stopped." Another reported from Clifton House: "There is some talk here of Dean Richmond being the nominee of the Chicago convention."

The *Philadelphia Inquirer* tossed a barb at Sanders and Beverly Tucker, another Confederate agent, branding them "tricksters and adventurers, political and pecuniary." It said: "For many years past they have been bankrupt in character and fortune, making all the debts they can and never paying a dollar. Such fellows can have no influence except among their whisky-drinking, poker-playing bottle companions." A "veteran observer" in the *New York Times* wrote: "The principal writer of the play is George N. Sanders, the Kentucky bloviator ... one of the Rebel agents in Europe." Sanders and the other "inimitable knaves" in Canada, he said, "are the genuine stock of Southern braggadocios."

Because the armies were stalled before Richmond and Atlanta, and as the cries for "peace" increased all over the North, the Democrats became bolder in their plan to beat Lincoln by presenting themselves as the only party that could win back the South and thus end the terrible bloodshed. They, therefore, asked the Confederate commissioners to state the terms they would accept for the deal.

Commissioner Clay told his superiors at Richmond that, when asked if the Southern states would consent to reunion, he replied: "Not now. You have shed so much blood, have desolated so many homes, inflicted so much injury, caused so much physical and mental agony. … You must wait till the blood of our slaughtered people has exhaled from the soil, till the homes which you have destroyed have been rebuilt, till our badges of mourning have been laid aside, and the memorials of our wrongs are no longer visible on every hand before you propose to rebuild a joint and common government."

However, Clay held out hope for a deal that would halt the slaughter: "I think the South will agree to an armistice of six or more months and to a treaty of amity and commerce … and possibly an alliance … both defensive and offensive." The notion of an armistice or "cessation of hostilities" quickly gained much credence in the Northern press.

Under the headline "The Great Conspiracy—the Rebels in Canada," the *Philadelphia Press* reported that the Confederate agents were "ready for a peace movement that should put a final stop to the war" under "any terms that would not be too humiliating." "The darling dream of a Confederacy they were still unwilling to give up and will cling to it till the last moment," the paper said, but they could reluctantly swallow even that bitter pill "if they would be reassured of a restoration of a Union with State powers as of old." ("State powers," presumably, meant that the states could continue slavery.)

The *New York Times* reported that the Confederate commissioners had drafted a proposition to the Democrats for the restoration of the Union on this basis:

"First, all negroes who have been actually freed by the war to remain so.

"Second, all negroes at present held as slaves to remain so.

"Third, the war debt of both parties to be paid by the United States.

"Fourth, the old doctrine of state rights to be recognized in reconstructing the Union."

"If the Democrats should win the presidency on this basis," the *Times* warned, "the army and the conduct of the war would be for four years in the hands of men to whom this war is detestable and the army is a nuisance, and the Union a doubtful good. It is to help bring about this desirable consummation that Messrs. Sanders and Co. have offered to negotiate."

Reporting a similar list of proposed platform planks, the *Philadelphia Inquirer* wrote: "If the Democratic party of the Northern states will insert these planks in its platform, the Secessionist emissaries hold out hopes of being able to secure so general an assent to them in the South as to give the party great strength in the election by promising the restoration of peace."

Editor James Gordon Bennett surmised in the *New York Herald* that the first design of the Confederate "conspirators" in Canada was "the overthrow of the present federal administration" and their second goal was to revise their scheme for reconstructing the Federal government by combining most of the Northern states with the South and leaving New England "out in the cold." This, he said, would create "a permanent Southern balance of power" by eliminating the twelve Republican senators from the six New England states.

Bennett recalled that when General Bragg led his army into Kentucky in 1862, he issued a proclamation prepared by Jefferson Davis inviting the Northwest states to "join the cause of the South" and assuring their access to the Mississippi River. Correctly, the editor predicted that "the first movement of these conspirators will be to secure, as the peace-at-any-price faction, control of the Democratic national convention." Bennett added: "The rebel ambassadors lately gathered at Niagara Falls under the manipulation of George Sanders have been trying the effect of a flank movement upon Old Abe in support of the Northern Peace Democracy. ... The Copperhead press organs from Maine to Missouri are turning the cold shoulder on General McClellan."

The *Rochester Democrat* also observed that "the Rebels at the Clifton House don't want McClellan nominated," preferring "anybody else but him. The whole pack of them would prefer Lincoln to McClellan. They want an out-and-out peace man nominated." As the result of Sanders' deals with the Democrats, it added, "a letter is to be prepared for the Chicago convention, in which the commissioners hold out strong assurances of a restoration of the Union under Democratic auspices."

Besides perfecting his arrangements with the Democrats to control their Chicago convention, Sanders achieved his most sensational coup by hornswoggling a Republican, editor Horace Greeley of the *New York Tribune*. He trapped Greeley and President Lincoln in a web of intrigue with the Confederate commissioners and a fast-talking confidence man named William Cornell "Colorado" Jewett, who sought to end the Civil War through foreign mediation. This incredible episode deserves to be narrated in a separate chapter: It began as a pipe dream and ended as a farce.

Chapter Twenty-Three
A Machiavellian Scheme

"THE McCLELLAN WING of the Democracy having possession of the press and machinery of the Democratic party, and evincing no very friendly disposition to the South, I determined to make a direct move on President Lincoln, and for the purpose I opened negotiations with Horace Greeley." In these words, written to Jefferson Davis, George Nicholas Sanders revealed that he was the chef who devised the menu and cooked up the plot to trap both Lincoln and Greeley with a bid for peace by the Confederate commissioners in Canada. It was a Machiavellian scheme, typical of the intriguer who had plotted with revolutionaries to hurl despots from the thrones of Europe and who now was aiming at his new target: Lincoln.

Greeley, originally a pacifist, had come around to supporting the Civil War while demanding that it be turned into a crusade to end slavery. As the influential editor of the *New York Tribune*, this emotionally unstable man swung wildly back and forth in his editorials, sometimes calling for all-out war to crush the Rebels and at other times crying for peace. Horrified by the awful loss of life in Grant's bogged-down campaign against Richmond, Greeley once more was crying for an armistice. He was secretly in correspondence with Colorado Jewett, a self-promoting adventurer who had been going back and forth to Europe making appeals to Napoleon III and other monarchs to mediate the Civil War. One critic called Jewett "an unmitigated ass." Thurlow Weed described Greeley, his former ally, as "a fanatic, crazed, muddle-headed aspirant for office." Clearly, Greeley and Jewett deserved each other.

Sanders first turned his hypnotic blue eyes and his silvery tongue upon Jewett, a fellow confidence man, and persuaded him to enlist Greeley in his scheme. On July 5, 1864, Jewett wrote to Greeley from Niagara Falls: "Having just left Hon. George Sanders of Kentucky on the Canada side, I am authorized to state to you, for your use only, not the public, that two ambassadors of Davis & Co. are now in Canada, with full and complete powers for a peace, and Mr. Sanders requests that you come on immediately to me, at Cataract House, to have a private interview, or if you will send the President's protection for him and two friends they will come on and meet you. He says the whole thing can be consummated by me, you, them, and President Lincoln."

On July 7, Greeley wrote to Lincoln, sending Jewett's note along with a passionate plea of his own: "Our bleeding, bankrupt, almost dying country also longs for peace—shudders at the prospect of fresh conscriptions and of new rivers of human blood, and a widespread conviction that the government and its prominent supporters are not anxious for peace and do not improve proffered opportunities to achieve it, is doing great harm now and is morally certain, unless removed, to do far greater in the approaching election." Greeley added this ominous note: "It may save us from a northern insurrection."

Lincoln replied July 9: "If you can find any person anywhere professing to have any proposition of Jefferson Davis, in writing, for peace, embracing the restoration of the Union and abandonment of slavery, he shall, at least, have safe conduct with the paper (and without publicity, if he chooses) to the point where you shall have met him."

On July 12, Greeley received this note from the wily Sanders at Clifton House at the Falls: "I am authorized to say that the Honorable Clement C. Clay of Alabama, Professor James P. Holcombe of Virginia and George N. Sanders of Dixie, are ready and willing to go at once to Washington, upon complete and unqualified protection being given either by the President or Secretary of War."

Greeley told Lincoln, the next day: "I have now information on which I can rely that two persons commissioned and empowered to negotiate for peace are at this moment not far from Niagara Falls, in Canada, and are desirous of conferring with yourself, or with such persons as you may appoint and empower to treat with them." The president fired back a telegram saying he was "disappointed": "I was not expecting you to send me a letter but to bring me a man, or men."

But Greeley made a mistake. He failed to inform the Confederates—as Lincoln had ordered him to do—that they were to come on the specific terms laid down by Lincoln, "embracing the restoration of the Union and the abandonment of slavery." Greeley had left the Rebels with the false impression that they were to have free-ranging negotiations with Lincoln about the peace terms, with no preconditions.

Greeley dreaded playing a public role in the drama but Lincoln forced him into it. So the editor went to Niagara Falls, rented hotel rooms on the U.S. side, and went forth to talk to Jewett at the Cataract House.

Through an exchange of telegrams with the White House, Lincoln's secretary, John Hay, arranged presidential safe conduct for Greeley and his Confederate associates, guaranteeing that "they shall be exempt from arrest or annoyance of any kind from any officer of the United States."

On July 16, Hay handed Greeley a note from the president: "I am disappointed that you have not already reached here with those commissioners." He told Greeley to show them his previous letters stating his terms for the meeting. "I not only intend a sincere effort for peace, but I intend that you shall be a personal witness that it is made." The next day, Greeley sent a note to Clay and Holcombe, saying that he had arranged their safe conduct to travel to Washington with him if they were duly accredited from Richmond as the bearers of "propositions looking to the establishment of peace." His message startled the Confederate agents because they had no such credentials and had never claimed to have them.

Reporting the whole affair to Secretary Benjamin, Clay said that Sanders, in dealing with his "ancient and intimate party friends and others," had arranged to have Greeley visit the Confederate agents.

Believing the editor to be "a sincere friend of peace, even with separation if necessary," they had authorized Sanders to say that they would be glad to receive him. But they were greatly surprised upon reading Greeley's note addressed to them as "duly accredited from Richmond" to carry on peace talks. They could not imagine where Greeley got that idea, except, perhaps, from the fertile imagination of Colorado Jewett or from "Dame Rumor." Clay did not mention another possible source: George Nicholas Sanders.

On July 18, Clay and Holcombe told Greeley that, although they were not accredited to make peace, "we are, however, in the confidential employment of our government" and could get such authority from Richmond or "other gentlemen clothed with full powers would be immediately sent to Washington" to seek the earliest possible end to "the calamities of the war."

When Greeley telegraphed this new turn of events to the White House, Lincoln immediately fired back this curt manifesto: "To whom it may concern: Any proposition which embraces the restoration of peace, the integrity of the whole Union, and the abandonment of slavery, and which comes by and with an authority that can control the armies now at war against the United States will be received and considered by the Executive Government of the United States and will be met by liberal terms on other substantial and collateral points, and the bearer or bearers thereof shall have safe conduct both ways."

John Hay personally delivered the message July 20, meeting Sanders at the door of the Cataract House. Hay described Sanders as "a seedy looking Rebel" with grizzled whiskers and the "flavor of old clo'" (apparently he meant "old clothes"). As they conversed for a few minutes, a crowd filled up the barrooms and halls to see the negotiators, especially Greeley. Then followed tea and toast with Holcombe in his room. Hay called Holcombe "a tall, spare, false-looking man with false teeth, false eyes, and false hair."

Greeley rushed back to New York by train, leaving Jewett to cope with the Confederate commissioners. With the aid of the clever Sanders, they prepared a reply intended to turn the whole fiasco into a propaganda victory for the South. Sanders made sure that a copy went to the Associated Press to be printed in newspapers all across the North. Addressing Greeley rather than Lincoln, the commissioners

said they had been misled into believing that the president, by a concil-
iatory message, had opened the door to "a free discussion of conflicting
opinions, and untrammeled effort to remove all causes of controversy
by liberal negotiations." "We feel confident," they told Greeley, "that
you must share our profound regret" that this promise of free negotiations did not continue in "the councils of your President." Instead, the
Confederates said, Lincoln had returned to his original policy of "no
bargaining, no concessions, no truce with rebels except to bury their
dead, until every man shall have laid down his arms, submitted to the
government, and sued for mercy." They could not explain "this sudden
and entire change in the views of the President, or his rude withdrawal
of a courteous overture." "We have no use whatever," they said, for
Lincoln's manifesto, which could not be presented to President Davis
without "offering him an indignity, dishonoring ourselves, and incur-
ring the well-merited scorn of our countrymen."

The Confederates closed with a subtle bid for the Northern
people to oust Lincoln: "If there be any patriots or Christians in your
land who shrink, appalled, from the illimitable vista of private misery
and public calamity that stretches before them, we pray that in their
bosoms a resolution may be quickened to recall the abused authority
and vindicate the outraged civilization of their country."

For George Nicholas Sanders, the bungled peace maneuver was
not a failure but a success. The clever old intriguer had achieved his
goal. He had tricked Lincoln into stating officially his non-negotiable
terms of peace: both Confederate surrender and the end of slavery.
Now the Democrats could claim that Lincoln intended to carry on
the war, with all its terrible toll of death and suffering, until he
achieved abolition, although he could end the bloodshed with a
compromise peace.

Assailing the trickery of Clay, Holcombe, and Sanders, the
Philadelphia Press figured out that their "actual object" was to cooperate with Northern Copperheads in their efforts to stop the war.
"They are exulting," wrote the *Press*, "over the fact that they drew a
proposition from Mr. Lincoln while they make none themselves."

The Democrats and their Confederate friends were delighted
that Lincoln caught much criticism from both parties over his iron
terms for surrender. C. C. Clay told Secretary Benjamin that both

Peace and War Democrats, visiting him in Canada, had assured him that they would benefit from the exposure of Lincoln's insistence upon the end of slavery. "All the Democratic presses denounce Lincoln's manifesto in strong terms," Clay wrote, "and many Republican presses (and among them the *New York Tribune*) admit it was a blunder."

Clay rejoiced, too, that the Canadian capers had widened the breach between Lincoln and Greeley. "Greeley curses all fools in high places and regards himself as deceived and maltreated by the administration," Clay told Benjamin. Bitterly, Lincoln compared Greeley to an old shoe made of leather too rotten to be mended any more. "Greeley is so rotten," he said, "that nothing can be done with him. He is not truthful; the stitches all tear out."

The president gave his cabinet a detailed account of the peace negotiations. "I am surprised," Attorney General Edward Bates wrote in his diary, "to find the President green enough to be entrapped" by Jewett, "that meddlesome block-head" and "crack-brained simpleton."

Greeley had feared that he would be "blackguarded" by his critics over the failure of his mission and, sure enough, an avalanche of ridicule in the press descended upon his silvery head. "It is lamentable that a person of Mr. Greeley's ability and position should be so destitute of common sense or discretion as to lend himself to the plots of a parcel of miserable tricksters," wrote the *New York Post*. "'Mr. Sanders of Dixie,' as the rogue impudently styled himself, who invited him to an interview with pretended rebel envoys at the Clifton House, he must have known as a low, cunning, debauched, and utterly irresponsible adventurer."

"That shuffle-gaited, peripatetic, old Greeley has gone on a peace mission to Niagara," crowed James Gordon Bennett in the *Herald*. Greeley, he said, had dealt with "desperate adventurers, noisy charlatans, and political donkeys."

"Greeley and Jewett—Jewett and Greeley," Manton Marble jeered in the *New York World*. "Which is Don Quixote and which Sancho Panza?"

"That dancing windbag of popinjay conceit, William Cornell Jewett, has achieved the immortality he covets," said the *Cincinnati Commercial*. "He got Greeley and the President's secretary to the Falls on a fool's errand and made the President an actor in this comedy. Sublime impudence of George Sanders! Enchanting simplicity of Colorado Jewett!"

Later, Senator Harlan of Iowa suggested to Lincoln that Greeley had not turned out to be the best choice as "ambassador to Niagara." "Well, I'll tell you about that," the president replied, "Greeley kept abusing me for not entering into peace negotiations. He believed we could have peace if I would do my part, and when he began to urge that I send an ambassador to Niagara to meet Confederate emissaries, I just thought I would let him go up and crack that nut for himself."

Chapter Twenty-Four
Lincoln Scents the Dark Intrigue

WHILE GEORGE NICHOLAS SANDERS WAS leading Horace Greeley down the primrose path, President Lincoln was quietly sponsoring a peace initiative of his own. He sent Col. James F. Jaquess, a Methodist minister of the Seventy-Third Regiment of Illinois Volunteers, and James R. Gilmore, a writer who used the pen name "Edmund Kirke," on a mission to Richmond. Gilmore and Jaquess had a political motive to help Lincoln's faltering bid for reelection. They wanted to prove that the Confederates' peace overtures were really concocted to embarrass Lincoln's government, to throw upon it the odium of continuing the war and thus to secure the triumph of the "peace-traitors" in the November election.

Gilmore feared that "the peace men, the Copperheads, and such of the Republicans as love peace better than principle" could unite and impose a peace "inconsistent with the safety and dignity of the country." Lincoln shared those fears and realized that he had to break up that coalition which was already threatening to give the presidency to the general he most disliked and distrusted, George B. McClellan.

With a personal note from Lincoln to General Grant, the two travelers crossed the battle lines at City Point, Virginia, and entered

Richmond via a mule-drawn army ambulance and found rooms at the Spottswood Hotel. They first met with Secretary of State Benjamin, described by Gilmore as "a short, plump, oily, little man in black, with a keen black eye, a Jew face, a yellow skin, curly black hair, closely trimmed black whiskers, and a ponderous gold watch chain."

When they asked to see President Davis, Benjamin demanded: "Do you bring any overtures to him from your government?"

"No, sir," Jaquess replied, "we bring no overtures and we have no authority from our government." They were informal messengers, as Benjamin understood it, "sent with a view to paving the way for a meeting of formal commissioners authorized to negotiate for peace." Gilmore said they came with the knowledge and at the desire of Mr. Lincoln, realizing that the war would never end without some sort of agreement.

On Sunday evening, July 17, Jaquess and Gilmore encountered President Davis, "a spare, thin featured man with iron gray hair and beard and a clear gray eye full of life and vigor," as Gilmore later described him. "He had a broad, massive forehead, and a mouth and chin denoting great energy and strength of will. His face was emaciated and much wrinkled."

"Our people want peace," Jaquess told Davis. "Your people do and your Congress has recently said that *you* do. We have come to ask how it can be brought about."

"In a very simple way," Davis answered, "Withdraw your armies from our territory, and peace will come of itself. We do not seek to subjugate you. We are not waging an offensive war. ... Let us alone and peace will come at once."

"But we cannot let you alone as long as you repudiate the Union. That is the one thing the Northern people will not surrender."

"I know. You would deny to us the one thing you exact for yourselves—the right of self-government," Davis retorted. "You have sown such bitterness at the South, you have put such an ocean of blood between the two sections, that I despair of seeing any harmony in my time. Our children may forget this war, but we cannot."

"We are both Christian men," the minister said. "Can *you*, as a Christian man, leave untried any means that may lead to peace?"

"No, I cannot," said Davis. "I desire peace as much as you do. I deplore bloodshed as much as you do; but I feel that not one drop of the blood shed in this war is on *my* hands—I can look up to my God and say this.

"I tried all in my power to avert this war. I saw it coming, and for twelve years I worked night and day to prevent it but I could not. The North was mad and blind; it would not let us govern ourselves, and so the war came. ...

"I would give my poor life gladly if it would bring peace and good will to the countries, but it would not. It is with your own people you should labor. It is they who desolate our homes, burn our wheat fields, break the wheels of wagons carrying away our women and children and destroy supplies meant for our sick and wounded. At your door lies all the misery and crime of this war—and it is a fearful, fearful account."

Benjamin interpreted the administration's peace terms as calling for the reconstruction of the Union, the abolition of slavery, and the grant of an amnesty to the Southern people as "repentant criminals." According to Benjamin, Davis said the offer meant that "the Confederate States should surrender at discretion, admit that they had been wrong from the beginning of the contest, submit to the mercy of their enemies, and avow themselves to be in need of pardon for crimes." Davis said "extermination was preferable to such dishonor."

Davis, in Gilmore's account, declared emphatically: "We are not fighting for slavery. We are fighting for independence—and that, or extermination, we will have."

"And slavery, you say, is no longer an element in the contest?" Gilmore asked.

"No, it is not," Davis replied. " ... You have already emancipated two million of our slaves—and if you will take care of them, you may emancipate the rest. I had a few when the war began. I was of some use to them; they never were of any use to me. Against their will you emancipated them; and you may emancipate every negro in the Confederacy but *we will be free!* We will govern ourselves. We will do it, if we have to see every Southern plantation sacked, and every Southern city in flames."

As the interview ended, the Confederate president said: "Say to Mr. Lincoln from me, that I shall at any time be pleased to receive proposals for peace on the basis of our independence. It will be useless to approach me with any other."

Under his pen name, "Edmund Kirke," Gilmore published a short version of the meeting in the Boston *Evening Transcript* July 22. A little later the *Atlantic Monthly* printed a detailed account, the author insisting that it was accurate because he had written down the president's precise remarks immediately after leaving him.

Why did Davis receive the two Yankees? The most logical surmise is that he intended to use them to prove to the world that the Southerners were fighting for the right of self-government, not to save slavery. The publication of his firm declaration on that point in the Northern press might, at long last, lead to intervention by Britain and France, which hesitated to help a nation based on slavery. The Richmond government was still seeking foreign mediation for a compromise peace that could lead to Southern independence.

Gilmore's motive in rushing his story into print was to prove, before the Democrats' convention, that all their talk about a peace deal with the Confederates was unreal as long as the iron-willed Davis insisted upon independence. But the Democrats were not deterred; they knew that Davis was not a dictator who could control all the people of the South; other leading Confederates had provided private assurances that a call for an armistice would yield a favorable response. So they continued their political cotillion with the Southerners about a platform acceptable to the South.

Somehow—perhaps through a double agent—Lincoln obtained a copy of a proposed Democratic platform prepared by Confederate Commissioner Clay in Canada and sent to certain Democrats in the North. In late July, the president wrote this memorandum showing that he was keenly aware of the dark intrigue going on between the Democrats and their Confederate friends.

Lincoln wrote:

"Hon. Clement C. Clay, one of the Confederate gentlemen who recently, at Niagara Falls, in a letter to Mr. Greeley, declared that they were not empowered to negotiate for peace, but that they were, however, in the confidential employment of their Government, has prepared a platform and an Address to be adopted by the Democrats at the Chicago convention; the preparing of these, and conferring with the Democratic leaders in regard to the same, being in the confidential employment of their government, in which he and his confreres are engaged."

Among the planks, Lincoln noted, was one saying: "The war to be further prosecuted, only to restore *the Union as it was*, and only in such manner that no further detriment to slave property shall be effected."

Lincoln wrote that he had found these paragraphs in Clay's proposed address: "Let all who are in favor of peace; of arresting the slaughter of our countrymen; of saving the country from bankruptcy and ruin; of securing food and raiment and good wages for the laboring classes; of disappointing the enemies of democratic and republican government who are rejoicing in the overthrow of our proudest monuments; of vindicating our capacity for self-government; arouse and sustain these principles and elect these candidates. ... "

Lincoln could not have enjoyed reading this comment by Clay: "The stupid tyrant who now disgraces the chair of Washington and Jackson could, any day, have peace and restoration of the Union; and would have them, only that he persists in the war merely to free the slaves."

To this, Lincoln adds these comments:

> The convention may not literally adopt Mr. Clay's Platform and Address, but we predict it will do so substantially. We shall see. Mr. Clay confesses to his Democratic friends that he is for *peace and disunion* but he says: "You cannot elect without a cry of war for the Union; but, once elected, we are friends, and can adjust matters somehow."
>
> He also says: "You will find some difficulty in proving that Lincoln could, if he would, have *peace* and *re-union* because Davis has not said so and will not say so; but you must assert it, and re-assert it, and stick to it, and it will pass as at least half proved."

Clay's proposed Democratic "Platform and Address," which mysteriously fell into Lincoln's hands, provides substantial evidence that the Confederate agents in Canada really were in cahoots with certain Democratic Party leaders in drafting a platform that would satisfy the Southerners and encourage them to return to the Union if assured of their states' rights—a euphemism, of course, for maintaining slavery.

To Abram Wakeman of New York, Lincoln wrote July 25:

The men of the South recently (and, perhaps still) at Niagara Falls, tell us distinctly that they are in the confidential employment of the rebellion; and they tell us as distinctly that they are not empowered to offer terms of peace. Does anyone doubt that what they *are* empowered to do is to assist in selecting and arranging a candidate and a platform for the Chicago convention? Who could have given them this confidential employment but he who only a week since declared to Jaquess and Gilmore that he had no terms of peace but the independence of the South—the dissolution of the Union? Thus the present presidential contest will almost certainly be no other than a contest between a Union and a Democratic candidate, disunion almost certainly following the latter. The issue is a mighty one for all people and all time; and whoever aids the right will be appreciated and remembered.

A. Lincoln.

Chapter Twenty-Five

A Spy Exposes Plot for Revolt

PRESIDENT LINCOLN'S CONCERNS about the machinations of the Confederates in Canada were justified. Indeed, he did not know the full extent of their schemes against his government. While Sanders, Clay, and Co, were romancing northern Democratic politicians at Niagara Falls, Jacob Thompson was pouring out a golden stream of cash to the Sons of Liberty, who promised to buy guns and ammunition for an armed revolt in Illinois, Indiana, and Ohio. Thompson believed these states could be organized into a Northwest Confederacy "to dictate terms of peace to the United States government." "If peace be not granted," he told his superiors in Richmond, "then it shall be war." He continued:

> Captain Thomas H. Hines shall command at Chicago and Captain John B. Castleman at Rock Island. If a movement could be made by our troops in Kentucky and Missouri, it could greatly facilitate matters in the West ... This would give courage and hope to the Northwestern people. The rank and file are weary of the war, but the violent abolitionists, preachers, contractors, and political press are all clamorous for its continuance.

If Lee can hold his own in front of Richmond and Johnston defeat Sherman in Georgia prior to the election, it seems probable that Lincoln will be defeated.

Thompson's grandiose dreams of victory were based upon the idea that thousands of Democrats in the Sons of Liberty were willing to risk their necks in a real, armed revolt instead of merely making bold speeches about how they would fight the "tyranny" of the Lincoln administration. But the premise was questionable. The Sons were never quite ready to fire the opening gun, so the date of the uprising had to be delayed several times. "Thus it was," Castleman recorded, "that the movement ... agreed for the Fourth of July, the sixteenth of July, for the twentieth of July, all alike indicated obvious timidity." Delegates who met July 20 in Chicago agreed upon a final date—August 16.

The postponement "was insisted upon the ground that it was necessary to have a series of public meetings to prepare the public mind," Thompson recalled, so immense "peace" rallies were staged at three Illinois cities, Peoria, Springfield, and Chicago—at Confederate expense. "To make the Peoria meeting a success, I agreed that so much money as was necessary would be furnished by me," Thompson told the Richmond authorities. "It was a decided success; the vast multitudes who attended seemed to be swayed by but one leading idea—peace." As they shouted for "peace, peace," the innocent masses never knew that the whole show was orchestrated and financed with Confederate gold.

The *Chicago Tribune* denounced the Peoria rally as "a convention of traitors" called by "Copperheads" including Chicago's own "Buck" Morris, "a flagrant Southern sympathizer who is identified body and soul with the Rebels." Judge Buckner Morris was a leader of the Peace Democrats in Illinois. His Chicago home was a haven for Confederates.

Thompson also got his money's worth from the Springfield assembly, which the *New York Herald* covered in an August 18 dispatch headlined: "Violent and Treasonable Speeches—Revolution Openly Recommended—Northwestern Confederacy Brewing." James W. Singleton told the crowd that there was but one issue, "war or peace." Henry Clay Dean said, "The way to correct the war was to refuse to vote supplies for the Union army."

All this time, Thompson and his fellow conspirators were blissfully unaware that their activities were being closely watched by Federal spies, some of whom had penetrated into the inner circles of the Sons of Liberty. General Carrington, commanding the Military District of Indiana, enlisted Felix Stidger, a young Kentuckian who had dropped out of the Union army after serving as a clerk, and persuaded him to become a Federal agent, with orders to worm his way into the secret order by posing as a Peace Democrat sympathetic to the South.

Stidger soon gained the confidence of Joshua Bullitt, chief justice of the Kentucky Supreme Court, who also secretly led the Sons of Liberty in that state. Judge Bullitt had hobnobbed with the Confederate agents at Niagara Falls. Favorably impressed by his young protégé, Bullitt named Stidger grand secretary of the order for Kentucky.

Stidger donned a gray "butternut" suit and a pair of spectacles and, posing as "J. J. Grundy," went to see Dr. William A. Bowles, the order's "major general" for Indiana. The spy visited the doctor's palatial health resort at French Lick Springs, a popular spa attended by throngs of people.

As commander of the Second Indiana Volunteers in the war with Mexico, Dr. Bowles was blamed for the rout of his troops in the battle of Buena Vista. Now, he was diligently arming a band of Butternut volunteers to take part in the revolt financed by the Confederates.

Dr. Bowles accepted the mild-mannered, bespectacled former clerk Stidger as a genuine Southerner and incautiously confided to him all his plans for the revolt. "He told me," Stidger reported, "that the forces of Indiana and Ohio would concentrate in Kentucky and make Kentucky their battleground, that the forces of Illinois would proceed to Saint Louis and cooperate with those of Missouri ... that the Rebel General Sterling Price would invade Missouri with 20,000 troops and that with 100,000 troops they could occupy and permanently hold Missouri."

Confederate Capt. T. N. Freeman, sent by Hines to help Dr. Bowles, described the ancient warrior as "a magnificent specimen of manhood, over six feet high, broad shouldered, straight as an arrow, very soldierly in bearing and as true to the South as his wife, a New

Orleans lady." Freeman went on: "While I was there, daily, men were coming to the Springs and reporting fully organized companies ready for service at his call. I was astonished … this grand old man had collected … quantities of arms and ammunition and, had two pieces of artillery concealed."

Stidger also learned that the forces in Indiana had arranged for help from Confederate Partisan Rangers in Kentucky, headed by Col. Adam Johnson. Captain Freeman was an officer in Johnson's Rangers.

The Confederate War Department knew about their plans for the revolt. Clerk John Beauchamp Jones noted in his diary that "the work" was to begin in August.

Stidger found out many secrets by becoming a trusted ally of Harrison Dodd, the Democratic politician who was the Grand Commander of the Sons of Liberty in Indiana. After meeting with the Confederate commissioners in Canada, Dodd attended the Chicago session, which set the date of the uprising at August 16. Dodd told Stidger that the armed Sons of Liberty would storm Camp Morton at Indianapolis, free the several thousand Rebel prisoners there and arm them with guns from the armories, hold Governor Morton as hostage "or kill him, as circumstances seemed best." With Morton out of the way, Indiana Secretary of State James Athon, a Democrat and a member of the Sons of Liberty, would take over as governor. If the members of the order did not soon rise in revolt, Dodd informed Stidger, "I will leave the country, for I'll be damned if I will live under such a government as the present administration."

On the night of July 29, Stidger met at the State House in Indianapolis with Governor Morton, Governor Thomas E. Bramblette of Kentucky, and Maj. Gen. Stephen G. Burbridge, the iron-fisted military boss of Kentucky. He told them all he had learned from Dodd about the plans made at Chicago for the revolt. The next day, Governor Bramblette and General Burbridge staged a statewide sweep of Kentucky, arresting about fifty men on suspicion of leading the Sons of Liberty. The same day, Judge Bullitt returned from a strategy session with the Confederates in Canada, carrying a leather satchel, which sagged. He said it was "god-damned heavy."

Soon after he stepped off the ferryboat at Louisville, Bullitt was arrested and his satchel was found to be loaded with gold coins. He had obtained the gold from a Montreal bank by cashing one of two $5,000 drafts which the Confederates had given him. The other draft was found in his pocket. When Stidger told Dodd about Bullitt's arrest and the exposure of the Rebel payoff, the spy recorded Dodd became so excited that he "gritted his teeth."

On an early August morning after his return to Indianapolis from his parley with the Confederates in Canada, Dodd visited Joseph J. Bingham, editor of the city's Democratic newspaper, the *State Sentinel*, swore him to secrecy, and told him about the plans for the revolt. Dodd demanded that Bingham, as acting chairman of the Democratic state central committee, call a mass meeting of Democrats in Indianapolis August 16, ostensibly for an antidraft protest but actually as a cover for the proposed attack to free Rebel prisoners at Camp Morton. Bingham flatly refused. He and Joseph E. McDonald, the Democrats' candidate for governor, agreed that "the thing must be stopped at all hazards."

Next, Michael Kerr, soon to be elected to Congress as a Democrat from southern Indiana, came to Bingham in a state of wild excitement and cried, "The devil's to pay in our section of the state!" Farmers were so frightened about the talk of revolution, Kerr said, that they were "selling the hay in the fields and their wheat in the stacks," and converting their property into greenbacks which, unlike grain, could not be confiscated or destroyed. Kerr, a fellow member of the Sons of Liberty, expressed fear that Governor Morton would be captured and Dr. Athon put in his place.

At an emergency meeting of state Democratic Party leaders called to stop the revolt, Dodd and J. C. Walker revealed that the plan was to strike simultaneously at Columbus, Cincinnati, and Chicago. They had recently met Sanders and Holcombe at the Clifton House in Niagara Falls and agreed upon the plot.

Gubernatorial candidate McDonald and others protested against the revolution as "madness" and prevailed upon Dodd to issue a circular ordering the various lodges to cancel it. The politicians feared that an attempted coup would ruin their party's chances of defeating Morton in the October election. The governor would cite it as proof of his oft-repeated charge that the Democrats were in cahoots with Rebel revolutionaries helping Jefferson Davis.

A *Cincinnati Gazette* correspondent, revealing the Democrats' decision to squelch the revolt, wrote: "I also learn on undoubted authority that one of the delegates to the Chicago convention, a peace man, states that terms of peace from the rebel government will be submitted to that convention." This report adds credence to Lincoln's suspicion that Clay, in Canada, was drafting a sample platform for the Democrats.

On August 11, Dr. Bowles sent Captain Freeman of the Partisan Rangers to tell Dodd that he was all set to move on New Albany, Indiana, with 5,000 men and two pieces of artillery, to carry out his part in the revolt.

"Well, it's too late," Dodd retorted. "The government knows all our plans. They are rushing reinforcements to the prison guards." Dodd told Freeman to inform Dr. Bowles that "the whole plan must be indefinitely postponed." When the captain delivered this message, he recalled, "Bowles was the maddest man I ever saw." Bowles shouted that Dodd was "the damnedest idiot" for failing to go ahead with the uprising anyway. "He should have ordered the attack at once. We were better prepared than they were. He has thrown away the best chance we will ever have."

Captain Hines, upon receiving Freeman's bad news, said the feisty old doctor was right. "Freeman," he said, "Bowles is the only soldier among the whole lot."

"I believe fully that had there been even half a dozen military men as Colonel Bowles among the leaders of the Sons of Liberty, the whole theater of war would have been transferred to Ohio, Indiana, and Illinois in the fall of 1864, and the final issue would have been a Southern, a Northwestern, and an Eastern Confederacy," Freeman commented.

More disasters for the Confederates' friends soon followed.

On August 20, Governor Morton received a letter from a woman in New York saying, "The Copperheads of Indiana have ordered and paid for thirty thousand revolvers and forty-two boxes of fixed ammunition to be distributed among the antagonists of the government for the purpose of controlling the presidential election. ... Thirty-two boxes of the above have been forwarded to J. J. Parsons, Indianapolis, via Merchants' Dispatch, and marked 'Sunday school books.'"

On the governor's orders, a detail of soldiers raided Dodd's printing office and found 32 boxes, containing 400 navy revolvers and 35,000 rounds of ammunition. "The pistols alone would cost close to one million dollars," the *Indianapolis Daily Journal* estimated.

At a mass meeting August 22, Governor Morton charged that the money for the weapons had been supplied either directly by Confederate officials or by their authorized agents in New York. "Some months ago," he noted,

> the Confederate authorities had borrowed fifteen million dollars in Europe, for which they issued cotton bonds, and every blockade runner carries out cotton to repay the loan. The object of the loan was primarily to purchase a navy in European ports, including the celebrated rams. That speculation having failed by the refusal of the governments of England and France to permit the rams to depart ... the Peace Commissioners are in funds and they could not make an investment more to the advantage of their masters than to purchase arms and ammunition for Northern traitors, and to pay Northern demagogues liberally for shrieking for peace, free speech and liberty.

"It is all one thing to Jefferson Davis whether we fall by means of a defeat in the coming elections or by the overthrow of the Union arms in the field," Morton told the crowd. "If we elect a candidate for the presidency who is in favor of withdrawing our armies from the field and recognizing the independence of the southern Confederates, they will gain their object just as effectually as if they had annihilated the last Union army."

A few days later came even sadder news for the Rebels and their friends: Col. Adam Johnson, who had counted upon leading his Kentucky Rangers in the Indiana uprising, was shot in the head and permanently blinded in a skirmish with Federal troops in Kentucky. The bullet entered directly behind one eye, severing the optic nerve, and came out through the other eyeball. Fortunately, Johnson's brain escaped injury. He recovered, returned to Richmond in a prisoner exchange, and was promoted to brigadier general.

Chapter Twenty-Six
Lincoln Fears Defeat

IN THE GLOOMY MONTH OF AUGUST, when Union armies were stalled before Richmond and Atlanta, President Lincoln was besieged by anxious Republicans who feared that he faced certain defeat in his bid for a second term.

Pennsylvania editor Alexander McClure, a friend of the administration, spent an hour with Lincoln in the White House and commented afterwards, "I never saw him more dejected in my life. His face, always sad in repose, was then saddened until it was a picture of despair, and he spoke of the want of sincere and earnest support from the Republican leaders. New York was regarded as almost hopelessly lost and Pennsylvania trembling in the balance."

Thurlow Weed told Lincoln, to his face, that his reelection was "an impossibility" because "the people are wild for peace."

"You think I don't know I am going to be beaten but *I do,*" the president told another visitor, "and unless some great change takes place, *badly beaten.*"

Henry J. Raymond, the Republican national chairman, told Lincoln, "I am in active correspondence with your friends in every state and from them all I hear but one report. The tide is setting strongly against us." Raymond, the *New York Times* editor, predicted that New York state "would go fifty thousand votes against us tomorrow, and so of the rest. Nothing but the most resolute and decided action on the part of the government and its friends can save the country from falling into hostile hands." Raymond noted two principal causes for the despair—"the want of military success" and the idea that "we are not to have peace *in any event* under this administration until Slavery is abandoned."

That suspicion arose from Lincoln's "To whom it may concern" letter, which specified that his peace terms called for not only Confederate surrender but also "the end of slavery." A correspondent told Gen. Benjamin F. Butler: "Mothers, sisters, wives who have husbands, brothers and sons in service are indignant at the prospect to prosecute the war on the solitary issue of abolition. ... The crafty politicians of the South have humbugged the ... Democratic leaders with the idea that peace may be had without fighting on the basis of the Union as it was and the Constitution as it is."

Horace Greeley wrote to Lincoln:

> Nine-tenths of the whole American people, North and South, are anxious for peace—peace on almost any terms—and utterly sick of human slaughter and devastation. I know that, to the general eye, it now seems that the rebels are anxious to negotiate and that we repulse their advances. I know that if this impression be not removed we shall be beaten out of sight next November. ... Your trusted advisers all think that I ought to go to Fort Lafayette. ... The cry has steadily been, No truce! No armistice! No negotiation! No mediation! ... I beg you, I implore you to inaugurate or invite proposals for peace forthwith; and in case peace cannot now be made, consent to an armistice for one year, each party to retain unmolested, all it now holds, but the rebel ports to be opened. Meantime let a national convention be held and there will surely be no more war at all events.

In this situation, a distinguished Democrat, Judge Jeremiah Sullivan Black, saw a ray of hope for a compromise peace. The tall

Pennsylvania jurist, with a loosely fitting wig of thick black hair, had been secretary of state in President Buchanan's cabinet and had arranged that his former job as attorney general be given to his friend, Edwin M. Stanton.

Although Stanton had gone over to the Republicans and become Lincoln's secretary of war, Black still considered him a friend, and paid him a visit. They talked about the political situation and Stanton's fears for his own future in case of a Lincoln defeat. A few days later, in mid-August, Black turned up in Canada to see a third member of the Buchanan cabinet, Jacob Thompson, former secretary of the interior and now heading the Confederate mission.

Black gave the impression that he came as an envoy from Stanton, who was extremely afraid that Lincoln would lose the election and that his cabinet members "would be treated with contumely and violence." It was typical of Stanton, the bully, to be afraid of suffering from "violence," in case of a Lincoln defeat.

Stanton, who had a morbid fear of death, had often displayed panic before. He paced about the White House like a crazy man in March 1862, fearing that the Confederate ironclad warship, the *Merrimac*, would soon steam up the Potomac and attack Washington. After the second battle of Bull Run, he was afraid that victorious Rebels would capture the capital and himself; he most recently had more jitters when Jubal Early's tatterdemalions had swooped down across Maryland in their surprise raid, threatening the capital's defenses before skedaddling back to Virginia.

According to the Confederates' accounts of Judge Black's conversations with them at Toronto, he said Stanton deplored Lincoln's manifesto, "To whom it may concern." Lincoln's declaration that his non-negotiable peace terms included "the end of slavery" led to charges that he would carry on the war indefinitely to free all the slaves. Stanton, Black said, called Lincoln's manifesto "a grave blunder," which would defeat him "unless he could countervail it by some demonstration of his willingness to accept other terms," Commissioner Clay reported to Richmond. Clay added: "Judge Black wished to know if Mr. Thompson would go to Washington to discuss terms of peace, and proceed thence to Richmond, saying that Mr. Stanton desired him to do so and would send him safe-conduct for that purpose. I doubt not that Judge Black came at the instance of Mr. Stanton."

Clay had good reason for trusting this report about Stanton's panicky desire to rescue Lincoln from the "grave blunder." Black had been Pennsylvania's chief justice, had a sterling reputation as a man of total integrity, and could be expected to give an accurate report about his old friend, Stanton.

"Mr. Stanton was not averse, therefore, to some negotiation which might be the basis of peace, and for that purpose he had desired Judge Black to confer with Mr. Thompson and ascertain his views," Hines and Castleman wrote in their account of "The Northwest Conspiracy." "Judge Black stated that his desire was to open some negotiations for peace without the condition ... of final and eternal separation" because the Northern people would not agree to an independent Confederacy. Mr. Thompson replied that he was not authorized to make any positive reply ... that they demanded the right of self-government."

Upon returning to his home in York, Pennsylvania, Judge Black sent Stanton a long report which began: "Agreeably to the wish expressed by you in our last conversation. ... I saw Mr. Thompson of Mississippi ..." The jurist interpreted Thompson's comments in these words, concerning his fellow Southerners: "They struck for independence because that was the simplest and readiest means of saving the rights of the states from violation. Independence was entirely a means to an end, the end being the security of state rights. If they could now have some absolutely certain guarantee that the same end might be accomplished in the Federal union, they are not so perverse as to fight an army of half a million men and expose their country to desolation for a punctilio."

Because Stanton had said Lincoln blundered by insisting upon "the end of slavery" as an essential precondition for peace, Black told Stanton: "If it be probable that the attitude of the government ... will change and negotiations can proceed upon the basis of a constitutional union, I am thoroughly convinced that peace, harmony, and a union never again to be broken are very near at hand. If I were in your place I would advise the President to suspend hostilities for three or six months and commence negotiations in good earnest, unless he has irrevocably made up his mind to fight it out on the emancipation issue." Echoing Commissioner Clay's views, Black concluded by saying: "It is perfectly certain that they will at once agree to a close commercial arrangement and to a military alliance offensive and defensive, for the protection of American interests."

Stanton sent a sharp reply to the suggestion that he urge Lincoln to accept an armistice. "You go for an armistice, which is nothing more and nothing else than what South Carolina wanted when the rebellion began," Stanton wrote. "You and I then opposed it as fatal to our government and our national existence; I still oppose it on the same ground."

Stanton was enraged and embarrassed because the *New York Herald* on August 22 said Judge Black had visited Thompson on behalf of the administration and that the idea of an armistice and a convention of the states had been discussed.

Black told Stanton that he had nothing to do with the newspaper article, but his disclaimer could not calm the secretary's rage. Stanton had been caught criticizing the president behind Lincoln's back and therefore he had to deny it to save face, or some other part of his anatomy. Stanton claimed that he had not sent Black to Canada to see the Confederates. In reply, Black insisted that he had visited Thompson in accordance with Stanton's wish and approval.

Defying calls for compromise, Lincoln made an emotional defense of his antislavery policy when visited August 19 by two Wisconsin men, former Governor Alexander Randall and J. T. Mills, a circuit judge. "There have been men base enough to have proposed to me to return to slavery the black warriors of Port Hudson and Olustee, and thus earn the respect of the masters they fought," Lincoln said. "Should I do so, I should deserve to be damned in time and eternity. Come what will I will keep my faith with friend and foe."

"My enemies pretend that I am now carrying on this war for the sole purpose of abolition," the president said. "So long as I am president, it shall be carried on for the sole purpose of restoring the Union. But no human power can subdue this rebellion without the use of the emancipation policy."

Lincoln estimated that nearly 200,000 former slaves were serving in the Union war effort, most of them in the army and navy. Democratic strategy, he said, required that all the blacks in the Union forces be disbanded. "Abandon all the posts now garrisoned by black men, take two hundred thousand men from our side and put them in the battlefield or the corn field against us," he said, "and we would be compelled to abandon the war in three weeks."

"There is no program offered by any wing of the Democratic party but that must result in the permanent destruction of the Union," the president asserted.

"But Mr. President," one of his guests protested, "General McClellan is in favor of crushing out the rebellion by force. He will be the Chicago candidate."

"Sir," Lincoln replied, "the slightest knowledge of arithmetic will prove to any man that the Rebel armies cannot be destroyed by strategy. It would sacrifice all the white men of the North to do it."

Judge Mills published an account of this interview in the Grant County, Wisconsin, *Herald* and it was later reprinted in Republican papers across the country.

Clearly, Lincoln was arguing that the blacks were indispensable to winning the war, and, without them, thousands more white men would have to join the army or be drafted. Lincoln was already having enough trouble with his call for half a million more troops and the prospect of conscription. Many of the recruits for Grant's army were criminals, bounty-jumpers, and reluctant warriors thrown into the ranks to replace soldiers killed in Virginia and others who had refused to reenlist when their terms of service expired.

Fortunately for Lincoln, Jefferson Davis was having even more trouble filling the thinning ranks of his armies, for he had no reserves. "The rebels have now in their ranks their last man," General Grant said in a mid-August letter to Congressman Elihu Washburne of Illinois. "The little boys and old men are guarding prisoners, guarding rail-road bridges, and forming a good part of their garrisons for intrenched positions. A man lost by them cannot be replaced. They have robbed the cradle and the grave equally to get their present force. Besides what they lose in frequent skirmishes and battles they are now loosing (sic) from desertions and other causes at least one regiment per day."

Grant had no doubt that the Confederates were "exceedingly anxious to hold out until after the presidential election," hoping for a "counter revolution" or the election of the "peace candidate."

Lincoln feared that McClellan, if elected, would be compelled by peace advocates to accept an armistice that must lead to a compromise peace. On August 23, he asked his cabinet members to sign the back of a memorandum that he had penned and folded up and pasted so that they could not read it. They could not know the text until after the election.

This was Lincoln's secret memorandum: "This morning, as for some days past, it seems exceedingly probable that this Administration will not be reelected. Then it will be my duty to so cooperate with the President elect, as to save the Union between the election and the inauguration as he will have secured his election on such ground that he cannot possibly save it afterwards."

On August 25, Henry J. Raymond came to pressure Lincoln into going along with a gesture for political purposes, to dispel the notion that he refused to accept any peace without the end of slavery. Backed by the Republican National Committee, Chairman Raymond proposed that the president send a commission to Jefferson Davis, offering peace on the one condition that the South give up its independence and accept the Constitution, all other issues—including slavery—to be settled by a national convention. Raymond feared that, without such an appeal, Lincoln would lose to McClellan.

"Hell is to pay," Nicolay wrote to Hay in Illinois that day. "The politicians and the National Committee are here today. R. thinks a commission to Richmond is about the only salt to save us—while the Tycoon sees and says it would be utter ruination ... Weak-kneed damned fools ... are in the movement for a new candidate to supplant the Tycoon. Everything is in darkness and doubt and discouragement."

Under pressure from panicky politicians, Lincoln reluctantly drafted a paper carrying out the idea of a peace commission to Richmond. But he hated the very idea of writing a letter to Jefferson Davis; he could not bring himself to go through with it. He concluded that sending an emissary to Davis would be worse than losing the election, because it would be surrendering it in advance. So he scrapped the whole thing, and Raymond returned to New York and set to work trying to head off the dump Lincoln plot.

The prime movers in the scheme, summoned by former mayor George Opdyke of New York, called for a new convention in

Cincinnati September 28 to combine all the Republican strength behind a single fresh candidate—assuming that both Lincoln and Frémont would drop out. Horace Greeley wrote: "Mr. Lincoln is already beaten. He cannot be elected. And we must have another ticket to save us from utter overthrow." He suggested General Butler, Grant, or Sherman for president and Adm. David Farragut for vice president. Farragut had become famous in August for driving his fleet into Mobile Bay, Alabama, shouting, "Damn the torpedoes—full speed ahead!"

General Butler was more than willing to be drafted for the White House. His chief of staff, J. W. Shaffer, was scouting the political arena for him in New York and wrote: "I have seen and talked with nearly all the leading men in the city and they are all of the opinion in regard to Lincoln. They consider him defeated. ... It is the judgment of all the best politicians in this city and elsewhere that he can't carry three states." One politician declared: "The country has gone to hell!"

Chapter Twenty-Seven
Peace Democrats Oppose McClellan

AS THE GLOOM OF LINCOLN and the Republicans deepened in late August, the Democrats enjoyed a surge of optimism and began to see bright visions of being ensconced once more in the White House. It looked as if the presidential nominee of their national convention at Chicago opening August 29 would surely beat Lincoln. So the war and peace factions, and others, waged intense battles to determine which would achieve control of the party.

The *Philadelphia Inquirer* accurately defined the rival groups: "First," it said, "one interest, composed of a large body of influential politicians of which Tammany Hall is the type, is in favor of a war policy with some popular general as a candidate"—obviously General McClellan.

"Another interest, also numerous and powerful, advocating such action at Chicago as will combine all the opposition to the present administration so as to make sure of its overthrow. ...

"The third interest is made up of out-and-out advocates of 'peace on any terms,' who are led by Fernando Wood, Vallandigham, and others of the same kidney. They want a 'peace' platform at Chicago and an unequivocal 'peace' candidate like Thomas H. Seymour for President."

Besides Seymour, a former governor of Connecticut, there was some support for two former presidents, Millard Fillmore and Franklin Pierce, and a Supreme Court justice—Samuel Nelson. But such fossils from the past could not arouse the enthusiasm expressed for McClellan, who was only thirty-seven. Little Mac had the appeal of youth as well as his charming personality and his status as a martyr who, according to his friends, had lost command of the Army of the Potomac because of Republican political intrigue.

Ever since S. L. M. Barlow had begun dreaming of the general in the presidency in 1861, the campaign machine had been moving swiftly and silently to lock up convention delegates. The New York State Democratic convention in February barred Fernando Wood and his brother, Ben, from the delegation because they advocated a negotiated peace. It placed Governor Horatio Seymour at the head of a strong delegation, officially noninstructed as a courtesy to the governor, who harbored presidential aspirations of his own. Under pressure, Seymour announced in the newspapers that he would not be a candidate, but he did not give up his ambitions.

The delegation from Pennsylvania, another crucial state, seemed assured for McClellan, who was a Philadelphia native, through the influence of the Eastern railroad executives and financiers who predominated in New York. McClellan now resided near Orange, New Jersey, having moved out of the spacious Manhattan house donated to him by his wealthy friends; the New Jersey delegates were sewn up for McClellan through the power of Camden and Amboy Railroad executives who dominated the politics of that Democratic state.

Manton Marble, editor of the *New York World*, the pro-Democratic newspaper largely bankrolled by Barlow, consistently banged the drum for McClellan in news stories and editorials. Congressman Samuel S. Cox of Ohio, who campaigned vigorously for McClellan, wrote to Marble from Columbus, Ohio: "There is but one voice among the masses of our party … that Lincoln must be beaten by McClellan."

Beyond the East, however, the general encountered fierce opposition from the "peace" faction, which controlled the Democratic Party apparatus in several states, notably Illinois, Indiana, and Ohio. Led by Clement Vallandigham, the "peace" men were demanding a platform and a candidate pledged to an immediate armistice and peace.

The power of the peace men was shown by the hero's welcome which greeted the return home of Cincinnati congressman Alexander Long, who had narrowly escaped expulsion from the House because he had called for recognition of the Southern Confederacy as an independent nation. When the "Hon. Aleck" arrived in Hamilton County, a reporter observed that he was surrounded by four hundred constituents, all eager to shake his hand. The Rev. G. W. Maley, praying for the end of "this cruel war, which has raged for over three long, dark and bloody years," praised the congressman for having the courage to stand up against "the clamorers for war, blood and carnage."

Those Democrats demanding peace at almost any price would have preferred Vallandigham to head the ticket but that was impossible because he was too divisive. It was too much to expect the party to name "a convicted felon"—as his enemies called him—for the presidency. Many Peace Democrats favored Thomas Seymour even though he was denounced by the *Cincinnati Commercial* as "a vain, brainless man."

Some of the strongest eastern Democrats were leading McClellan's campaign, so he had only to rest at his New Jersey home and receive their advice. In addition to Barlow, the general had powerful sponsors in Dean Richmond, boss of the New York Central Railroad, and August Belmont, the Democratic national chairman, who wielded considerable influence as the American representative of the Rothschild financial empire in Europe.

Enemies, envious of his wealth and power, sneered at Belmont as an "Austrian Jew" speculator, typical of the financial "nabobs" controlling McClellan. Born in the Palatinate in Western Europe in 1816, Belmont entered the House of Rothschild at age fourteen, his first job being to sweep out the office in Frankfurt-am-Main. Through his industry and intelligence, he rose quickly to positions of trust in Naples and Havana. After the 1837 financial crash in the U. S., he sailed from Cuba to New York, rented a small office in Wall Street, and founded the firm that eventually grew into the great banking house of August Belmont and Company.

At age twenty-five, the hot-blooded financier fought a duel with William Heyward of South Carolina after an argument at the theater. Belmont deliberately fired into the air but his opponent's shot inflicted a severe leg wound, which caused Belmont to limp for the rest of his life. In 1849, the banker enhanced his prestige in New York society by marrying Caroline Perry, daughter of Commodore Matthew Perry, and a niece of John Slidell, a former senator from Louisiana and following secession, the Confederate envoy to Paris.

A *New York Times* editorial observed that McClellan was being boomed by a "Mutual Admiration Association," of which "the chief bottle-washers are Messrs. Barlow, Marble, Belmont and the other acknowledged friends of the Little Giant."

To show New York's strong support for McClellan, his promoters staged a mass meeting that filled much of Union Square in Manhattan on August 10. Former congressman John B. Haskin praised him as the victor at Antietam who had received a telegram of fervent thanks from President Lincoln after the battle and yet was summarily sacked because he opposed emancipation. (Hisses, groans, and cheers.) William D. Murphy called the war "unnecessary and unholy" and denounced Lincoln as "a … criminal whose garments were dripping with the blood of his countrymen." (Cheers.) C. C. Eagan, amid "hisses and groans," said that if Lincoln had not "perverted the war from war for the Union to a war for the abolition of slavery … we should have had peace long ago."

To their dismay, the New York Democratic chieftains supporting McClellan found opposition right on their own doorstep. A huge crowd at a Syracuse peace rally August 18 cheered Vallandigham, Fernando Wood, and former California Governor John Weller because they demanded an immediate armistice and a national convention to make a compromise peace.

Noting that Lincoln had vowed to carry on the war for three more years, if necessary, Vallandigham predicted that the Democratic convention would nominate a candidate "who will be committed to a suspension of hostilities and a convention of states." "The South has proposed, through her press and agents, to meet us to see if we cannot agree, so that peace and prosperity will be once more restored to our country," Vallandigham said. "They, too, are tired and weary of war.

They too, want an armistice and a convention." If he had possessed the power, Vallandigham said, "not one drop of blood would have been shed" in this unnecessary war. "Ruin is impending and now, in the fourth year of the war, what better is the prospect of success? The campaign of 1864 opened with the largest armies the war had yet seen … and with what result? The record of carnage and blood."

A man named O. P. Rookes, who attended the Syracuse peace rally, reported one speaker as saying, "I tell you, gentlemen, Jefferson Davis is fighting the battles for the liberties of this country and he must and shall succeed." New York's Governor Seymour was quoted as declaring: "Gentlemen, we have got to stop this war. It must be stopped, and if Old Abe should finally be re-elected, we have got to raise a counterrevolution and overthrow the entire cursed abolition horde." His call for a "counter-revolution" indicated that the New York governor was angling for the support of the antiwar forces in a bid for the Democratic presidential nomination although he had officially declined to be a candidate.

Soon Vallandigham and Weller would be on their way to the Chicago convention to write a Democratic Party platform calling the war "a failure," and some of their followers hoped that McClellan, whose reputation was based entirely upon his wartime services, would refuse to run on such a platform. They would then be free to name an all-out "peace" candidate for the presidency, probably one of the Seymours.

McClellan's hopes for a quick and easy nomination were dimmed by the harsh reality that the advocates of a peace candidate on a peace platform probably would dominate the convention. "The majority of the delegates … are 'Peace Democrats' and the rest have not enough war spirit in them to scare a sheep," commented the *Sacramento Union*. This pro-Lincoln newspaper could see little difference between the openly pro-Confederate Congressmen Long and Benjamin Gwinn Harris and "such men as Horatio Seymour and S. S. Cox." "It is just the difference between rebel soldiers in butternut uniforms and rebel soldiers disguised in Union blue." At Chicago, it surmised, "such lovers of masquerade as Horatio Seymour may persuade that delectable conclave to manufacture a kind of loyal harness for 'the war horse of Antietam.'"

McClellan's chief strategist, Barlow, stayed away from the convention and relied upon the strong men in the New York delegation to protect McClellan's interests against the mounting threats to his bandwagon. Marble, the *New York World* editor, although not a delegate, became an influential force at Chicago. Arriving there several days before the convention's opening day, he noted all the latest twists and turns of events and reported them to Barlow, who relayed the bulletins quickly to McClellan at his home in New Jersey. Barlow peppered Marble with dispatches urging the greatest vigilance. "The conviction now seems to be almost universal that no one but McClellan can control any large portion of the army vote in the field and at home, that he alone can prevent the use of the army by Mr. Lincoln to deprive us of an opportunity of voting freely in November," Barlow advised Marble August 21.

Confidently predicting that McClellan would be nominated on the first ballot, Barlow said he had "no doubt" that Governor Seymour could "control the honest peace men of the West and show them that our only safety lies in success, and that with McClellan peace is certain. This ought to make them willing to so frame the platform as to enable all who are in opposition to Mr. Lincoln's policy to unite with us as, after all, mere platforms cannot control as against events, either for peace or for war."

"As to the Vice Presidency, great care must be taken to prevent a nomination that will weaken the ticket," Barlow cautioned. "If a Border State man is presented by his friends who is otherwise unobjectionable, I think we should gain by such a nomination." "If our friends are wise, and do not absolutely throw away success, I have no doubt of our ability to elect McClellan and to restore the Union," Barlow wrote. "With any other man, we utterly lose the army vote. We lose the support of tens of thousands of honest Republicans who will support him but will not support any other man unless we take a Republican pure and simple."

On August 24, Barlow ordered Marble to see Washington McLean, boss of the pro-Southern *Cincinnati Enquirer*, "to head off an attempt to give the Democratic nomination" to John Charles Frémont "on the basis of a promise from F. to declare for an immediate armistice and a convention." Frémont, the deposed Union general running as an independent presidential candidate, had friends who were trying to foist him onto the Democrats. Barlow said McLean was "entirely satisfied" that McClellan "is for peace, not war, that, if he is nominated, he would prefer to restore the Union by peaceful means, rather than by war ... and with these assurances he professes to be entirely convinced that McClellan should be nominated as the strongest man.

"We have all sorts of rumors as to bargains and tricks, first with Seymour, then with Fremont, then with Guthrie. I place no credence upon any of them."

Marble telegraphed some disturbing reports that the New York governor was angling for the presidency. Admitting "some uneasiness" over this news, Barlow replied: "I think you will be able to counteract the Seymour movement by convincing the doubters that we cannot carry this state or Pa. with Seymour."

Such was the mood of McClellan's friends—outwardly confident but inwardly worried about the "peace" men and the tricks they could play against him.

Meanwhile, the Confederates in Canada kept a close eye on Democratic delegates who just happened to pass through Niagara Falls on their way to Chicago for consultation about the candidates and the platform. "The rebels in Canada prefer to bring about a settlement through the Democracy and are inclined to wait for the action of the Chicago convention," the *New York Herald* revealed in a dispatch from Clifton House August 22. "Delegates and outsiders are passing Niagara now on every train for Chicago," the paper said. "The delegations from the New England states went to New York to consult tonight and tomorrow night. There was an immense crowd at the Falls yesterday, among them several delegates."

Chapter Twenty-Eight
Mint Juleps and Sherry Cobblers

Two slightly "tight" Democrats at the Chicago convention met on the steps of the Sherman House and set forth for an evening's entertainment. According to the *Cincinnati Commercial*, this conversation occurred:

"'Let's go and see the women tonight.'"

"'Why, they've run them all out o' town. There ain't a whore in Chicago. They arrest every one they find.'"

"'Well, by God! I don't know what this country will come to if Lincoln is in four more years. Personal liberty is gone to hell!'"

→ • ←

CHICAGO, IN THE SIZZLING DAYS of late August, throbbed with excitement as a throng of shouting, cheering, drinking Democrats descended upon the booming rail center on Lake Michigan. Trains of eleven railroads, chuffing, clanging, rattling, and befouling the air with clouds of coal smoke and cinders, delivered mobs of politicians, ward heelers and ruffians from Eastern cities, all determined to name the next president of the United States and to have a grand time doing it amid the temptations of the city.

"The city is swarming like a huge beehive," the *Chicago Tribune* observed. The hotels were all jammed, so men slept four to a room when they slept at all, and some had to rest on cots in the lobbies. One observer called it a convention of "red noses," noting that many delegates "promise impetus to the retail liquor trade."

The saloons were crowded with thirsty men swallowing mint juleps and sherry cobblers although it cost "a five-dollar Treasury note" for a fellow to treat his friends. "But," said the *Tribune,* "there are men in Chicago just now who have plenty of greenbacks and 'don't give a damn about expenses.'"

One delegation arriving from the East on Saturday night, August 27, found flags and fireworks on Courthouse Square and noisy spectators surrounding speakers at various places around the square who were shouting for Seymour, Vallandigham, and Fernando Wood. All night long, the uproar raged on and one sleepy traveler saw "Sunday morning dawning on a vast mob, gone mad and yelling for more speeches."

The Sabbath day was spent, not in quiet religious meditation, but in "a perfect saturnalia" of politicians caucusing and quarreling over rival candidates. Much of the "outside pressure" was exerted for McClellan, "the Grave-digger of the Chickahominy," as his critics called him. "Thousands of short boys, plug uglies, shoulder hitters, Blood Tubs"— riotous fighters from the gangs of New York—were brought in at the expense of wealthy Democrats such as August Belmont. Against them were arrayed thousands of the plain people from Illinois and Indiana farms who camped with their wagons on the edge of the city and prepared to storm the convention hall and cheer for a "peace" candidate and platform.

Into the maelstrom of seething Chicago, slipping in quietly by twos and threes, came seventy tough Confederate soldiers who had escaped from Yankee prisons, fled to Canada, and were returning in a daring campaign to free a potential army of other Rebel prisoners in the vicinity of Chicago. Riding in on trains from Toronto, they were disguised in civilian clothes to look like just another bunch of countrified Butternuts, coming to see the convention.

These Rebels were running a great risk, for they could be captured and possibly even shot as spies. They were under the command of Capt. Thomas H. Hines, who traveled under the name of "Dr. Hunter." "These courageous men were as if over dynamite mines likely to explode at any moment," said the commander's right-hand man, Capt. John B. Castleman.

Hines and Castleman expected about 5,000 men of the Sons of Liberty—all Democrats—to be mingling in the throngs of the convention city. Many had received guns at the expense of the generous Confederate Jacob Thompson, who had poured out a stream of gold to arm the Sons and transport them to Chicago.

Rumors about the presence of Confederate soldiers in Chicago caused great uneasiness among the citizens. "There is a feverish anxiety all over the city, especially among the women," the *New York Times* reported, continuing,

> There are so many stories afloat as to the purpose of the Copperheads, that it creates much excitement. It is feared that one part of the plot is to release the Rebel prisoners in Camp Douglas, in which case all expect the city to be fired and plundered. … The wives and families of all the officers have been removed from the camp. … The seizure of arms in Indianapolis and the general belief that the Irish are armed here, adds not a little to the general concern. Never was a political convention held in this country around which cluster so many omens of evil.

"There are now nine thousand Rebel prisoners in the barracks at Rock Island, Illinois, and 5,577 at Camp Douglas, Chicago," according to a newspaper report. "There are also several hundred at Alton. Thus, there is a considerable Rebel army in Illinois."

Col. B. J. Sweet, the Camp Douglas commandant, appealed for more troops and warned his superiors that the Confederates coming in squads from Toronto would try to free the prisoners and that would be the signal for "a general insurrection in Indiana and Illinois." Captain Hines certainly hoped to prove the colonel an accurate prophet.

Despite all their brave boasts about being ready to battle against Old Abe Lincoln's tyranny, the Sons were not soldiers hardened by war or well disciplined; they were only civilians, so they had to be coerced into a clash with Federal troops. How to do that? Castleman wrote: "It was understood that any arrest would mean such overt act of oppression must be resisted. We knew that an arrest by troops would supply our hopes of success … an inflammable crowd might thus be led beyond retreat."

On Sunday night, August 28, Hines and Castleman assembled their seventy veteran Rebel soldiers with some of the Sons of Liberty in their rooms in the Richmond House. The suite bore a sign, "Missouri Delegation." The Camp Douglas prisoners had been tipped off that their rescuers were coming, so they were all set to attack the guards and fight their way to freedom whenever their saviors would storm the gates.

However, Castleman recorded, the commanders of the Sons of Liberty were "appalled" by the actual demand for overt action against armed forces. And when Hines called for 5,000 men to assault Camp Douglas, the commanders' excuses "made evident a hesitancy about the sacrifice of life." This was far more than the Sons of Liberty had bargained for. They had not expected to be called upon to risk their lives. They feared that the Camp Douglas guards had been lately increased to 7,000 soldiers—not 3,000 as Hines insisted—and those Yankee troops would fire real bullets that could kill!

Hines gave the chieftains twenty-four hours to assemble their men, who were scattered all over Chicago and in no semblance of military order. But when they met again the following night, the faint-hearted were even more frightened than ever. So the attack on Camp Douglas—which had aroused so much trepidation all over Chicago—had to be abandoned. Then the Confederates asked for a mere 500 men to help them take the prison at nearby Rock Island, where the chances of success would be better and the risks of casualties much smaller. There, only 700 Yankees were guarding 9,000 captive Rebels.

Castleman recalled: "Captain Hines agreed that if, with five hundred Western men and twenty Confederate soldiers, I would run through on the regular train to Rock Island, he would, with fifty Confederate soldiers, control all the wires and railroads out of

Chicago ... and take possession of the arsenal at Springfield." But even such a small force could not be mustered from the timorous civilians, so the Confederates realized that their glorious plans were hopeless.

They also became aware that, if they stayed any longer in Chicago they could be risking their lives for nothing. So Hines called the seventy Rebel soldiers together at the Richmond House and offered them three choices. Of the seventy soldiers, twenty chose to go South to rejoin their old regiments; twenty-three returned to Canada; and the rest stayed in Illinois to follow their two captains on a rampage of sabotage. In the ensuing weeks, they moved around central and southern Illinois as a band of partisan marauders and burned several steamboats carrying supplies for Federal troops and government installations.

In the National Archives is a letter written by one of the Confederate soldiers, apparently to Commissioner C. C. Clay in Canada, explaining why the raid on Camp Douglas had to be called off:

> In accordance with your orders I left Saint Catharines Friday evening Aug. 27th for Chicago to engage with my company in the enterprise contemplated by yourself and Col. Thompson for the release of Camp Douglas prisoners. Upon reaching Chicago, we found that already a strong guard had been collected and veteran regiments were still arriving. One regiment was placed in the enclosure with the Confederates and 16 (sixteen) pieces of field artillery were parked, ready to open upon those defenseless men in case an attack was made. ...
>
> Caps. Hines & Castleman decided to make no effort in that direction. We quietly waited ... hoping something would turn up by which we could benefit our suffering comrades and enhance the glory of the Confederacy. It was then determined to make an attempt upon Rock Island if the Copperheads would furnish a small portion of the long promised aid. When brought to the test Walker, Barrett, Dodd & Co. could not furnish fifty (50) men for the purpose. Hines and Castleman then admitted the thing a failure and gave the men a choice of returning to Canada or accompanying them to Egypt [southern Illinois]."

This Confederate soldier's letter is but one of many pieces of direct, contemporary evidence proving that the plot to free Rebel prisoners in the Northwest was real. Stephen Z. Starr, in his 1971 book *Colonel Grenfell's Wars*, ridicules Prof. Frank Klement's claim that the stories of the prison raids were "a myth, invented for their own profit by detectives and agents provocateurs in the employ of the government, by partisans, or merely gullible state governors and army officers eager for promotion."

So the grand Confederate scheme of freeing Rebel prisoners in Illinois and elsewhere in the Northwest, and forming them into the nucleus of an army for a second front in the North, fizzled out. It had been based on the erroneous belief that the loud-mouthed Sons of Liberty who talked so bravely of providing thousands of men to resist Federal oppression, would put their bodies where their mouths were when called upon to act. They chickened out.

Chapter Twenty-Nine
"This Damned War Must Be Stopped!"

DEAN RICHMOND STOOD IN THE LOBBY of the Sherman House in Chicago on the eve of the Democratic national convention and swore: "By God, McClellan shall be nominated and this damned war must be stopped!"

Reporters surrounding this arrogant "railroad king" viewed him with a mixture of awe and respect because he controlled the largest bloc of delegates—sixty-six New Yorkers with half a vote each—and he had "the pins so fixed" to deliver them to the general. "Richmond, S. L. M. Barlow, Manton Marble, August Belmont and a few others are involved in trying to make McClellan president," the *Philadelphia Press* correctly observed. "He is all their own, this little McClellan, as absolutely as their watches or pocketbooks."

"Do you see that portly, large-headed man with a gold-headed cane and wearing a jaunty blue coat that might become a man twenty years younger?" asked one correspondent. "That is Dean Richmond of New York, the resident manager of conventions, legislatures and rail-roads. ... He is just now swearing, by many holy names, that 'it's got to be did.'"

"He stands with his hands in his breeches pockets, with his head slightly turned to the right side in a knowing sort of way," another newsman noted. "His lower lip protrudes ... the facial lines all indicate strong passions, strong will ... force, cunning, acquisitiveness and cool calculation."

A third correspondent viewed Richmond as "a man of ponderous make-up, of short answers and grunts. His head is large and round and thinly covered with gray hair. ... His nose is hideously large and surmounted by two large warts. ... His face is an expression of coarseness and sensuality, especially ... a pair of thick protruding lips that import an air of ferocity to the whole countenance."

Dean Richmond was accustomed to controlling political events, whether they were in the New York legislature or in the councils of the Democratic Party. He had risen from a poor childhood to build a fortune in the shipping business at Buffalo, then persuaded the state legislature to merge several railroad lines into the New York Central, and now he ruled as its president. He was accused of running the railway and the Democratic Party in the same ruthless way. He even found himself mentioned as a possible choice for the presidency.

"He would make, beyond doubt, a strong candidate," the *New York Tribune* commented. "He is regarded as a War Democrat with very pronounced views but, as he never speaks in public and never writes letters, he has no record to alienate ... the Wood-Vallandigham Copperheads of his party." But Richmond refused to run, and one reason was that he was well aware of his personal handicaps. "He had little education and no cultural opportunities," one biographer wrote. "All his life he swore to excess, he could not make a speech or even converse in grammatical language; and his handwriting was practically illegible."

With single-minded drive, the railroad executive set out to make McClellan president, regardless of the platform or any other factor. He opposed writing any platform at all, knowing that it would only cause trouble, and he suggested that the Democrats take the title of the "true Union party" rather than letting Lincoln and the Republicans claim it. He wanted his party to insist upon ending "this damned war" but only on terms of a united country.

Waging the most expensive campaign yet seen in U.S. politics, Richmond and his allies spent money freely to bring pro-McClellan politicians to Chicago from all over the East, either as delegates to vote for the general, or as throngs of people cheering for him as a form of "outside pressure." "'Little Mac' is run by the bloated aristocrats of the Democratic party," said the hostile *Chicago Tribune*. "He is the candidate of the money brokers of Wall Street and the great railroad corporations of New York and New England. The Democratic party used to boast, in Jefferson's and Jackson's times, that it was the poor man's party. It denounced banks and corporations bitterly and unceasingly. Now ... it is controlled by Austrian Jew banker Belmont and codfish aristocrats and railway kings like Dean Richmond ... Never in the history of this country was so much money expended to influence, by outside pressure. ... The satellites of the shoddy aristocracy have no modesty. They are shameless."

Besides having his grip on the delegations from New York, New Jersey, and Pennsylvania, Richmond had allies in New England. A reporter interviewed William B. Converse, "a tough, uncouth specimen of Connecticut Yankee" who had also worked his way up to wealth. What, asked the reporter, did the delegates hope to achieve in the convention?" "By God, sir," came the reply, "we are going to shut-pan on this damned war!"

On the eve of the convention, Richmond faced trouble engineered by the "peace" mavericks of his own state, notably Fernando Wood and his brother, Ben, both having risen from obscurity to their present eminence as members of Congress. An unfriendly observer caught a glimpse of Ex-Mayor Fernando cruising along Michigan Avenue in a buggy: "There he sat, as sleek and slimy as ever in closely buttoned broadcloth, his neatly fitting black wig deceiving everybody as to his age, and his look of virtuous coolness and indifference leading the uninitiated to take him for an honest man. ... He would be more at home as the proprietor of a rat pit or umpire at a prize fight."

Fernando Wood had often expressed sympathy with the South, and now he rivaled Vallandigham in demanding an armistice and a compromise to end the war. Brother Ben went even further, working hand in glove with the Confederates, his newspaper, the *New York Daily News*, serving as a go-between for the Rebels and their friends in the North, printing "personal" items that were really coded messages, some of them between the Richmond authorities and their agents in Canada.

The *New York Times* revealed on August 25 that the *Daily News* had cashed a $25,000 check from the Confederates in Montreal "and this is but one of many remittances from the same source for the sustenance of the *Daily News*." The August pay-off was later confirmed by Confederate agent John B. Castleman in his memoir *Active Service.*

A bystander who watched Ben at the Chicago convention described him thus: "He is a short, heavily built, broad-shouldered man about forty years of age. His head is large and covered with short frizzly hair of a light hue. He wears a heavy moustache, which serves in part to conceal an extremely large mouth. His eyes are small and sunken and not at all expressive of benignity or amiability." His large nose gave him a "bulldog" look.

Ben wielded less influence than his older brother, partly because of a keen interest in concerns other than politics. At one Chicago caucus, Fernando made an ardent speech for peace, but when Ben's time came to speak, he was nowhere to be seen. "He had stepped out," someone explained, "to take a sherry cobbler and to get the latest numbers from the Delaware lottery."

The Woods were deep into a dark intrigue to make Horatio Seymour the presidential candidate of the peace bloc, although he had told the press that he would not run. The sudden courtship of the wavering New York governor seemed an obvious maneuver to spike Dean Richmond's plan to have the Empire State's delegation united and to nominate McClellan on the first ballot. Belmont and Marble also began to pick up rumors that Seymour was being wooed by the Wood crowd, and they began to worry. Writing to Barlow in New York, Belmont said Seymour "blows hot and cold. ... He professes not to be a candidate and will not be one if I can help it."

Barlow, waiting eagerly in New York for the latest news from Chicago, expressed uneasiness over a telegram from Marble about the governor's pirouettes and advised that he be blocked, by "convincing the doubters that we cannot carry this state or Pennsylvania with Seymour." Barlow gave Richmond, Marble, and Samuel J. Tilden "full authority to control" the New York delegation—if they could.

The New Yorkers caucused about their choice of candidates on the Sunday before the convention's opening day, to decide how they would cast their big bloc of thirty-three votes. As the suspense increased and Barlow awaited the next telegram from Chicago, he told Marble, "I am almost used up by excitement."

Dean Richmond moved to the forefront of the caucus and threw his considerable weight around where it could be most effective. He had a heart-to-heart talk with the vacillating Seymour—some might call it "career counseling"—and the governor at last saw the light. He realized that, for the sake of his future in politics, he should bow out gracefully and let the delegation go for McClellan. So Belmont was able to send Barlow a joyful telegram that McClellan had received fifty-three of the sixty-six half-votes. "All going well, success sure," the banker declared.

Barlow then transmitted the good news to McClellan who was anxiously awaiting every bulletin at his home in New Jersey. The general's nomination seemed assured now after a very hard fight against a combination of enemies. "It is plain to me," Barlow wrote, "that but for Richmond, Tilden, and Marble, the peace men, the Lincoln men and Seymour men would have had it all their way. As it stands, if we win at all, we win everything; and we shall have a wise platform and a good v. p."

McClellan replied: "If we win, we win everything and are as free as air. If we lose, we lose like gentlemen. I would not for the world have given any powers to make bargains."

Having disposed of the Seymour problem for the moment, Richmond turned to a second source of headaches: Clement L. Vallandigham. Back from his exile in Canada, and apparently unafraid of being arrested again for his bold speeches against the war, the Ohio "martyr" roamed about Chicago, followed by cheering crowds clamoring to hear his voice. When he yielded on one occasion, the *New York Tribune* reported in disgust, "his speech gave the opportunity to several hundred open Rebel sympathizers to hurray for Jeff Davis, which they did with a gusto."

"The truth is, the masses of the party sympathize with radical men like Vallandigham," confessed the *Daily Missouri Democrat*. "He is today the idol of the crowds. He is the great favorite of the masses of the country precincts, who crowd the convention and the city. Today, were they allowed their preference, they would nominate him unanimously for the presidency."

That, in Dean Richmond's view, was just the trouble. Vallandigham could sway the thousands of spectators who far outnumbered the regular delegates and even intimidated them. Although well aware that he was too "hot" to have a place on the national ticket, himself, Vallandigham was hell-bent on getting a platform that would call for an armistice and a negotiated peace while McClellan's men believed the Democrats must insist that the Confederates first agree to come back to the Union.

Samuel S. Cox, busily rounding up votes for McClellan, obtained a promise from his friend, Vallandigham, and Fernando Wood that they would support the nominee of the convention in return for concessions on the platform. Without a platform they considered satisfactory, the peace advocates could stage a walk-out from the convention or even run a separate ticket, thus guaranteeing another Lincoln victory. This was the nightmare that haunted the dreams of the men controlling the McClellan campaign.

They also had to worry about the Sons of Liberty who had flocked to Chicago. The *Chicago Tribune* greeted the arrival of Dick Dodd, the grand commander of the secret order in Indiana, who was also a delegate, and said a large number of "midnight assassins" accompanied him. Vallandigham, the national commander of the Sons of Liberty, addressed the brethren at the Richmond House, where the Confederate visitors' fifth-floor rooms were thrown together to form an auditorium.

James B. Wilson, who was there, would later testify that he heard Vallandigham say he no longer thought the convention would break up as in 1860 because "he had found a wonderful unanimity of feeling" for peace. Vallandigham already had his own version of the peace platform prepared and said that, if the convention adopted it, he could accept McClellan as the presidential nominee.

McClellan's men also were concerned about the violent antiwar tone of speeches to crowds packing the streets of Chicago who cheered every mention of Vallandigham's name. Many of the tirades were racist diatribes and personal attacks upon President Lincoln.

"They could search Hell over," cried Ohio delegate Stambaugh, "and not find a worse President than Abraham Lincoln."

Judge Miller, also of Ohio, charged: "A bloody war has been waged to elevate the negro to an equality with the white man. There is no difference between a War Democrat and an abolitionist. They are both links in the same sausage, made from the same dog."

"What is this war for?' asked Sanderson of Pennsylvania. "The nigger! It is for the nigger against the white man ... We don't want our bosoms stuffed so much with damned niggers in this warm weather." (Cheers and laughter.)

"Do the people want a draft?" demanded Paine of Missouri.

"Not by a damned sight!" shouted someone in the crowd.

"Then they must upset the present government at Washington. This dynasty has already placed in the field 2,200,000 men to be offered on the altar of the negro and now it demands 500,000 more ... all to elevate the flat-nosed, woolley-headed, long-heeled, cursed of God, damned of men, descendants of Africa!"

Senator Thomas Hendricks of Indiana told a street crowd that the people, oppressed by Lincoln, "will rise and crush out abolitionism and hurl the smutty old tyrant out of political existence!"

Senator William H. Richardson of Illinois, haranguing a cheering crowd at Bryan Hall, declared: "We are going to end the war. As soon as our President is elected, he will issue a declaration of freedom, opening all the Bastilles where prisoners are confined for mere political expressions of opinion. ... I say to Abraham Lincoln, if there is not to be a free election, there will be a free fight! We demand, and we must restore, this government to the white race!"

W. W. O'Brien of Peoria, Illinois, predicted that "a true Democrat" would be elected president and "on the Fourth of March he will apply his boot to the posterior of Old Abe and kick him out of the presidential chair."

Ohio Congressman Samuel S. Cox charged: "Abraham Lincoln has deluged the country with blood ... filled the land with grief and mourning."

A voice from the crowd responded: "God damn him!"

Benjamin Allen of New York prophesied: "The people will soon rise, and if they cannot put Lincoln out of power by the ballot, they will by the bullet." This outrageous proposal to assassinate the president drew loud cheers from the crowd on the Chicago streets.

Some Democratic orators assailed not only Lincoln, but also McClellan. A speaker named Trainor from Butler County, Ohio, asked his listeners if they would vote for Lincoln and they shouted back, "No, no!"

"Neither would I, gentlemen," said he, "and much less would I support his dog, McClellan, who has barked and bitten for him, who has slain thousands of as good Democrats as the Lord ever made, at his bidding."

Shouting from the Sherman House balcony, the eccentric Henry Clay Dean named several men who could get his vote for the presidency, but he left out McClellan. Some in the crowd asked him if he would not vote for Little Mac.

"Before God, gentlemen," Dean cried, "we have one idiot in the presidential chair; do not elect another!"

Chapter Thirty
Democrats Promise Armistice

FOLLOWING A WEEKEND OF REVELRY in the hotels, saloons, and streets of Chicago, the Democrats opened their national convention on Monday, August 29, in the Wigwam, an enormous wooden barn about a mile from the hotels, on the shore of Lake Michigan. The amphitheater was built to hold 15,000 people, and an even larger mob stormed through the doors to grab the spectators' seats, leading one reporter to comment that they all seemed "as crazy as bedbugs."

The Butternuts, mostly country people from southern Illinois and Indiana, who had come to demand a peace platform and a peace candidate, outnumbered the McClellan forces imported from the Eastern cities to cheer for Little Mac. "The farmers of the rural districts ... have completely squelched the Blood Tubs, Short Boys and Dead Rabbits of the large cities," the *Chicago Tribune* said, quoting the nicknames of Manhattan's most notorious gangs.

When the band blared "The Star Spangled Banner" and "Yankee Doodle," the throng applauded with gusto; but the real favorite tune of the convention was "Dixie." Every time this quick-step from the minstrel shows, transformed into the Confederate fight song, burst forth, it "was received with the most uproarious shouts and cheers." Whenever the Butternut masses heard it, they made the rafters ring.

To open the convention, August Belmont limped to the rostrum and gaveled the crowd to order at noon. "He has a rather Broadway look," one newsman reported. "Below the medium height, with a broad Hebrew face trimmed in the English style, a large head and an expression of earnestness and sagacity—what might be called a counting-house expression. He proceeds to make a brief and earnest speech in a tone of voice sufficiently distinct to be heard and sufficiently German to make it piquant."

Belmont, the party's national chairman, appealed for unity and peace. Reminding the battling factions that their disputes four years before had split the party and placed Lincoln in the White House, he warned that the same mistakes must not be made this time. "We are not here as War Democrats or Peace Democrats but as citizens of the great Republic, which we will strive to bring back to its former greatness and prosperity without one single star taken from the brilliant constellation that once encircled its youthful brow," he said. "The cause of 'the Union, the Constitution and the Laws' must triumph over fanaticism and treason."

Belmont needed all of his persuasive eloquence to unite the "peace men" and the "policy men," the *Daily Missouri Democrat* said. In a blistering editorial, the paper explained how the two factions worked together at the convention. It declared:

> "McClellan and Peace" are to be blazoned on the debauched and demoralized Democratic party of 1864. Under the livery of war they seek to hide the cloven foot of peace and disunion. Oh, how mean, how contemptible, how unworthy of the once great party of Jefferson and Jackson. ...
>
> There are two factions of the Democratic party here, both working their devilish scheme of peace and disunion. ... The peace men are nothing more or less than agents of the Jeff Davis Government. The policy men are their cat's paws. The peace men ... communicate with the rebels. The policy men communicate with the peace men.
>
> The work begun at Charleston will be consummated at Chicago unless the Union people of the country arise in their majesty and might and bury these political tricksters and

gamblers, these thimble-rigging politicians, these rebels and outlaws, these assassins of their country in a … grave so deep that the hand of the resurrection can never reach them.

William Bigler, a former Pennsylvania governor and U.S. senator, took over as temporary chairman and led the delegates through a tedious round of business, including the appointment of committees. With a mighty effort led by Samuel J. Tilden, a sharp New York lawyer and future presidential nominee, the McClellan forces blocked Vallandigham from becoming chairman of the resolutions committee, which would write the platform. They won the chairmanship for James Guthrie of Kentucky, a War Democrat, president of the Louisville and Nashville Railroad, and treasury secretary in Franklin Pierce's presidency. Guthrie was also the Easterners' choice to be McClellan's running mate.

Nevertheless, the dauntless Vallandigham won a place on the resolutions committee and on its subcommittee, which would actually do the hammering and sawing that would build the platform. He worked hand-in-glove with former California governor John B. Weller, who had often been accused of advocating that the Pacific Coast states should form their own republic and ally it with the Southern Confederacy.

Only a month earlier, his brother, C. L. Weller, the postmaster of San Francisco, had been arrested and imprisoned on Alcatraz on charges of inciting armed resistance to the war. Federal authorities were alarmed by his "peace" speeches and saw visions of an antiwar revolt by Democrats in California.

On the second day of the convention, Horatio Seymour took charge as its permanent chairman. He ripped into Lincoln with a speech blaming fanatical Republicans for continuing the war, which the Democrats had tried to prevent. "They will not let the shedding of blood cease even for a little time," he railed, "to see if Christian charity or the wisdom of statesmanship may not work out a method to save our country" "This administration cannot Save the Union," Seymour said. "We can."

After two days and nights of wrangling, the resolutions committee produced the platform. It was mercifully brief—only six planks in all. It promised that the Democrats would be true to the Union under the Constitution; that the Lincoln administration's interference in state elections must be resisted; that Federal, state, and individual rights must be protected; that the administration should be condemned for refusing to exchange military prisoners; that the Democrats, once back into power, would give Union soldiers and sailors all the care and protection they so justly deserved.

All of these statements were hardly controversial. The explosives were packed into the second plank.

It charged that the Lincoln administration had failed to restore the Union "by the experiment of war" and that "justice, humanity, liberty and the public welfare" require "immediate efforts ... for a cessation of hostilities, with a view to an ultimate convention of the states or other peaceable means, to the end that, at the earliest practicable moment, peace may be restored on the basis of the Federal Union of the States."

Clearly, Vallandigham and Weller had drafted the platform along the lines of the gentleman's agreement reached between the Democrats and the Confederate commissioners with whom they had had their chummy chats at Niagara Falls, just as Lincoln had said they would. While the resolutions committee penned the final draft in Chicago, it carried out the essence of the understandings reached with the Rebels in Canada. Whether the Democrats realized it or not, they were actually playing the enemy's game—for the one thing the Rebels wanted was an armistice or a "cessation of hostilities." They won this in the final draft.

Guthrie, Tilden, and others in the McClellan camp struggled to water down this "war failure" plank through one amendment after another in the resolutions committee, but they could not prevail. Guthrie was seventy years old, white-haired, with trembling hands, and when he tottered forward to make his report, the McClellan men realized that he was no match for the hard-driving Vallandigham.

The *Chicago Tribune* quickly realized why the Peace Democrats campaigned for the platform plank pledging the "cessation of hostilities" because those were merely fancy words for "armistice." The *Tribune* said: "Stop the war for a month, they say, and it will never be resumed again. ... The armistice plank is the plank for them. Let them secure this to Jeff Davis and he will take care of the balance. The proposition of Dean Richmond—to whip the South if it cannot be coaxed back—is laughed at." The New York boss could round up the votes for McClellan, but he could not control the platform-drafting committee.

Noah Brooks of the *Sacramento Union* observed that the plank calling for "cessation of hostilities" was greeted with "most vociferous applause, outsiders and delegates cheering, roaring and hallooing like madmen for the space of five minutes. Sunset Cox looked black and sad, but Wood and Vallandigham rubbed their hands together gleefully."

The Easterners could have made a floor fight against the plank and perhaps defeated it. But they had a deathly fear that such a battle would have split the party and led to a walkout of the peace delegates just as the Southerners had bolted in 1860. McClellan's managers were intent upon nominating him quickly, without any fuss, although they feared that this "war failure" plank would be a heavy load for him to carry.

Eagerly anticipating almost certain return to the White House, the Democrats did not dare throw all the spoils away and let the hated Lincoln win again. So the entire platform sailed through without debate amid wild cheers. Many delegates had no idea that they had made a fatal mistake.

Then came the nominations for the presidency. John Stockton of New Jersey's Camden and Amboy Railroad nominated McClellan and Samuel S. "Sunset" Cox made a seconding speech. Also offered as contenders were former President Franklin Pierce and the Seymour cousins.

Benjamin Harris, a Maryland congressman, made a seconding speech for Thomas Seymour and assailed McClellan for having ordered the arrest of the Maryland legislature in 1861, ostensibly to prevent its secessionist members from taking Maryland out of the Union. Amid cries of "No! No!" he shouted that McClellan was Lincoln's "assassin of state rights." He continued: "You ask me to go home and see my friends in the Maryland legislature—men who were put in prison, whose property was destroyed, whose families were left beggars upon the world and by the orders of this man, and yet, remembering their imprisonment and suffering, to walk up to the polls and vote for him. I cannot do it! I never will do it!"

An uproar of shouting and cursing ensued. Charles W. Carrigan of Pennsylvania charged that any man who says he will not vote for the convention's nominee is "not fit to be a member of it." That set off shouts of "Put him out!" "Kick him out!" and "You're a damned traitor!" all aimed at Harris. As he returned to his seat, a McClellan delegate struck him across the mouth and Harris knocked his assailant over the benches. One eyewitness said Harris "put his hand to his vest, as if to draw a pistol," but the police intervened. "As it is well known that about every third man in the convention is armed," one reporter commented, the fracas "might have been enlarged to formidable dimensions."

George Morgan, an Ohio delegate and friend of McClellan, claimed that the Maryland legislature was on the point of adopting a secession ordinance when McClellan blocked that by arresting the pro-Southern members. But several Maryland delegates angrily retorted that their legislature had never intended to turn the state over to the Confederacy, that McClellan had made the arrests on the basis of false testimony, and that the lawmakers had suffered in prison for many months although they were innocent.

By this time, the long, hot summer day was over, and it was too dark in the unlighted Wigwam for the delegates to see what they were doing. So the balloting for president was postponed until the following morning.

When the voting began, Dean Richmond, in his tall white hat and his blue tailcoat, was seen towering far above little August Belmont for a last-minute check on the delegates, and it soon became clear that the New York chieftain indeed had "the pins so fixed" for McClellan to win. The general picked up the solid votes of New York, Pennsylvania, and Illinois and began adding support from Ohio, New England states, and New Jersey. As the roll call droned on, McClellan finished the first ballot with 174 votes; then, as various other candidates dropped out, he reached 202.5, clinching his victory.

"Instantly, the pent-up feelings of the mob broke forth in the most rapturous manner; cheers, yells, music and screams indescribable rent the air, and a brace of cannon volleyed a salute to the welkin in honor of the hero of the Chickahominy," Noah Brooks reported. "The long agony was over and men split their throats, threw up their caps and behaved as much like bedlamites as men well can."

Then came another dramatic moment: Vallandigham stepped up to the rostrum and moved that McClellan's nomination be made unanimous. Astonished reporters credited him with being a martyr

HARPER'S WEEKLY. [September 3, 1864.

This cartoon is an attack upon the Democratic Party's platform calling the Civil War a "failure" and demanding a "cessation of hostilities" that would lead to a compromise peace, not a Union victory. "Dedicated to the Chicago convention," which nominated General McClellan on the "peace" platform, the cartoon shows a triumphant Jefferson Davis shaking hands with a crippled Union soldier while standing on the grave where Columbia is weeping over the war dead. The tombstone reads: "In memory of the Union Heroes who fell in a useless war." The cartoon, by Thomas Nast, appeared in *Harper's Weekly* September 3, 1864. It is from the collections of the Library of Congress.

once more by swallowing this bitter pill. But perhaps Vallandigham was not such a martyr after all. His Confederate friends understood that he had been assured of becoming secretary of war, and that suited them just fine. They could imagine just how vigorously he would carry on the war against the South, since he had opposed the conflict from its very first day.

"Mirabile dictu! It is even said that Vallandigham can have the War portfolio," one reporter exclaimed. "Angels and ministers of grace defend us. ... The shamelessness with which the McClellan men cast their pearls before the swinish peace men is a matter of surprise even in these days of political degeneracy."

Next came the nominations for vice president. Ohio presented Congressman George Pendleton, youthful, suave and personable, a "smart and sharp" lawyer, scion of an old Virginia family, a crony of Vallandigham's, and even more of a Copperhead and fierce opponent of the war. McClellan men distrusted him; they thought they had the tracks all cleared for their favorite, the Kentucky railroad man, James Guthrie. Like Belmont, Guthrie also had been lamed for life by a bullet wound in a duel. Barlow had urged the Democrats to name an acceptable border state man to round out the ticket.

But Guthrie could not be accepted by the crowd of Democrats who hated the war and who cheered the platform plank calling for a cessation of hostilities. They insisted that, since they had swallowed McClellan, they were entitled to have their own man on the slate with him. So, despite the bitter protests of Belmont, the deal was struck. New York added its votes to those for Pendleton, and he emerged victorious. The peace men, therefore, staged no walkout and there was no party split.

George Francis Train* claimed that, at the outset of the convention, the peace delegates were counting on Vallandigham and Pendleton to help them block McClellan's nomination on the first ballot. Train said that Pendleton told him then, "So help me God, I will do all I can to beat McClellan." But then, said Train, "they offered him the vice-presidency and he went!"

---

* Train has been called by one historian the "crank of cranks" among the eccentrics at the Chicago convention who demanded immediate and unconditional peace.

The morning after the balloting, Train added, "I saw Vallandigham at the breakfast table and I said to him: 'You have sold out this concern and if I can find it out I'll burst the whole thing.' Vallandigham said, 'Train, you talk too loud.'"

The peace men took one more trick in the political card game when the delegates accepted a resolution offered by former Kentucky governor Charles A. Wickliffe. Tall, white-haired, and crippled by rheumatism, Wickliffe was known as "the leader of the rebel wing of the Kentucky Copperheads, the largest slave holder in Kentucky, having three sons in the Rebel army." He proposed that "the convention shall not be dissolved by the adjournment at the close of business, but shall remain as organized, subject to be called together at any time and place as the executive committee shall designate."

The purpose of Wickliffe's maneuver puzzled some newsmen. One surmised that since "that hoary old rebel Wickliffe ... is an original secessionist," his resolution actually "may be for the purpose of throwing Little Mac overboard." If McClellan refused to run on the "war failure" platform, the Democrats would reconvene and choose another nominee more suitable to the peace crowd.

Wickliffe also won approval of a resolution stating that the first act of "president" McClellan "will be to open Lincoln's prison doors and set the captives free." He charged that many of the best and most loyal citizens of Kentucky, including twenty or thirty ladies, were imprisoned in Louisville in damp and dirty cells with only straw to lie upon and the coarsest prison food, and the newspapers were forbidden, under martial law, to print the truth about their mistreatment. He proclaimed this truth, he said, at the risk of his own liberty perhaps of his life. His proposal passed unanimously amid cries of "Bully for Wickliffe!" Then the convention adjourned.

As the crowd filed out of the Wigwam, one Indiana delegate commented bitterly that the nominee for president was a nobody and the nominee for vice president was "a putty head." But the *Daily Missouri Democrat* said Pendleton "is a stronger peace man than even Vallandigham," so his selection gave the Democrats "a kangaroo ticket, all of the strength being in the tail."

The *Chicago Tribune* proclaimed in a headline: "The Peace-Sneaks Got All But the Head of the Ticket."

Chapter Thirty-One
Seward Proves the Dark Intrigue

ON SEPTEMBER 3, THE PEOPLE of Auburn, New York, gathered at a rally to hear their most famous neighbor, William Henry Seward, make a notable speech officially opening President Lincoln's reelection campaign. To the citizens of the upstate town, Seward was a familiar figure and a source of great community pride for his achievements as governor, United States senator, and now secretary of state. He should have been president, too, they believed, if he had not lost the prize to Lincoln.

Five feet, six inches tall, with a rather slight, stooping body, Seward did not look like a towering statesman. His clothes were often disheveled, sometimes powdered with ash from the cigars he smoked at the rate of a dozen a day; his thatch of hair, flaming red in his youth, had faded in sixty-three years to silvery white. His face was sallow, his ears stuck out, and his nose resembled an eagle's beak. But his bright blue eyes flashed intelligence and good humor. He was fond of good food, fine wines, lively dinner table conversation, and late night card games; he shared the president's love of jokes.

Seward was especially vivacious this day and for an excellent reason. He had just received a telegram from the War Department, relaying a joyous wire which General Sherman had flashed to Lincoln: "Atlanta is ours, and fairly won."

The good news provided an inspiring theme for the secretary, as he began by praising Sherman's soldiers as well as Adm. David Farragut and his sailors who had recently captured the forts protecting Mobile, Alabama, one of the few ports still open to the struggling Confederacy. These victories brought rays of hope for the eventual triumph of the Union and a great relief from the gloom that had oppressed the North throughout August—except for the Democrats. After nominating General McClellan as Lincoln's opponent, the Democrats acted as if they had already won the November election.

Now, with the fall of Atlanta, Lincoln's prospects for reelection no longer seemed hopeless. But Seward did not take success for granted. In his speech, he hit the Democrats with a sensational charge intended to brand them as allies of the Confederacy in a dark intrigue to stop the war, not to win it. This is how Seward built his case, in the text published September 7 by the *New York Herald:* First, he harked back to 1860 when Lincoln won the presidency by battling three opposing forces: The "states' rights" Democrats who supported John C. Breckinridge; the national Democrats who backed Stephen A. Douglas; and the Constitutional Union faction that endorsed John Bell. Now, Seward said, the same three forces are again in the field: "The Southern Democracy is still in arms under the usurper in Richmond; the Douglas and Bell columns, consolidated, are found in Chicago; and all three … compassing the rejection of the constitutional president of the United States.

"The Richmond Democrats and the Chicago Democrats have lately come to act very much alike," the secretary continued. "I shall go further and prove to you that they not only have a common policy and a common way of defending it, but they have even adopted that policy in common with each other." Seward recalled that Confederate agents George Nicholas Sanders, Clement C. Clay, and J. P. Holcombe had appeared at the Clifton House on the Canadian side of Niagara Falls and "the Chicago Democrats resorted there in considerable numbers to confer with these emissaries of Jefferson Davis." He quoted a *London Times* dispatch of August 8 that said: "Clifton House has become a centre of negotiations between the Northern friends of

Peace and Southern agents which propose a withdrawal of differences from the arbitrament of the sword."

"Mark now, that on the eighth of August, 1864," Seward went on, "Northern Democrats and Richmond agents agreed upon three things to be done at Chicago: First a withdrawal of the differences between the government and the insurgents from the arbitrament of the sword; second, a nomination for President of the United States on a platform of an armistice and ultimately a convention of the states; third, to thwart by all possible means the re-election of Abraham Lincoln."

"Such a conference, held in a neutral country between professedly loyal citizens of the United States and agents of the Richmond traitors in arms, has a very suspicious look," Seward charged. Here, he quoted the Democrats' platform plank, which declared the war a "failure" and called for an immediate "cessation of hostilities" and an ultimate convention of the states for peace. "The Democracy of Chicago did there just what had been agreed upon with the Richmond agents at Niagara—namely, they pronounced for an abandonment of the military defense of the United States against the insurgents, with a view to an ultimate national convention and the defeat of Abraham Lincoln," Seward emphasized.

Next, Seward offered evidence that the Niagara agreement had been carried out at the Chicago convention "in full execution of the previous contract." He quoted a telegram sent by George Nicholas Sanders from Saint Catharines, in Canada, September 1, to the Hon. D. Wier at Halifax, Nova Scotia: "Platform and presidential nominee unsatisfactory, Vice President and speeches satisfactory. Tell Phillmore not to oppose."

Seward did not reveal exactly how the United States government had intercepted this telegram sent by one Confederate agent to another in Canada. He identified "D. Wier" as "a Richmond accomplice at Halifax" and "Phillmore" as the editor of the pro-Confederate newspaper in London, the *Index*.

"Here we have a nomination and a platform which were made by a treaty formally contracted between the Democratic traitors at Richmond and the Democratic opposition at Chicago, signed, sealed, attested and delivered in the presence of the *London Times* and already ratified at Richmond," Seward proclaimed.

"By heavens, we've got 'em!" shouted someone in the Auburn audience.

"Got them!" Seward replied. "To be sure you've got them, my friends. ... The last hope of the rebellion hangs upon the ratification of this abominable and detestable compact by the American people."

For some strange reason, Seward's detailed indictment of the Democrats' dark intrigue with the Confederate agents in drafting the party's "war failure" platform is missing from nearly every book mentioning the Democrats and their Confederate connection. Either the authors did not read the evidence, or they ignored it, or covered it up.

Coverage of his speech in most books usually concentrates on a passage that noted that the Emancipation Proclamation was a wartime measure, indicating that the final abolition of slavery might be delayed until after the war. The abolitionists protested that this indicated a Lincoln retreat from his demand that the peace terms must include the end of slavery. The White House hastily explained that Seward was not speaking for the president.

Approving Seward's charges of the dark intrigue between the Democrats and the Rebels, the *Sacramento Union* commented: "Here the Copperheads were caught in the act. They were proved to have been intriguing with the emissaries of the enemy who had declared at all times and all places that they would accept no peace that was not based upon a recognition of the 'Confederate' government. Their tracks were traced and were found to lead straight into the camp of Jefferson Davis."

Even more convincing proof of the Confederates' happiness over the Democrats' decisions at Chicago can be found in a letter written by Commissioner Clay to Secretary of State Benjamin on September 12 after receiving encouraging first-hand reports from various friends who stopped by his Canadian retreat on their way home from the convention. Seward would have been delighted to cite this letter as evidence of the dark intrigue, but it did not come to light until years later in the *The War of the Rebellion: A Compilation of the Official Records of the Union and Confederate Armies*.

In backing McClellan, Clay's Democratic comrades assured him, "Peace may be made with him on terms you may accept. He is committed to the platform to cease hostilities and to try negotiations.

That is a great concession from him and the War Democracy. An armistice will inevitably result in peace. The war cannot be renewed if once stopped, even for a short time."

"The platform means peace, unconditionally," Clay assured Benjamin. "Vallandigham and Weller framed it. McClellan will be under the control of the true peace men. Horatio, or T. H. Seymour is to be Secretary of State; Vallandigham Secretary of War. McClellan is privately pledged to make peace even at the expense of separation, if the South cannot be induced to reconstruct any common government."

How Seward would have loved to lay his hands on this written proof that the Democrats intended to turn the War Department over to Vallandigham, of all people, the national commander of the Sons of Liberty, who had opposed the war from its first day!

Also, how could Confederate Commissioner Clay be so sure that McClellan was "privately pledged to peace" even at the cost of letting the South separate? One piece of evidence on that score can be found in the National Archives. It is a letter from a businessman named James Harrison to Col. L. V. Bogy in St. Louis, written August 24 at the Metropolitan Hotel in New York. This is the text:

> I had an interview today with Gen. McClellan with a view of ascertaining his status on the Peace question. He is a strong Peace man, but still wishes to see the Union preserved. His own words are: "If I should be elected, I will recommend an immediate armistice, and a call for a convention of all the states, and insist upon exhausting all and every means to procure peace without further bloodshed, and shall not wait for the call to come from the other side, but that we should make the call first." ...
>
> I then asked this question: "When the proper time arrives for treaty negotiations, will you be governed by what you then conceive to be the views of the majority of the Democratic party?" To which he answered me emphatically that that should or would be his policy. I feel and know that we can trust him.

With such private assurances as this from McClellan, the peace delegates at Chicago had accepted him as the presidential nominee, and they believed that he would be bound by the platform. But the Eastern financiers, who had railroaded his nomination through the convention, were horrified by the "war failure" plank pledging the immediate quest for a "cessation of hostilities," and they demanded that he must repudiate that language in his letter accepting the nomination. August Belmont, for instance, advised him: "It is absolutely necessary that in your reply of acceptance you must place yourself squarely and unequivocally on the ground that you will never surrender one foot of soil and that peace can only be based upon the reconstruction of the Union. In other words, cessation of hostilities or an armistice can only be agreed upon after we have sufficient guarantees from the South that they are ready for a peace under the Union."

Editor James Gordon Bennett of the *New York Herald* was convinced that the plank had been drafted by the Confederates and that the Peace Democrats had "foisted it on the convention as the price for their endorsement of McClellan." The *Herald* asserted that it could not continue supporting him unless he would repudiate the "secessionist" platform plank and "come out boldly as a Jackson Democrat."

But Vallandigham warned McClellan, in a letter hinting at a bolt: "Do not listen to your Eastern friends who in an evil hour may advise you *to insinuate* even a little war in your letter of acceptance. If anything implying war is presented, two hundred thousand men in the West will withhold their support and they may go even further." This was a thinly veiled threat that the disgruntled peace men might run their own candidate while many could just stay at home on Election Day.

With the help of Belmont, Barlow, and other friends in New York, the general struggled through six drafts of his acceptance letter before settling upon the final version, released September 8. He rejected an unconditional armistice and said reunion must come before any settlement with the Confederacy. Without this, he wrote, "I could not look in the faces of my gallant comrades of the Army and Navy, who have survived so many bloody battles, and tell them that their labors and the sacrifice of so many of our slain and wounded comrades had been in vain."

If he had not rejected the "war failure" plank, McClellan explained to S. S. Cox, "there was no chance whatever" for carrying

New York State and Pennsylvania. "More than that," he added, "I could not have run on the platform as everybody interpreted it in this part of the world without violating all my antecedents, which I would not do for a thousand presidencies."

Well aware of Vallandigham's warnings, McClellan left the word "war" completely out of his final draft, along with the word "slavery." He desperately tried to please both the Peace Democrats and those in the East who would not stop the fighting until Southerners accepted reunion first. His prose was so vague that George Templeton Strong ridiculed it as "platitudes floating in mucilage, without a single plain word against treason and rebellion."

Nevertheless, George Nicholas Sanders denounced McClellan's acceptance letter as "an arrogant, war-spitting letter" that wrecked all the Confederate agents' plans for an early peace. He told Jefferson Davis: "In a letter to Gov. Seymour and the Hon. Benjamin Wood, immediately after the appearance of the McClellan letter of accept-ance, I endeavored in vain to move Gen. McClellan and his advisers from their disastrous position and I demonstrated that if they would come into an understanding with us ... they could carry the whole country. I told them plainly that, if they continued to cry out for a more vigorous prosecution of the war, when the whole affair could have been settled in a day, they would not, and ought not, carry a single state."

It is fascinating to note how Sanders, a Confederate agent, worked through Governor Seymour and the proprietor of the pro-Confederate *New York Daily News*, in an attempt to steer the McClellan men into the direction of a compromise peace.

Vallandigham cancelled his speaking engagements in protest against the apparent double-cross on the war failure plank. Later, however, he stopped sulking in his tent and resumed campaigning for the party ticket. After all, he had to remember the assurances he had received at Chicago about making him secretary of war.

For the rank-and-file of the Peace Democrats, it was not so easy to swallow their disappointment and go out and work for McClellan. Writing from Springfield, Illinois, September 12, a newspaperman reported: "The Peace Democracy of this state are indignant at McClellan's letter in which he spits upon the platform under the instructions of the Shoddy Democrats headed by Belmont and Dean Richmond. The Peace men say they have been cheated. ... The masses of the Democratic party in this state and in the Northwest generally are for peace. Those of this belief form the backbone of the Democratic party."

Some unhappy Peace Democrats, meeting in Columbus, Ohio, tried to float an independent ticket with Alexander Long as its presidential candidate. But the Cincinnati congressman had sense enough to refuse the dubious honor, so the revolt went nowhere.

While the Democrats were thus falling into disarray, the fractured Republicans began coming together after the fall of Atlanta, causing the masses to believe that there really was hope that Lincoln would finally win the war. Leonard Swett, a major Illinois politician and friend of the president, had shared the general gloom of August. Now he told his wife: "God gave us the victory at Atlanta, which made the ship right itself as a ship in a storm does after a great wave has nearly capsized it."

The politicians who had scampered off Lincoln's craft in August, like rats deserting a sinking ship, began climbing back aboard in September. Those who were conspiring to dump the president at a new convention and substitute a Union general had to give up their plot. Thurlow Weed told Secretary Seward on September 20 that the conspiracy collapsed on the twelfth. "It was equally formidable and vicious, embracing a larger number of leading men than I supposed possible," Weed wrote. "Knowing that I was not satisfied with the President, they came to see me for cooperation but my objection to Mr. Lincoln is that he has done too much for those who now seek to drive him from the field."

John Hay, in a diary entry of September 29, also quoted Weed as revealing that the ambitious, but militarily incompetent, Gen. Benjamin F. Butler "spent several hours with him" in New York seeking his support for a Butler-for-president ticket to be chosen at the new convention in Buffalo or Cincinnati. But Weed refused.

Horace Greeley, who had proposed Grant, Butler, or Sherman for president, because "Mr. Lincoln is already beaten," now changed his tune and began singing hymns of praise for the president in the columns of the *Tribune*. Senator Ben Wade of Ohio and Congressman

Henry Winter Davis of Maryland had denounced Lincoln as a dictator in their notorious "Wade-Davis Manifesto" in their fury over his pocket veto of their bill for reorganizing the South. Now, late in the game, they came out for him at last.

Senator Zachariah Chandler of Michigan, a constant radical critic of Lincoln, also switched. Chandler exerted great personal efforts to persuade General Frémont to give up his independent race for the White House. Although he had no chance of winning, Frémont could have diverted enough votes—especially among German Americans—to swing several key states to McClellan. Chandler and his fellow radicals concluded that they must stop McClellan, that "tool" of the "traitors," at any cost, and so they had to back Lincoln. Chandler thought he had struck a bargain with the president on these terms: Frémont would withdraw if Lincoln would fire Montgomery Blair, the postmaster general, hated by the radicals. Frémont withdrew September 21. The next day, Lincoln asked Blair to resign and Blair did so. Was it a deal? It certainly looked like one.

Frémont departed with a singular lack of grace. He was withdrawing, he wrote, "not to aid in the triumph of Mr. Lincoln, but to do my part towards preventing the election of the Democratic candidate" who, in his view, would restore the Union with slavery. But the Pathfinder still considered that Lincoln's administration "has been politically, militarily, and financially a failure and that its necessary continuance is a cause of regret for the country."

Chapter Thirty-Two
Pendleton and Belmont Assailed

ALL THROUGH THE EARLY AUTUMN, Republicans hammered away on their central themes—that the Democrats were the party of "Dixie, Davis, and the Devil" and that they must be defeated, at all hazards, to avert a dishonorable peace deal with the Confederacy.

Montgomery Blair, at a Union ratification meeting in New York September 27, charged:

> The Chicago convention was a direct co-operation with rebel emissaries in Canada. Vallandigham came directly from this focus of the Southern intrigue ... Vallandigham, the unblushing advocate in Congress of the secession party until discarded by his constituents, the emissary in connection with Thompson and Clay and others of the Davis government at Richmond, made a principal figure at the convention.
>
> His adhesion to the platform silenced all opposition to it. On his motion, every voice that had been raised to fury against the nomination of McClellan was silenced and the vote in his favor made unanimous. There was a potent spell in his voice that made 'a cessation of hostilities,' 'a convention of the

states'—of course, as equal and independent—and a quondam chief of the Union army ... to lead the last assault pressed by the Southern conspirators, countenanced by foreign powers, against the institutions of the country.

Blair warned that "secret Jacobin clubs, upon the plan of the Knights of the Golden Circle, are found in the free states and are preparing to use arms, as well as all the means of corruption, to carry the election." Jefferson Davis, he said, would pledge his last bale of cotton to help his "Knights in the North."

Besides assailing General McClellan as a mere tool of the Copperheads, in league with the Confederacy, the Republicans denounced his running mate, George Pendleton, as a worse secessionist than his dear friend "Val."

At first, they depicted the elegant Cincinnati congressman as a young dandy, too superior in dress and manners to appeal to red-blooded American voters. "He is one of those fellows who keep their moustaches cleanly scissored and highly polished and he carries a scented pocket handkerchief and a bottle of smelling salts in his hand when he travels," jeered Senator Jim Lane of Kansas, a veteran of the bloody border wars.

"George H. Pendleton is a fine-looking man with dark hair, inclined to curl, dark, expressive eyes, a handsome face," the *Daily Missouri Democrat* reported. "His speeches are perfect specimens of oratory." "I could name fifty young barristers in Philadelphia who are his superior," wrote a *Philadelphia Press* correspondent, who said Pendleton was chosen for vice president because, "after Vallandigham, who is his bosom friend and with whom he resided in the city of Washington ... he is the most determined and bitter enemy of the war in the national legislature."

Both men on the Democratic ticket were open to challenge on the basis of youth and limited political experience. Indeed, the Democrats had chosen the most youthful combined national slate ever presented by a major U.S. political party.

Pendleton had reached his thirty-ninth birthday July 19 while McClellan would not turn thirty-eight until December 3. No other national ticket has ever consisted of both nominees in their thirties.

Incidentally, the pair could also be called "the Cincinnati ticket" because Pendleton lived in the Ohio city and so had McClellan in his prewar days as a railroad executive. They were not residents of the same state at the time of the campaign—that would have presented legal problems—because McClellan now resided in New Jersey.

The light-hearted ridicule of Pendleton soon changed to more sinister tones. His foes began portraying him as a bogeyman who could actually move into the White House in case of President McClellan's death in office—by accident or design—and then, as commander in chief, the villain would have the power to disband the army and stop the war! "An apoplexy, catarrh, or cough of the lungs may carry off the valiant McClellan any day and then Vice President Pendleton would become President of the United States," wrote the diarist George Templeton Strong, who called Pendleton "a cold-blooded traitor."

"Suppose, in one of the powerful intellectual efforts of McClellan, his vessel of clay should burst," said a speaker at a Union political rally in Columbus, Ohio, September 15. "Then Pendleton becomes President. He would issue a proclamation that all the armies of the United States be disbanded."

To prove their charge that Pendleton was pro-secessionist, the Republicans claimed in a pamphlet that he had told Congress in 1861: "If you find conciliation impossible, if your differences are so great that you cannot or will not reconcile them, then, gentlemen, let them establish their government and empire, and work out their destiny according to the wisdom that God has given them."

The peace men who distrusted McClellan as a War Democrat had no fears about Pendleton, the *Sacramento Union* commented:

> Why, Vallandigham himself has not been a more constant enemy of the government nor a more persistent apologist for Jeff Davis. He could be trusted and might eventually become President. … He is a thorough-going secessionist. He assisted Vallandigham in organizing the Copperhead faction out of the traitorous element of the old Democratic party and after their formidable demonstration in the Fall of 1862 became bolder than ever in demands for a disunion …

In the opinion of Pendleton the war on the part of the government was wrong in its inception, and it has increased in iniquity as it has approached its legitimate end. The majority of the people of the loyal states have been wrong throughout the struggle, and our brave soldiers achieved no glory because they have been fighting in a dishonorable, unholy, and unnatural cause.

The Democrats tried to answer the charges of disloyalty against Pendleton by presenting him as a strong advocate of the Union, not the Confederacy. A crowd of thousands at the New York Hotel, October 24, serenaded him at a rally sponsored by the McClellan Legion, an organization of soldiers who had fought in the Army of the Potomac. Denying charges that he was a native Southerner, he declared: "I was born in Ohio; I have lived all my life in the Northwest. I know the sentiment of the people; I sympathize entirely with it. They are attached by every tie of affection and interest to the Union (loud cheering). ... The Democratic party is pledged to an unswerving fidelity to the Union under the Constitution (cheers). It is pledged to the restoration of peace on the basis of the Federal Union of the states (loud applause)."

Besides attacking McClellan and Pendleton, the Republicans had another favorite target in August Belmont, the American agent of the Rothschilds. His enemies charged that he, along with other Eastern financiers and railroad "kings," had taken over the Democratic Party lock, stock, and barrel and forced the nomination of their puppet, Little Mac. Thus the *New York Times* called upon the rank and file of the Democratic Party "to rebuke the demagogues pretending to be of their faith, who, by the construction of such a platform and choosing such a plastic manikin to stand upon it as the representative of the American people in a crisis such as this, who have humiliated that party beyond measure, and seek to make it the jackal to the lion of general rebellion."

Belmont also suffered crass appeals to jealousy of the rich, fear of foreigners, and hatred of the Jews. One hostile newsman described him as "a pale, sleek-headed man, dapper and smooth, with a game leg." Another said: "He is a small, dark complexioned man, walks lame in consequence of a duel ... and speaks with a German accent."

A Republican newspaper sarcastically praised the Democratic Party for selecting

> August Belmont, the gorgeous and fastidious agent of the Rothschilds in America, as the proper person for chairman of the national Democratic committee, and doubtless expects the plethoric speculator in Confederate bonds to furnish the money to be used in buying up the mudsills of society in the North. …
>
> The noble Belmont can quit his elegant mansion to encounter the terrific odor of a Five Points crowd. The silky Seymour can leave his parlor to address a heaving threatening mass of his friends. Other notable Democrats can pause in the princely game of gold speculation in Wall Street to stir the blood of the working men by dilating upon the evils of a depreciated currency.

Some Peace Democrats likewise assailed Belmont, who had guided the party to its nomination of McClellan in Chicago. Samuel Medary, the fiery editor of the *Crisis* newspaper in Columbus, Ohio, who had led the crusade against the war since its first day, refused to place McClellan's name on his paper's masthead. He also savagely attacked Belmont in editorials.

Medary vented his rage over McClellan's repudiation of the platform plank, which the peace men had carefully crafted to Confederate specifications to assure an immediate armistice. Belmont "is a foreigner," Medary wrote. "He lives in the style of the European nobility, feeds and drinks well, and is put up by the money mongers and shoddy contractors of Wall Street."

Medary described the elaborate chariot of "His Democratic Majesty," Belmont, as "[a] low barouche, drawn by four elegant and fiery thoroughbreds, with postillions mounted onto the left, or near, horse of the pair. Two footmen in extreme livery are suspended from a high seat on the back of the carriage. … The barouche is lined in red satin damask, and the outside trimmings are of heavy gilt. The postillions are dressed in buckskin breeches and high top boots, with black silk velvet jackets; and capes highly ornamented with gold lace."

"The rabble think they nominated McClellan, but it was Belmont and the money of the Rothschilds," the *Chicago Tribune* charged. "McClellan is Belmont's tool, the instrument of his selfish purposes. He furnished the money to carry on the political campaign for Mac. ... The Jew banker owns him, body, soul, and breeches. Belmont ... runs the Democratic machine and makes the puppets dance."

George Francis Train, in a Philadelphia speech, sounded a similar theme:

> George B. McClellan is simply the chattel of Sam Barlow and Sam Barlow is the mere chattel of August Belmont, and Belmont is the agent of the Rothschilds, who are the agents of the Confederate Government in England. They were ... sending money through these agents, to try to carry the state of Pennsylvania in November (cries of: "They can't do it!"). I found the Regency and the Rothschilds ruled the entire destiny of the convention.
>
> I know of no more pitiful sight than to see the Pennsylvania delegation cringing before these New York men. When New York took snuff, all Pennsylvania sneezed ...

"Why did Belmont urge the nomination of McClellan for President?" asked the relentless *Chicago Tribune*. "Because he could use him, if elected, to saddle the Rebel debt on the government, and thus get par value for the Confederate bonds which the Rothschilds have been purchasing at about one dollar a bushel."

"The question before the country," the Republican paper declared, "is: Will we have a dishonorable peace, in order to enrich Belmont, the Rothschilds, and the whole tribe of Jews, who have been buying up Confederate bonds, or an honorable peace, won by Grant and Sherman at the cannon's mouth?"

Belmont bore most of the libelous assaults upon his character with dignified silence. His conscience was clear; he had aided the Union war effort financially throughout the conflict; while traveling in Europe, he had encouraged support for the United States government and had discouraged speculation in Confederate bonds. The evidence tending to refute the charges of speculating in Confederate bonds can be found in a letter from Belmont to Baron Lionel de Rothschild, M. P. of London, sent from New York on April 14, 1863: "I am glad to hear from you that you have not taken any interest in the Confederate loan. It is a most reckless speculation, and I do not believe that the first dollar will ever be paid on it."

The U.S. Jewish press emphatically denied the charges of speculating in Confederate bonds. The *Israelite* and the *Jewish Messenger* of New York denied that the Rothschilds "had assisted the rebel treasury to the extent of a dollar."

Belmont finally lost his temper when the *New York Evening Post* insinuated that he was an illegitimate son of the Rothschilds. That was

This pro-Lincoln cartoon depicts President Lincoln holding a tiny figure of General McClellan in his hand and saying, "This reminds me of a little joke." McClellan is holding a spade, symbolic of the entrenchments his army dug outside Richmond that led to his being ridiculed as "the Grave-digger of the Chickahominy." This cartoon appeared in *Harper's Weekly* September 17, 1864. It is from the collections of the Library of Congress.

really a blow below the belt. The *Post* said October 6, 1864: "Prominent among the intriguers who sought to shape the convention was Mr. August Belmont … a reputed son and accredited agent of the Rothschilds." Belmont hit the *Post* with a civil lawsuit for libel about the words "reputed son." Former New York County District Attorney A. Oakey Hall and other friends filed a criminal libel suit. The *Post* apologized October 11 for its "unfounded remarks" and the libel suits never came to trial.

Chapter Thirty-Three

Hood Moves North

TRYING TO RALLY THE SPIRITS of his people, who were dismayed and dejected by the loss of Atlanta, Jefferson Davis made a swing around the South delivering a fusillade of defiant speeches calling for one last effort to win independence. He also revealed that the Confederates were counting on the Democrats' Peace Party to beat Lincoln in the election and thus end the war, not win it for the North.

At Macon, Georgia, Davis revealed that two-thirds of the Confederate soldiers were absent, "some sick, some wounded, but most of them absent without leave." This was a scandalous admission but the president apparently felt compelled to make it public in order to spur laggards into doing their duty. If only a fourth of the absentees would return, he said at Columbia, South Carolina, "we could plant our banners on the banks of the Ohio."

"Let fresh victories crown our arms and the peace party, if there be such at the North, can elect its candidates," he said. "But whether a peace candidate is elected or not, Yankee instinct will teach him that it is better to end this war and leave us to the enjoyment of our rights."

Davis visited the Army of Tennessee and its crippled young commander, John Bell Hood, who had replaced Joe Johnston and then lost Atlanta. Davis promised the Kentucky and Tennessee soldiers that they would soon march northward and their feet would touch their home soil again.

He thus tipped off the latest Southern strategy—to offset the loss of Atlanta by having Hood's army move north and capture Nashville and Middle Tennessee, then dash into Kentucky to free it from the Yankee yoke. After a series of skirmishes along the railroads north of Atlanta, Hood's soldiers entered Alabama while Sherman turned southward and began his notorious March to the Sea, vowing "to make Georgia howl."

Although his left arm had been crippled at Gettysburg and he had lost his right leg at Chickamauga, Hood pressed ahead with his grandiose scheme to recapture the offensive in the war in the West. His idea has usually been derided as the wild pipe dream of a reckless gambler who never had a chance of success. Hood's plan, however, was basically sound—if he could carry it out quickly.

Sherman had left only about 18,000 men, commanded by Gen. George Thomas, to protect Nashville. Hood had 40,000 and believed that, with the aid of Nathan Bedford Forrest's cavalry, they could take the Tennessee capital before Thomas could stop them. Hood intended to cross the Tennessee River at Tuscumbia, Alabama. Here, however, he encountered a disappointment that wrecked his entire timetable.

"He had expected to find—and had ordered weeks ago—ample supplies and the railroad in operation to Corinth," Mississippi, Union Col. Henry Stone recalled in his article, "Repelling Gen. Hood's Invasion of Tennessee," in *Battles and Leaders of the Civil War.* "Instead of the rapid and triumphant march with which he had inflamed his troops, he was delayed three weeks, a delay fatal to his hopes." Thus Hood's ragged Rebels were stalled on the border of Tennessee, their battle for Nashville delayed for weeks, while their morale suffered and desertions increased. The delay gave General Thomas time to round up thousands of additional troops to defend Nashville.

At the same time, Capt. Tom Hines was plotting a new effort to free the Confederate prisoners at Chicago, Indianapolis, and Columbus, Ohio, and march them to Louisville to form a new army and ignite "a fire in the rear" of General Thomas. This was more than a mere theory. The evidence has remained obscure for years and only came to light with the recent rediscovery of a long-forgotten book. The book is *Reminiscences of the Boys in Gray, 1861–1865,* a collection of interviews with Confederate veterans by Miss Mamie Yeary of McGregor, Texas, published in 1912.

H. G. Damon, a Florida native, remembered being involved with Hines and Captain Castleman after the failure of their plan to raid Camp Douglas during the Democratic convention. Their new plan, Damon said, was to free the Rebels in several prisons, form them into an army, and "cross the Ohio and attack General Thomas in the rear." This force of ex-prisoners, even if only a few thousand, could have placed Thomas in a box between two Confederate armies—the Hines troops coming down across Kentucky and Hood's coming up from Alabama.

While Castleman and Damon were rounding up recruits in Indiana in October for the new enterprise, they were arrested by a band of militiamen who were looking for horse thieves. Discovered in Castleman's pockets were his record books proving that he had paid out funds from the Confederates to finance the men who had gone to Chicago for the aborted August raid. So he was tossed into a Federal prison as a suspected spy, and Damon landed in jail in Indiana.

Hood's disappointing delays caused much disaffection among his troops, and the *Chicago Tribune* printed a significant dialogue between Federal interrogators and some Confederate deserters who had lately arrived at Nashville. These are samples:

Sgt. Brent, Fourteenth Alabama Infantry.
  Q. You are tired of service, I presume?
  A. Yes, I have fired the last gun for Jeff Davis.
  Q. Are the men dissatisfied?
  A. Yes, they would desert if they could. Thousands have deserted. Those that make the Union lines do not constitute all that leave.
  Q. Where do they go?
  A. To the woods, where they gather in gangs and live by plundering the men who brought war and then wanted the poor people to do the fighting.

Q. Is this generally regarded as a rich man's war and a poor man's fight?

A. Yes, by everybody. We went into it thinking our rights were in danger, but since we entered the service, we have been perfect slaves ourselves, worse off than niggers.

Q. How long do you think the leaders will hold out?

A. Till after the presidential election. They think a peace man will be elected and the Union armies will be withdrawn.

Q. What do they think of McClellan?

A. They say he is all right, at least they are not afraid of him.

A soldier of the First Tennessee regiment said: Hood's whole fighting force consists of ten divisions averaging 2,300 men each. The Georgia militia was deserting so badly that they were allowed to go home.

Q. Are your men discontented?

A. Our officers tell us that if we will hold out until McClellan is elected, the North will give up the struggle.

Q. Have they any other hope?

A. None.

Q. What, in your opinion, will be the effect on the masses of the army if Lincoln is successful?

A. They will stand no longer, they will tell the officers they have been deceived and the mutiny will be so general, it will be a success.

A soldier named Glover of the 23rd Georgia regiment said the woods were full of deserters, that a great many others, at the solicitation of their officers, had resolved to continue in the field until the result of the presidential election was known.

Q. What would be the effect of Mr. Lincoln's reelection?

A. They would lose all hope and give up.

Q. What is the thought among your officers about McClellan?

A. They say if he is elected, the South will come out safe but, if beaten, they might as well give up.

Chapter Thirty-Four

"Treason" Trials in Indiana

INDIANA AND ILLINOIS LOOMED as the greatest danger to President Lincoln as he fought to win a second term and to keep subversive elements from trying to take the two states out of the war. Republican governors in both states had to battle legislatures controlled by Democrats bent on aiding the peace movement. If the Democrats won, their Copperhead governors could control state militias and weapons in the state arsenals.

John Hay, the president's secretary, worried that "the defection of the executive governments of those two great states, Illinois and Indiana, from the general administration" could be "disastrous and paralyzing."

Governor Oliver P. Morton held Indiana in the Union almost single-handedly by ruling as a virtual dictator for two years. Governor Richard Yates had few financial troubles in Illinois but constantly feared seditious activities of guerrilla bands, especially in the southern part of the state. There "bushwhackers" allied with the Sons of Liberty claimed to control several counties full of "Secesh" sympathizers and constantly engaged in civil strife.

Then, in Indiana, came the shocking revelation of the plot for an armed uprising to free Confederate prisoners at Indianapolis and to depose Governor Morton, a scheme foiled in August only when Democratic Party leaders scotched it because they feared that it would hurt their chances of beating Morton in the October election and carrying the state for McClellan in November.

The president was so worried about losing Indiana that he appealed to General Sherman in September to send home as many Indiana soldiers as he could spare from the battlefront in Georgia so that they could vote in October. Lincoln feared that a Democratic victory would amount to giving the state government over to men who opposed the war.

Lincoln's concern showed that the Civil War was no longer popular with the Northern masses. It had become such a bloody burden that he was afraid the people in the Northwest would simply give up and let the South go.

Indiana Republicans charged that Democrats would stuff the ballot boxes by bringing in men from outside the state to vote illegally. "A very large number of men are coming to this state from Kentucky and farther South," wrote Col. James G. Jones from Indianapolis September 12 to Brig. Gen. James G. Fry, the provost marshal general in Washington. "With scarcely an exception they are in sentiment and feeling rebels." Those armed men intend to vote the Democratic ticket and thus commit "a stupendous fraud," said Jones, the state's acting assistant provost marshal general. "We are on the verge of civil war in Indiana," the panic-stricken colonel warned.

Thoroughly alarmed by the aborted August uprising, Secretary of War Stanton and Governor Morton agreed, according to the governor's biographer, that drastic measures were needed "to strike terror into the hearts of the conspirators" and "prevent a repetition of the plots." They also intended that ties between certain Democrats and Confederates must be fully publicized in time to help Republicans win the October 11 state election. So they decided to rush the accused ringleaders before a military commission rather than risk hauling them before a civil court where the jury probably would include some Democrats who would hesitate to convict.

On September 27 the court, composed of several U. S. Army colonels, convened in Indianapolis and began the trial of Harrison Dodd, the grand commander of the Sons of Liberty in Indiana. Dodd had been a delegate to the Democratic convention in Chicago and was arrested soon after his return home. The judge advocate, Col. H. L. Burnett, presented five charges: 1. Conspiracy against the government of the United States; 2. Affording aid and comfort to rebels; 3. Inciting insurrection; 4. Disloyal practices; and 5. Violation of the laws of war. Dodd pleaded "not guilty" to all counts.

Dodd suffered a shock when he saw the government's first witness take the stand. It was Felix Stidger. "Dodd turned a deathly pale, or white, as I approached the witness chair," Stidger recalled. "He stared at me in bewilderment as though he found it difficult to believe his own senses of sight and hearing."

Dodd had confided all of his revolutionary plans to Stidger, the meek-looking former clerk who had become secretary of the Sons of Liberty in Kentucky and posed as a friend of the South. Now, Dodd realized that his confidante was really a Federal spy.

Stidger's damning testimony made front-page headlines all across the North. Typical was the display in the *Troy Times* in Miami County, Ohio:

"Treason!"

"Startling Disclosures!"

"Assassination!"

In devastating detail, Stidger recounted all the plans Dodd had told him about preparations for the uprising of August 16 when Governor Morton was to be taken hostage or possibly killed and Confederate prisoners released at Indianapolis. In addition, the government tried to tie the Sons of Liberty to the Democrats and the Confederacy through the words of other witnesses.

Wesley Trantor, a former private in Sherman's army, said he joined the secret order because he was a lifelong Democrat. He said he was told that "Indiana, Illinois, and Missouri would join the Southern Confederacy" and "they would lick 'old Abe' and his bluecoats."

William Clayton, a farmer, said his oath as a member of the order bound him "to assist the South" and "to shake hands with the rebels" if they should invade Illinois.

Steven Teney, a cooper, said the members were sworn to "support Jeff Davis, North or South" and "we were to suffer ourselves to be torn into four pieces if we did not."

Dodd had been confined in the military prison at Indianapolis. Upon his word of honor that he would not try to escape, he was transferred to a third-story room in the United States court building. In the early morning darkness of October 7, he escaped through a window by sliding down a rope conveniently provided by friends on the outside and slipped across the border into Canada.

Naturally, the Republicans raised a great uproar over Dodd's mysterious departure only four days before the state election, and they pounded the Democrats over new evidence of treachery. Gen. Henry B. Carrington called Dodd's escape a confession of guilt and warned the voters: "Testimony every day shows that you are upon the threshold of revolution. You can rebuke this treason. The traitors intend to bring war to your homes. Meet them at the ballot box, while Grant and Sherman meet them in the field."

"If the rebels in arms could vote in Indiana today, every one of them would cast his ballot for Joseph E. McDonald and the Democratic state ticket," the *Indianapolis Journal* declared in a last minute appeal on Election Day. "Let voters remember that Joseph Ristine, James S. Athon, Oscar B. Hord and Napoleon B. Taylor, all candidates on the Democratic state ticket, are third degree members of the treasonable order, Sons of Liberty."

On Election Day, in response to Lincoln's urgent appeals to General Sherman, Union soldiers voted by the thousands for Governor Morton and not all of them were from Indiana. Soldiers from Vermont and Massachusetts, according to some reports, followed the dictum of "come early and vote often" in Indiana.

Morton won reelection over McDonald by a margin of 22,000.

"I am deeply thankful for the result in Indiana," John Hay recorded. "I believe it rescues Indiana from sedition and civil war. A Copperhead Governor would have afforded a grand central rallying point for lurking treason whose existence Carrington has already so clearly demonstrated, which, growing bolder by the popular zeal and sanction, would have dared to lift its head from the dust and measure strength with the government."

In Pennsylvania the Union ticket prevailed but by a smaller margin than in Indiana, causing Lincoln to worry about losing that key state in November. The Republican state ticket swept Ohio by

54,000, a sure sign that it would stick with Lincoln in November.

After a recess to celebrate Republican victories, the military commission at Indianapolis reconvened October 24 to provide more sensational campaign material for the November election. Several more prominent Democrats were brought to trial: Dr. William A. Bowles, Lambdin P. Milligan, Joseph Bingham, Stephen Horsey, Andrew Humphreys, and Horace Heffren.

A most unlikely hero was Heffren, the "deputy grand Commander" of the Sons of Liberty in Indiana, whom the *Indianapolis Journal* had earlier ridiculed as "that disgusting compound of whisky, grease, vulgarity and cowardice." The Republican paper chronicled Heffren's career: As a member of the legislature in 1861, "he was so carried away by the exhilarating extract of corn, that he actually talked of fighting ... on behalf of the South." Instead, he raised a company for the Union army and became its lieutenant colonel. His regiment, "strung along the line of the Louisville and Nashville railroad," was "gobbled up by the Rebel raider John Morgan," but Heffren escaped because he had "stowed himself safely away in Nashville." He saved himself from a court martial by resigning. If he should lead the secret order into a fight against the government, the *Journal* surmised, this "blatherskite" would be "a formidable enemy to all the hen roosts and whisky on the line of his march."

But the whisky-soaked warrior did not lead his "Gophers" into any fight at all. He struck a deal with the prosecutors whereby all the charges against him were dropped, and he turned state's evidence, telling tales that astonished the spectators in the courtroom.

General Carrington exultantly telegraphed to Judge Advocate Gen. Joseph Holt in Washington November 4: "Heffren ... has turned state's evidence and has sworn this afternoon that their object was a Northwestern Confederacy and that a committee of ten was appointed to assassinate or hold as hostage Governor Morton."

The *Indianapolis Journal* quoted Heffren as saying that "half a million dollars was sent by rebel agents in Canada to Indiana, Illinois, and Kentucky to purchase arms for the order, of which amount Dodd and John C. Walker received one hundred thousand dollars each."

The trial transcript shows that Heffren testified: "The order members were to march under the banner of the Confederate army. If they could not win a Northwestern Confederacy they were to join their forces with the South."

"How would you know when you could not get a Northwestern Confederacy?" Heffren was asked. He shot back:

"As any fool would know when he got whipped."

Commenting editorially on Heffren's testimony, the *Journal* declared:

> It has often been charged that there was a design on the part of prominent Democrats of Ohio, Indiana, Illinois, and other Western states, to establish a Northwestern Confederacy with a view to an ultimate union with the South. This has been denied with every appearance of candor by the Democratic press, and those who have asserted it have been unsparingly denounced as slanderers of the Democratic party. Yet Mr. Heffren testifies that it was the main purpose of the order. He says:
>
> > "The military organization, as I learned, was for the purpose of separating the Northwestern States from the East, and establishing a Northwestern Confederacy; and, failing in that, to unite with the South."

With relish, the *Chicago Tribune* reported: "Heffren said the O. A. K. was composed entirely of Democrats. He never knew a member who was not a Democrat. It was understood that the administration party would not allow the Democrats a fair vote, and they had determined to have a free vote or a free fight."

Colonel Burnett, the judge advocate, charged in a campaign speech that, when the mid-August uprising was being plotted in Indiana, "three Rebel colonels came to the Bates House in this city for the purpose of having a consultation with leaders of the conspiracy." They were "going to Chicago to take charge of the rebel prisoners who were to be released from confinement there and take an active part in the revolution."

Colonel Burnett accused editor Joseph Bingham of the *Sentinel* of doing nothing to have the three Rebel colonels arrested. "No! He counseled and assisted their escape by his silence and allowed them to return to their friends and engage in shooting down your fathers and brothers and sons."Colonel Burnett's oratory was so passionate that it evoked shouts from the audience, "Hang him! Hang him! Hang him!" Bingham escaped harm, however. For turning state's evidence, like Heffren, he walked out of the courtroom a free man.

The revelations in the Indianapolis trials delighted Republicans, who believed the testimony tying Democrats directly to the treason plots would guarantee a Lincoln victory. Indeed, the whole treason issue was so loaded with political dynamite that the Republicans made it a central feature of their entire national campaign against McClellan.

At the behest of Secretary Stanton, Judge Advocate General Holt concocted the official "Report" on the secret orders, wildly exaggerating their strength at about half a million and accusing them of plotting revolution and civil war in the North. The report mainly combined the earlier versions by General Carrington and Colonel Sanderson and, bearing the official seal of the United States government, it had a powerful effect upon many voters. The Republicans spread the *Holt Report* all across the North in pamphlet form and their party newspapers gave it front-page play.

Holt accused the Sons of Liberty of: "Aiding soldiers to desert; discouraging enlistments and resisting the draft; communicating with the enemy; helping them to recruit within our lines; furnishing the rebels with arms and ammunition; cooperating with the enemy in raids; destroying government property; persecuting loyal men; assassination and murder" and attempts to set up a Northwestern Confederacy.

"Although its capacity for fatal mischief has … been seriously impaired" by the arrest of its leaders and the seizure of its arms, Holt warned that the secret order was still plotting against the government "in aid of the Southern rebellion." He said: "Its members assert that foul means will be used to prevent the success of the Administration at the coming election, and threaten an extended revolt in the event of the re-election of President Lincoln."

In his peroration, Judge Holt declared: "Judea produced but one Judas Iscariot and Rome, from the sinks of demoralization, produced but one Catiline; and yet … there has risen together in our land an entire brood of such traitors, all animated by the same parricidal spirit and all struggling with the same relentless malignancy for the dismemberment of our Union. ... All these blackened and fetid streams of crime may be traced to the same common fountain ... slavery."

Holt made an especially partisan attempt to link the backers of General McClellan to the "Order of American Knights," saying, without evidence: "In the state of New York and other parts of the North, the secret political association known as the 'McClellan Minute Guard' would seem to be a branch of the O.A.K."

The McClellan Guard's secretary, Dr. R. F. Stevens, fired back in a letter to the *New York World*, asserting that "nothing of a secret or traitorous nature was ever connected with it." Holt's charges, he wrote, "are absolute and entire falsehoods." Dr. Stevens asserted: "The Minute Guard is an association for ordinary political campaign work. On election days, they work for votes and the result of their work will be seen all over the Union as it has been seen in the recent election in Pennsylvania."

Then he leveled this withering blast at the campaign tactics of some of Lincoln's men: "In the unparalleled election frauds in Indiana; in the open boasts of a company of Massachusetts soldiers that they voted at several of the polls in Pennsylvania; in the discharge of workers at the navy yard for being in favor of McClellan; in the thousands of arbitrary arrests and the hundreds of suppressions of a hitherto free press, all men may see that the re-election of Mr. Lincoln and the continuance in power of such men as support him, will be the most unmitigated curse ever inflicted upon a free people."

In vain did the Democrats protest their innocence of the treason charges and insist that Holt's report was a partisan election-eering device, a mishmash of a few truths, some half truths, much fiction, and many outright lies. They accused Holt, a former Democrat, of turning his back on his old party in pursuit of personal gain under the Lincoln regime. Holt had been postmaster general and secretary of war under Buchanan and, as late as 1860, he had sounded like a conservative who opposed Federal "coercion" of the states.

During the prewar cotton boom in Mississippi, Holt had amassed a fortune as a lawyer, and then returned to his native state, Kentucky. He labored successfully to keep Kentucky from joining the Confederacy, and, as a result, his relatives in the South branded him a turncoat. With the zeal of a convert, Holt became increasingly strident in his support of the war and his hatred of "rebels" and "traitors" and "the slave power."

Lincoln appointed him judge advocate general in September 1862, finding him exactly the right kind of merciless prosecutor who would expand the power of military commissions to convict many civilians charged with "disloyalty" in various forms, depending upon the whims of the accusers.

Holt received many letters denouncing him for defaming the Democrats and becoming a traitor to his old party. Typical was this one from Oswego, New York: "A man who, once a Democrat, and who has received so many favors and high honors at the hands of the Democracy as you have, and will stoop to such depths of infamy to curry favor, as manifested by the publication herein enclosed, merits the scorn, the contempt, and ignominy which will forever after attach to the name of Joseph Holt." Enclosed was a newspaper clipping calling the report "a despicable slander against the friends of McClellan" and "the fabrications of a defamer and a scoundrel."

B. W. Dennis wrote from Canandaigua, New York, backing Holt against the "Copperhead tirades" of his critics. "The unnatural situation of four years exclusion from office" seems to have maddened the Democrats, he wrote, "and they are entering into this contest like a pack of ravenous wolves."

A letter addressed to "My dear Josey" and signed "Your loving aunt till death," praised Holt's report and warned him to look out for assassins. "I believe," his "aunt" wrote, "they will send emissaries to Washington city in disguise on purpose to poison or kill you."

Chapter Thirty-Five

Illinois Democrat Takes Rebel Gold

ON THE EVENING OF OCTOBER 13, two days after the elections in the "October" states, President Lincoln jotted down his own prediction of the outcome of the voting in November. He conceded to McClellan eight states: New York, Pennsylvania, Illinois, New Jersey, Missouri, Kentucky, Delaware, and Maryland. Total: 114 electoral votes. For himself, the president claimed all of New England, Ohio, Indiana, Michigan, Wisconsin, Minnesota, Iowa, West Virginia, Kansas, California, Oregon, and Nevada. Total: 120. Needed for victory: 118, a majority of the 234 electoral votes. Thus Lincoln expected to keep the presidency by a margin of two electoral votes.

Clearly, the president had not succumbed to the rosy notion that the fall of Atlanta, Farragut's victory in Mobile Bay, and Sheridan's devastation of Virginia's Shenandoah Valley would automatically ensure a Republican triumph. Those events saved Lincoln from ruin, but his followers still had to work hard against the Democrats, who were waging strong, even desperate, campaigns in New York, Pennsylvania, and Illinois. So the Republicans intensified their efforts to brand McClellan as the captive of crafty politicians who intended to use him to achieve an armistice that would end the war on terms acceptable to the South.

Illinois was especially in peril. The Confederates were planning a double assault on Lincoln's home state for the purpose of taking it out of the Union war effort. First, the Confederates were pouring thousands of dollars from their gold fund in Canada into the campaign of the Democratic candidate for governor of Illinois, the notorious peace advocate, Congressman James C. Robinson. Second, Capt. Tom Hines, undeterred by the failure of his first attempt to free several thousand Rebel prisoners at Camp Douglas during the Democratic convention in Chicago, was secretly preparing for a second attempt—on election night, November 8—this time, not with weak, timid Sons of Liberty but with a band of ruthless bushwhackers famous for their guerrilla warfare tactics in southern Illinois.

Hines and John B. Castleman knew about the Illinois Democrats' appeal to Confederate Commissioner Jacob Thompson in Toronto for gold to finance Robinson's campaign against Republican candidate Gen. Richard J. Oglesby, a Union war veteran disabled by a wound in the battle of Corinth. Castleman recorded in his memoirs that a committee of Democrats called upon Thompson in October, bringing assurances from Clement Vallandigham and others, asking money, "stating that Robinson had pledged himself to them that if elected he would place control of the militia and the sixty thousand stand of arms of that state in the hands of the order of the Sons of Liberty.

"Mr. Thompson agreed that whenever proper committees were formed of responsible persons to use the money effectually and in good faith to secure that end, he would furnish the money." "Proper committees" were at once designated by the Illinois Democratic central committee—Castleman even lists the names of the two dozen members and the counties they covered—and the gold began to flow. He estimated that at least $50,000 in gold—the equivalent of about $140,000 in greenbacks—went out from the Confederate funds, plus at least two more gifts of $20,000 apiece were granted on the basis of written assurances from the candidate himself.

Robinson wrote these pledges to his Confederate financial friends: "If elected governor of the state, I will see that its sovereignty is maintained, the laws faithfully enforced, and its citizens protected from arbitrary arrest, and if necessary for these purposes will, after exhausting the civil, employ the military force of the state.

"I will also be happy to avail myself of the counsel and aid of the executive committee of the Peace Democracy in the conduct and organization of the militia of the state, recognizing the fact that a well organized militia is necessary for the maintenance of the rights as well as the liberties of the people."

Anyone versed in the euphemisms of politicians can easily see that Robinson was using familiar code words, such as "state rights," to promise that he would use the Illinois militia to carry out the policies of the Peace Democrats and their money men, the Confederates. Castleman includes a picture of the promissory letter in his memoirs and quotes a comment by his comrade Hines, who wrote:

"Verbal assurances from Mr. Robinson, fully committing himself to our movement, had already been had. A large amount of money was furnished on these assurances."

It is important to note that Hines says Robinson made private verbal assurances "fully committing himself to our movement." Now, what did this Confederate agent mean by "our movement"? Evidently, he meant the "movement" financed by the Confederates for a compromise peace. The Confederates were determined to get their money's worth when they financed Robinson as part of their last gasp effort to win independence.

David E. Long, author of *The Jewel of Liberty, Abraham Lincoln's Re-Election and the End of Slavery*, cites the Robinson letter in his excellent book to refute some historians who try to whitewash the Democrats' collaboration with the Confederates. Long asserts: "If it was not treasonous for an Illinois gubernatorial candidate to do business with enemy agents, then the definition of treason has been narrowed tremendously." A similar statement could apply to those Democrats who met with Confederate agents in Canada and welcomed their aid in drafting their party's platform.

Fortunately for Robinson and the Democrats, his gifts of gold from the Confederates remained a secret for years after the 1864 election. The Republicans already had dark suspicions of the congressman because of his record as a peace advocate; Republican newspapers greeted his nomination by the "Copperhead Convention" at Springfield as a total victory for the "O. A. K." or Sons of Liberty. Quoth the *Daily Missouri Democrat*:

The Democracy of the state was cheated at Chicago. The Northwestern states were beaten there by the capitalists of New England and New York—the shoddy manufacturers and railroad shareholders. But they were determined not to be beaten in the state nominations, so the societies went to work and everybody in the shape of shoulder straps or War Democracy was ruthlessly slaughtered. ... The ticket is an unconditional peace one ...

From the head to the tail there is not a man on it whose voice is for war, under any possible circumstance. Jim Robinson's votes in Congress tell the story of his treasonable instincts.

S. Corning Judd, nominated for lieutenant governor, was an officer in the Sons of Liberty and "the worst bargain in the lot," the newspaper claimed. Jim Allen, seeking another term as congressman at large, it said, "is the most unremitting peace-sneak and humbug generally in the state. If you were to search rebellion over, from one end of it to the other, you could not find more devoted tools of Jeff Davis and Company than this precious lot of Copperhead candidates,"

Figuratively dipping his pen in acid, the St. Louis correspondent then etched this brutally frank word portrait of Congressman Robinson: "In person, he is large, coarse looking and vulgar. His face is sensual in expression, round, fat and florid; his eyes are blue, his hair yellow and lank-looking. He chews tobacco and never cleans his teeth. ... He would make a fair-looking enough bartender in a lager-beer saloon but, as governor of the state of Illinois, it looks like putting a pig in a parlor."

In contrast to the fat, sloppy Copperhead Robinson, the *Indianapolis Daily Journal* warmly endorsed his opponent, General Oglesby, a severely wounded hero. In the capture of Fort Donelson and the battle of Shiloh, this Mexican War veteran showed great leadership and cool courage, the *Journal* said. In the battle of Corinth, October 4, 1862, "he was severely wounded by a ball lodging near the spine. The gallant old soldier still carries the ball in his body. ... Its painful effects, from which he has never fully recovered, incapacitate him from further service."

Backing Oglesby, the *Chicago Tribune* warned Illinois voters: "If you would throw the great weight of Illinois against the vigorous prosecution of the war, and in favor of a dishonorable prosecution of peace, vote for James C. Robinson. If you would bring disgrace to the Illinois dead on the field and shame to the cheeks of our boys that remain in the ranks, make your governor out of James C. Robinson, the confirmed Copperhead and Chicago platform peace-sneak."

The *Tribune* thus paid its respects to S. Corning Judd as a shifty politician who had been identified with three different parties: "Originally a Whig and an office-holder under Fillmore, he became a violent Native American in 1856 and edited a Know-Nothing paper in Syracuse, New York, called *The Daily Star*. The transition from the 'K.N.' to the 'O.A.K.' where we find him now, was easy and natural. None were more vociferous than he in crying, 'Put none but Americans on guard.' None are more obsequious now in soliciting the support of persons of foreign birth."

As late as mid-October, despite the evident Republican gains since the dark days of despair in August, President Lincoln feared that he would lose Illinois. So he called in the most powerful campaigner he could imagine to swing Democrats over to the Union cause. Lincoln personally called Gen. John A. Logan from Sherman's army in Georgia to bring wavering Democrats back to support the war and to make sure that General Oglesby would keep the loathsome Jim Robinson from becoming governor.

"Black Jack" Logan had not always been a zealous friend of the Republican president. A Democratic congressman when the war began, he had railed against Senator Stephen A. Douglas for backing Lincoln's decision in favor of waging war against the seceding Southern states. Logan opposed coercing the South, and he accused Douglas of selling out the Democrats to the Republicans. He was so ferociously antiwar then that his friends had to defend him against "cowardly slanders" that he had even aided in recruiting Illinois soldiers for the Southern army.

Later, however, Black Jack saw a great light. He agreed with Douglas that in the war there could be only two classes of Americans, "patriots and traitors." He resigned his seat in Congress and joined the Union army as a colonel of Illinois volunteers. He stayed on active duty throughout the war.

When Democrats controlling the Illinois legislature demanded an armistice in 1863 and some Illinois troops mutinied in opposition to the Emancipation Proclamation, Logan issued a stirring address to his soldiers, demanding that they stand firm to save the Union. "Intriguing political tricksters," he warned, were trying to produce "general demoralization of the army ... and aid those arch traitors in the South to dismember our mighty republic."

When Gen. James G. McPherson was killed in the fighting before Atlanta, General Sherman ordered General Logan to take command of the Army of the Tennessee and later commended him for having maintained his reputation "as a brave and gallant" soldier. It was from the field of victory at Atlanta that Black Jack returned to Illinois in the autumn of 1864 to assail the peace advocates in his own party and to rally Democrats to help carry the state for Lincoln and Oglesby.

Logan ripped into McClellan, Pendleton, and Robinson in a fiery speech to a cheering crowd at Carbondale, Illinois, declaring that, although he had long been a Democrat, he would not vote for any man who would not "put down this accursed rebellion." The Democrats, he said "would send commissioners to Jeff Davis, who has charge of the most gigantic conspiracy against the best government on earth, and say ... 'We beg of Your Worship that you give us an audience so that we can make propositions for peace.' (laughter). ...

"I would rather have my heart torn from my body and hung upon a tree for vultures to feed upon than bend my knee to that infamous traitor," (applause) ...

As for McClellan, Logan said: "There is no excuse for him except that he is so craving and anxious for power that he is willing to accept it from traitors and cowards." Black Jack warned that McClellan, as president, could die in office and Vice President Pendleton, "an infamous traitor," would then move into the White House and carry out his own policy of appeasing the South. Logan roared:

> I would not vote for Pendleton for vice president or any other
> office if the devil were a candidate against him. Why do I say so?
> I served with him in Congress. ... I have heard from his lips
> words of treason and disloyalty. He has denounced this war

from the time it commenced. He has never voted a solitary dollar, not a cent, in favor of prosecuting the war. ... He has advocated state rights and said that he believed the people of the South had a right to secede and the government had no right to coerce them back into the Union.

Logan would not call McClellan a traitor but predicted that, if elected president, "he would have around him such men as Wood, Vallandigham, Richmond, and the Israelite Belmont. He would be only a tool in the hands of these men who ... would give the Southern Confederacy its independence," (applause).

Logan quoted Alabama congressman J. L. M. Curry as saying the Southerners should pray for the success of the Democrats in the election, for that would mean "our independence would be established." "How does Curry know this?" the general asked. The answer, he said, is this: "These communications that have been going constantly between the rebels of the Southern Confederacy and the Northern rebels—all assembled at Niagara Falls—might possibly explain how he knows so much about what the Confederacy can expect from the peace men if elected."

Then Logan turned his guns on Robinson.

Jim Robinson, he said, has been voting with the peace men throughout his career in Congress while his opponent, General Oglesby, "has been devoting his whole time and energy to the cause of his country in the army" until he was wounded. Robinson's associations are with disloyal men, "his sympathies are with rebels and traitors," Logan charged. "He sustains and supports the men of the party who are determined to destroy the government."

"When November comes," Logan concluded, "let us cast our votes as though we were casting the fate of the nation; for I do humbly believe that the success of the so-called Democratic ticket for the nation will be but the success of the rebellion."

Black Jack stormed around Illinois, electrifying crowds with his tirades against the Peace Democrats and rallying the voters to stand firm for the Union with Lincoln and Oglesby. The powerful effect of his oratory can be seen in two messages from Congressman Elihu Washburne to the president.

In the first letter, Washburne mourned: "It is no use to deceive ourselves about this state. ... Everything is at sixes and sevens and no head or tail to anything. There is an imminent danger of losing the state."

Ten days later, the Republican congressman wrote to Lincoln about the results of General Logan's campaigning in the Democrats' stronghold, southern Illinois: "Logan is carrying all before him in Egypt."

If he had known that Jim Robinson was being bankrolled with Confederate gold, Logan would have hurled even more damning indictments against him. His worst fears would have been realized if he had known that the Confederates, led by Tom Hines, were secretly preparing to take over Chicago on Election Night, November 8, in an effort to free the prisoners at Camp Douglas and form a separate little Rebel army in the North.

Chapter Thirty-Six
Rebels Betrayed in Chicago

A FEW DAYS BEFORE THE NOVEMBER election, large numbers of seedy-looking men with bushy hair and beards, dressed in homespun clothing that marked them as Butternuts, began arriving on trains from southern Illinois. They streamed into depots in Chicago, carrying no baggage except revolvers and refusing to tell anybody who they were or why they had come to the city.

One gang of "mysterious passengers in tattered uniforms" created the suspicion that they were "rebel spies or raiders en route to Chicago to make an attack on Camp Douglas or to fire the city on Election Day in accordance with the plan concocted in Canada" and thwarted at the time of the Democratic national convention, the *Chicago Tribune* surmised. "Last night, more than sixty guerrillas arrived at Chicago and proceeded from the Alton depot to the Sherman House, where they liquored pretty freely and dispersed. Their unusual attire, their sinister expressions, and their general resemblance to the prisoners in Camp Douglas sent a feeling of mingled horror and animosity through the crowd. Chicago has never seen birds of this feather except under the arrest of Federal troops."

"What are these men here for?" the Republican newspaper asked.

"Are they here for the purpose of making a hole in the wall at Camp Douglas, or have they come merely to take possession of the polls and stuff the ballot boxes next Tuesday? Who pays their expenses?"

Some of the "Butternut ruffians" who had kept their mouths tightly shut upon their arrival, became more talkative after visiting local saloons. "After they had drunk freely of poor whisky, their tongues became loose and they boasted among themselves how they would 'choke off the damned abolitionists at the poll' and 'burn down the damned abolitionist town,'" the *Tribune* reported. It felt sure these were all "emissaries of Jeff Davis," come to Chicago to commit some dastardly deeds.

Noting the arrival of eighty more suspicious-looking men from southern Illinois, the paper told its readers: "We are sounding no false alarm. It is the startling truth that large numbers of Butternut ruffians from abroad are pouring into our city for some unlawful purpose. They have no business here but have come to perpetrate villainy."

Actually, the *Tribune*'s editors were striking close to the truth. The new wave of rednecks on the city streets made up the vanguard of a private army recruited by the tireless Confederate Capt. Thomas Henry Hines, who was back in Chicago undercover. He was determined to carry out his long-cherished plan to free several thousand Rebel prisoners at Camp Douglas, form them into the nucleus of a new Rebel army, and open a second front in the war, this time in the North.

He would no longer rely upon the timid souls of the Sons of Liberty, who had panicked in August and refused to furnish even 500 men for his revolutionary scheme. Now he had a different force of tough, well-paid desperadoes who liked to fight and who were unafraid of battling bluecoats. They scheduled their coup for Election Night, November 8, when they could mingle easily among the throngs of excited people in the streets.

Disguised in civilian clothes and traveling under the name of "Dr. Hunter," Captain Hines came by rail from Toronto to Chicago in early November and registered at the Richmond House along with several other Confederates, including Lt. J. F. Bettersworth, Col. Vincent Marmaduke, and Richard T. Semmes. Col. George St. Leger

Grenfell, a British soldier of fortune who had officially retired from the Confederate army, showed up at the Richmond House along with his hunting dogs and gun, saying that he had just come from several days of shooting game in southern Illinois. He was eager to have a front-row seat in the drama soon to begin in Chicago. He wrote to relatives in England that they could expect to hear of a revolution in the Northwest United States soon.

Rumors of a new Confederate plot alarmed the commander at Camp Douglas, Col. B. J. Sweet, a Union army veteran who had been wounded in the battle of Perryville, Kentucky, when a Rebel bullet had crushed the bones of his right arm. Disabled for further combat, he commanded a guard of 800 soldiers protecting the camp on the outskirts of Chicago. About 250 of his guards were also disabled and thus unable to fight.

Appealing for reinforcements, Colonel Sweet told Brig. Gen. John Cook at Springfield: "This city is filling up with suspicious characters, some of whom are known to be escaped prisoners; and others who were here from Canada during the Chicago convention, plotting to release the prisoners at Camp Douglas. … My force is, as you know, too weak and much overworked, only eight hundred men to guard between eight thousand and nine thousand prisoners. I ought to have more force here at once."

Besides beefing up his force of guards, Colonel Sweet made a deal with a Confederate prisoner named John T. Shanks, a Texan with a checkered past. Shanks was allowed to fake an "escape"; he went directly to the home of Judge Buckner Morris in Chicago and pleaded for help in making his way back to the Confederacy. The judge's wife gave him $30 as well as some clothing and advised him to take the next train for Cincinnati.

Instead of fleeing south, Shanks wormed his way into the confidence of a Confederate in the Tom Hines group—identified by Hines later as J. F. Bettersworth—and plied him with plenty of liquor. While intoxicated, Bettersworth blabbed the whole plan for the attack on the prison, and Shanks immediately relayed the information to Colonel Sweet. The colonel also questioned another prisoner, Maurice Langhorne, and learned further details of the plot. Hines later identified the talkative Langhorne as the "infamous traitor who sold his comrades for blood money." Hines had an equally low opinion of Shanks—"a blacker-hearted villain never lived."

Armed with the information from his spies, Colonel Sweet threw out a dragnet on Sunday night, November 6, swooping down on the Confederates and arresting most of the leaders and their allies. He protected his informer, Shanks, by having him arrested along with Grenfell at the Richmond House. The Federal patrols caught Col. Vincent Marmaduke at the home of Dr. E. W. Edwards; Brig. Gen. Charles Walsh of the local Sons of Liberty, Capt. George Cantrill of Morgan's command, and Charles Travers, all at the Walsh house; and Judge Morris at his residence. At Walsh's house, not far from Camp Douglas, the Federals found an arsenal of guns and ammunition. Colonel Sweet recorded the arrests of "106 bushwhackers, guerrillas and rebel soldiers, among them many of the notorious Clingman gang of Fayette and Christian counties, with their captain, Sears, and lieutenant, Garland, all of whom are now in custody at Camp Douglas."

But Captain Hines, the mastermind of the whole show, escaped. When the soldiers stormed the home of Dr. Edwards, seeking "two Confederate spies," they arrested only one, Colonel Marmaduke. They never found the other, Captain Hines. He had hidden in a large box mattress on the same bed where the doctor's wife lay seriously ill. Many well-wishers came to cheer up the ailing lady. One rainy day, Hines locked arms with a departing visitor and, sheltered by his umbrella, walked to the railroad depot, boarded the train to Cincinnati, and eventually arrived at Richmond.

In Chicago, more arrests followed and Home Guards patrolled the streets to make sure that no riots would interfere with the election. Mayor Sherman, who had been reelected in April with strong Copperhead support, promised to secure everyone the right to vote and "to preserve the peace." He thus sorely disappointed the Rebels and their Democratic allies, who had been counting on him to give them free rein in carrying out their schemes.

"The course of Mayor Sherman is the explosion of a bombshell in the very heart of the Chicago rebel camp," the *Tribune* gloated. "There was deep and bitter swearing in secesh circles yesterday. The Sons of Liberty, the K. G. C. and all the banded traitors in our midst grew white with wrath, while the Butternut strangers ... cursed Mayor

Sherman ... as having brought them here to betray them. The rebel prisoners in Camp Douglas, who had been led to believe that the mayor would aid their cause, made the air blue with frantic rage."

In a final appeal for Lincoln and the Republicans on election eve, the *Tribune* blamed the Democrats for the Camp Douglas plot and a scheme to burn the city. "Every one of those raiders was a Democrat," it charged. No doubt the Republicans exaggerated their claims of Chicago's narrow escape from being burned to the ground, and they did so for obvious partisan reasons. But the Hines plan was indeed a serious plot by desperate and determined men, and it could have succeeded had it not been betrayed.

In a magazine article praising Colonel Sweet, James B. Gilmore (Edmund Kirke) said the Confederates had planned to assemble an army of 100,000 by freeing prisoners of war in Illinois and Indiana; that the theater of war would have moved from the South to the heart of the free states "and Southern independence would have followed." The author obviously indulged in fiction in claiming that the prisoners would have made up an army of 100,000. That is a ludicrous exaggeration. But a much smaller force of even 20,000 battle-hardened Confederates, armed and quickly mobilized into a tough fighting force, could have caused plenty of trouble. Horace Greeley, in his massive narrative, *The American Conflict*, wrote that the arrests by Colonel Sweet broke up a conspiracy, which was intended to "lift the siege of Richmond ... and set off civil war in the North."

Colonel Sweet, in his own official report to Washington, expressed no doubt that the Confederates and their allies had come heavily armed to Chicago to free the prisoners at Camp Douglas and to light the spark of an uprising in Illinois and Indiana. They had gathered

> a force considerably larger than the little garrison then guarding between eight thousand and nine thousand prisoners of war at Camp Douglas, ... and they intended to make a night attack on and surprise this camp, release and arm the prisoners of war, cut the telegraph wires, burn the railroad depots, seize the banks and stores containing arms and ammunitions, take possession of the city, and commence a campaign for the release of other prisoners of war in the states of Illinois and

Indiana, thus organizing an army to effect and give success to the general uprising so long contemplated by the Sons of Liberty.

Those writers who have dismissed the entire Chicago plot as mere Republican propaganda must have neglected, or covered up, a large amount of evidence available in Confederate records, the National Archives, and the *Official Records* proving that the scheme was real. Ignoring such evidence, or whitewashing it, is poor scholarship.

Gilmore also wrote that the Chicago coup was linked to simultaneous advances by other Confederate forces, and that was true. They included Gen. Sterling Price's autumn campaign to regain Missouri and Gen. John B. Hood's drive to make up for his loss of Atlanta by leading his tattered army from Georgia northward through Alabama to Middle Tennessee with the goal of recapturing Nashville.

A few of Hood's stragglers, captured during the earlier fighting, arrived as prisoners in Nashville shortly before Election Day, while the bulk of Hood's army was stalled farther south. "I sometimes pity the poor devils," a newspaperman commented. "The first thing they ask, on getting into the corporate limits of the 'subjugated city,' is, 'Will McClellan be elected?'" It was sad to see their dejected faces, he added, "when they are told that Small Mac had not a ghost of a chance."

Chapter Thirty-Seven

New York in the Balance

THE PRESIDENTIAL CAMPAIGN reached the height of intensity in New York, a state which both parties considered vital to victory. Lincoln had carried the state by 50,000 votes in his 1860 sweep, but realistic politicians believed that majority had vanished. New York City, the strongest center of pro-Southern sympathy in the North, was certain to turn in its usual Democratic majority. But the Republicans were dismayed to find that their most loyal voters in upstate New York were also weary of the war and ready for a change. The people had poured out their men and their money freely in the early days of the conflict, but now they were weary of the endless carnage and responding coldly to Lincoln's call for half a million more men with the threat of a draft if the states failed to meet their quotas.

The *Albany Atlas and Argus* published a typical letter from a country reader saying that upstate residents were going to vote against the tyrannical Lincoln in November. Conceding that the army needed more men, they objected to raising any more of them from the native population.

"There is hardly a county in the North," said the *New York Times*, "that is not busy selling bonds in order to buy up for service in the army the worst military material to be found in the Western World—foreign mercenaries and liberated slaves.

"The call of the government for men is the signal, not for a rush to arms, but for a prodigious scratching of pens and issuing of 'evidences of indebtedness.' Everybody who can, takes up his check-book, not his sword, and meets the Provost Marshal with a smiling patriotic face." Judging from all the efforts of the towns, counties, and states to escape the draft, the *Times* asserted, the United States Army might soon be "entirely composed of the sweepings of emigrant ships, of Negro slaves, and any other refuse we could pick up; and—here is the worst of it—of that noble remnant of the old army who, faithful to the last, have gone back, after three years of hardship and danger, to face the storm once more."

The *Philadelphia Press* published a letter from a Union soldier, who had survived Confederate prisons, calling for the Northern people to send more fighting men to win the war. Half the new recruits, he said, are "the miserable sweepings of the cities. … Massachusetts sends agents to Europe to buy up the offal of the worn-out countries of the Continent, or seeks to fill her quota with emancipated Negroes. She devotes herself to educating the Negroes and making shoddy."

A. Dudley Mann, a Confederate diplomat in Belgium, wrote to Secretary of State Benjamin: "Europe is bankrupt of criminals and paupers. All the houses of correction and poorhouses have been drained. The fact that immigrants of this description were acceptable to the Lincoln government has a tendency to deter emigrating persons who can make a living by industry."

George Templeton Strong, the New York lawyer whose diary was filled with blood-thirsty verbal attacks upon the damned rebels and slave drivers and calls for ruthless war against the South, wrote this entry August 25: "To office of Provost Marshal of my district this morning. … where, after waiting an hour, I purveyed myself a substitute, a big 'Dutch' boy of twenty or so, for the moderate consideration of eleven hundred dollars. … Got myself exempted at this high price because I felt all day that some attack of illness were at hand."

Strong was typical of well-to-do Northerners who bought their way out of the army and let poor emigrants take their places while the stay-at-homes enjoyed the fruits of wartime prosperity.

The New York correspondent of the *Philadelphia Inquirer* wrote October 3: "The men are running mad with speculations in stocks, gold, oil, and politics; the women with costly apparel, public amusements, and the entire catalogue of vanities. The gambling houses are thronged every night with able-bodied young men between the ages of twenty and forty-five who would be doing themselves, their country, and the Moral Reform Society a service by shouldering a musket and moving off to the front with General Grant. The gilded saloons of Fourteenth Street and the subterranean hells of the Bowery and Houston Street would likewise furnish their quotas if the Provost Marshal would only be authorized to do his duty."

Not only in New York, but throughout the Northern states, young men eligible for the draft were seeking ways to avoid it. E. B. Wolcott wrote from Milwaukee to Wisconsin's Governor James T. Lewis: "Are there no means for arresting the stampede from our state of the miserable, cowardly, Copperhead scoundrels? They are leaving by the thousands to avoid the draft. ... Thousands of these shameless vagabonds are passing through our state from Minnesota ... but the worst of all is that these men will all be back in time to vote." Presumably—horror of horrors!—these "cowardly Copperheads" would vote for McClellan.

In New York City, the prospects for General McClellan looked bright because, as one newspaper explained: "The Democratic majority, which rules the city, is down on the 'abolition war' and believes in Lee and McClellan and would rejoice over the enthronement of Jeff Davis in the national capital."

Secessionists are all over Manhattan, "in omnibuses and cars, on the steamboats and in the large hotels—especially the hotels at that particular class where board is to be had for 'two dollars and fifty cents a day in gold and four dollars in currency'" the *New York Herald* said. Many of the "Northern men with southern principles," the paper said, "were the bands of affluent mercantile houses ... who got rich in Southern trade and who think ... that it is 'a pitiable sight to see Southern gentlemen crushed by the Northern scum!' They are all Southern agents and men directly in the interest of the leaders of the rebellion."

Lincoln's prospects for carrying New York State improved October 13 when Thurlow Weed overcame his strong opposition to the president's abolition policy and came out for his reelection. Earlier, Weed had called for the war to be waged strictly to restore the Union without regard to slavery—in essence General McClellan's position—but the former Albany editor stayed with the Union ticket because the peace faction had placed McClellan on a "war failure" platform and given him Pendleton as his running mate.

"The platform offended McClellan and all War Democrats," Weed said. "There is no word of condemnation, or censure, either of secession or rebellion in it. ... Indeed, so tender is rebellion touched that strong color is given to the charge that Washington Hunt's 'armistice' plank was inserted at the suggestion of the Confederate Commissioners with whom he conferred in Canada." Hunt, a former governor of New York, did indeed meet with Rebel agents in Canada. Weed gave his own great prestige to the charge that the Democrats' platform was actually crafted to suit the Confederates and gave them the one thing they desired above all—a "cessation of hostilities," or armistice, to stop the war. Weed also noted that nearly all the Democrats in Congress and their leading newspapers "are committed to an 'armistice' or peace party."

Remembering the terrible draft riots of 1863, which they blamed on the Democrats and their Confederate friends, the Republicans arranged for military surveillance of the voting booths in New York City on Election Day. The army was to prevent a repetition of the riots.

Actually, eight Confederate soldiers in civilian clothes slipped over the border from Canada in late October and were in New York City planning an uprising there on November 8. Col. Robert Martin and his second in command, Lt. John Headley, had orders to provide military direction for a crowd to stage a riot surpassing the violence against the draft. Washington authorities received reports indicating that gangs of Democrats would try to frighten Lincoln voters away from the polls and even count the city's entire vote for McClellan.

Headley, in his memoirs, recalled that James McMasters, the undercover head of the proposed revolt, talked boldly about sending 20,000 men into the streets to take over the city on Election Day, "release the prisoners at Fort Lafayette and unite them with our forces."

In the closing days of the presidential campaign, the Confederate visitors enjoyed attending the theater and Democratic political meetings at Tammany Hall. They watched a monster torch-light procession of Democrats, the full length of Broadway, and saw General McClellan reviewing his followers from the balcony of the Fifth Avenue Hotel. The Rebels joined the thousands who packed Madison Square, cheering orators who praised McClellan and denounced the president. They heard hisses and groans for Lincoln and shouts showing "a vicious sentiment against the draft and everyone connected with the management of the war."

When he looked out his hotel window the next morning, Headley saw Federal troops marching up Broadway. He soon learned that Gen. Benjamin F. Butler had arrived with 10,000 soldiers to make sure that there would be no disturbance of any kind to mar Election Day. Butler had plainclothes officers stationed at every polling place, clearly intending to intimidate Democrats and not let them intimidate Republicans. Butler had gunboats aiming at the toughest parts of the city, the haunts of the Blood Tubs, the Goats, and sundry other gangs, and a brigade of infantry all set to arrive on the Battery.

This show of force worked wonders for Lincoln.

"The leaders in our conspiracy were at once demoralized by this sudden advent of General Butler and his troops," Lt. Headley recalled. McMasters—once so confident of seizing the city—expressed fears that his uprising would be a dismal failure, so he called it off.

The polling places in New York City were so crowded on Election Day that George Templeton Strong had to stand in line for two hours before being allowed to vote. Standing a little in front of him was August Belmont. The Democratic national chairman was refused a ballot because he had bet on the election. (He bet on McClellan to win.) So one of the chief promoters of the general's presidential bid was denied an opportunity to vote for him. "Belmont went off in a rage," Strong recorded. "This foreign money-dealer has made himself uncommonly odious and the by-standers, mostly of the Union persuasion, chuckled over his discomfiture."

Chapter Thirty-Eight

Lincoln's Great Victory

ABRAHAM LINCOLN SCORED an extraordinary victory, winning reelection with 212 electoral votes to 21 for General McClellan, who carried only three states, New Jersey, Delaware, and Kentucky. Out of a total turnout of about 4 million popular votes, the president triumphed with roughly 2.2 million to 1.8 million for McClellan.

In a nationwide sweep, the Republicans recaptured the legislatures they had lost in 1862, increased their control of both houses of Congress, and left the Democrats with only one Northern governor, Joel Parker of New Jersey. In House seats, the Republicans moved up from 106 to 143 in the new Congress while the Democrats dropped from 77 to a little band of 41.

Lincoln's lopsided lead in electoral votes seemed to indicate an overwhelming tide in his favor, but that was not true. He polled about 55 percent of the popular vote to McClellan's 45 percent. The Democrats could say they did well to reach even 45 percent against the tremendous power of the incumbent president, the army, the War Department, and the war contractors who favored carrying on the profitable conflict.

In theory, Lincoln could have lost to McClellan, very narrowly, in electoral votes if only one percent of the total popular vote, in precisely the right states, had switched to the Democrats. The authority for this startling statement is none other than General Benjamin F. Butler, who personally delivered New York to Lincoln by having his troops at the polls in New York City intimidate potential troublemakers. Lincoln carried the Empire State by a mere 6,700 votes.

About "25,000 votes in three great states," if switched from Lincoln to McClellan, would have been just barely enough to "change the result of the late presidential elections" Butler wrote to Wendell Phillips from Wilmington, North Carolina, December 20, 1864. Butler explained: "The Nation tired of war; a specious offer looking to peace; 25,000 votes in three great states able to change the result of the late presidential election. ... A single disaster or a single victory, as did Atlanta, may turn your majority."

Presumably Butler's "three great states" were New York, Pennsylvania, and Illinois. In mid-October, even after the improvement in his fortunes caused by the fall of Atlanta, Lincoln had expected to lose all three. He carried Pennsylvania by about 20,000 and Illinois by about 30,000. These, added to New York's, would have made his victory margin in all three states combined roughly 56,000. Half of that would have been 28,000, so Butler came close to the mark with his figure of 25,000.

These three key states had a total of seventy-five electoral votes, which added to McClellan's twenty-one from New Jersey, Kentucky, and Delaware, would have raised his total to ninety-six. This would have been short of the 118 required to win—that is, half of the 234 electoral votes, plus 1. So Butler's statement is not quite correct. However, Lincoln squeaked through in several smaller states, which if switched, could have given McClellan barely enough to win a majority of the electoral votes. Among them were Connecticut, New Hampshire, Maryland, Oregon, and Minnesota.

As a practical matter, of course, the votes in precisely the right number in precisely the right states would not have switched. If they had given McClellan an apparent victory, it would have been contrary to the wishes of a majority of the voters, and no one can say that such a travesty of justice would have been tolerated. Lincoln and his supporters would have used their power to make sure that Congress would not accept the returns. It must be remembered that Congress, in the end, counts and certifies the electoral votes submitted by the states. The Republicans dominated both houses of Congress. They could have thrown out enough disputed returns to ensure Lincoln's triumph.

The Democrats could not successfully charge that they were "robbed" in 1864, but there is much evidence showing that Lincoln's administration misused executive powers ruthlessly to guarantee that the secessionists and their Northern allies would not take over the government and impose an armistice and a peace favorable to the South. In particular, the War Department became the great engine for Lincoln's success. Secretary Stanton excelled in his zeal to reelect the president, by hook or by crook.

One of his biographers asserts that Stanton carried the election for Lincoln by dispatching troops and Federal marshals to quell Confederate schemes for Election Day violence in several cities. Frank Abial Flower writes that Stanton found out in advance about the Rebels' plans to create "desperate disturbances" in the cities, "so distracting public attention that the election of McClellan could be accomplished by stuffing ballot boxes and other frauds. Stanton … sent military reinforcements to New York and elsewhere, swore in thousands of extra marshals, and took such other precautions that the plot was wholly thwarted," the author asserts. He adds: "Provost Marshal Fry states, and so does C. A. Dana, that Stanton carried the election for Lincoln, and insisted from the first that he would do so."

C. (Charles) A. Dana, assistant secretary of war, wrote: "All the power and influence of the War Department … was employed to secure the re-election of Mr. Lincoln. The political struggle was most intense, and the interest taken in it, both in the White House and in the War Department, was almost painful."

Ambitious army officers were advised that those who openly backed McClellan could not expect promotions. Officers at the front could hardly fault McClellan's courage as a soldier, but they told the troops to vote against him anyway because he had fallen into bad company with such "peace sneaks" as Vallandigham, Pendleton, and Fernando Wood.

William B. Hesseltine, in *Lincoln and the War Governors*, writes: "Without the soldier vote in six crucial states, Lincoln would have lost the election." Hesseltine contends that Lincoln's majorities in Illinois and

Indiana "were probably due to the presence of soldiers as guards and as voters at the polls. ... Maryland's vote was clearly the product of Federal bayonets." He also says 10,000 soldiers were sent to Pennsylvania for the November election "and Lincoln carried the state by nearly a 6,000 majority, while the soldiers in the field added 14,000 more."

McClellan's managers—S. L. M. Barlow in particular—had expected the soldiers to vote for him by huge margins, since he had been idolized by the men of the Army of the Potomac. One of their chief arguments, in seeking his nomination as the "most available" candidate, was their assurance that he could sweep the soldier vote. But the actual result of the election proved a crushing disappointment. While the civilians' votes tipped to Lincoln by about 53 percent to 47 percent, the president carried about four out of every five soldier votes.

McClellan did not realize that the men who had loved him and cheered him as no other Union general had ever been loved—those who danced with delight when he regained his command after Pope's disaster at the second battle of Bull Run and who followed him to victory at Antietam—were not the same men now confronting General Lee in Virginia under General Grant. Many of McClellan's favorites were no longer in the army; Stanton had gotten rid of them, and others had been wounded or killed. In their places were Irish and German boys who had enlisted for the bounty or as substitutes for rich men dodging the draft; they were immigrant mercenaries and former slaves. It was a polyglot army now, and its hero was not McClellan, it was Grant.

McClellan had never been idolized by the men of the Western armies who had followed Grant and Sherman, so he could not expect those soldiers to vote for him because of auld lang syne. Furthermore, some soldiers who respected McClellan shied away from voting for him because of the Chicago "war failure" platform drafted by Vallandigham and slanting toward an armistice and a negotiated peace.

Thousands of Union soldiers were furloughed home to key states to vote, while the wounded and convalescents in hospitals were sent back whenever possible to swell the vote for Lincoln and the state Republican ticket. In Illinois, Governor Yates pleaded repeatedly to Washington for more soldiers, not only to help Lincoln carry his home state, but also to crush the Democratic candidate for governor,

James C. Robinson, branded by the Republican press as a "peace sneak." Robinson, as previously noted, was being secretly bankrolled with at least $50,000 in cash from Confederate agents in Canada. So, when the Republicans charged that his election would aid the enemy, they were telling the truth, but they could not prove it.

By carrying Lincoln and their entire ticket to victory by a margin of 30,000 votes, the Illinois Republicans ended the threat that their state might fall under the influence of the Confederacy. A switch of only 15,000 votes to the Democrats might have taken Illinois out of the war and elected a governor who would have been a paid puppet of the Confederacy. Luckily for Robinson, his payoff by the Rebels in Canada did not become known in his lifetime, so he escaped political ruin.

Lincoln's victory marked a remarkable comeback from the depths of despair in late August, when many Republican leaders had given up on him and intrigued to dump him from the ticket. The Union victories at Atlanta, Mobile Bay, and the Shenandoah Valley all helped to strengthen the claim that the war was almost won and one more great offensive would win an honorable peace.

The improved military picture alone, however, could not have guaranteed Lincoln's reelection and his party leaders knew it. They feared that war weariness, resistance to the draft, the terrible death toll, and McClellan's personal popularity could yet combine to hurl them from power. So they waged a tremendous campaign depicting McClellan as the weak tool of the Copperheads who surrounded him; they depicted the Democratic platform as a sellout to the South, and the Democrats as skating on the edge of treason. The Democrats who fraternized with the Confederate agents in Canada and who discussed drafting the platform with them lent credence to their enemies' accusations.

The "treason" charges made many Democrats ashamed of their old party, especially in such crucial states as Illinois, Indiana, and Ohio, where the peace advocates controlled the party. McClellan's repudiation of the platform's call for an armistice infuriated the most ardent peace advocates in that same Northwest region, and they turned their backs on him. There is no way of telling how many simply refused to vote. The results of their mutiny are clear in Ohio, where the Republicans won by 60,000 votes in a sweep that completely turned around the state's congressional delegation. From fourteen Democrats and five Republicans, it switched to seventeen Republicans and only two Democrats. Ohio voters repudiated George Pendleton, the vice-presidential nominee from Cincinnati, and S. S. Cox, the Democratic congressman from Columbus, lost his seat.

Lincoln lost his native state, Kentucky, by a huge margin, polling only 27,786 votes to McClellan's 64,301. This represents a mighty protest by Kentuckians, who were close to revolt against the ruthless military control of their state. Even innocent hostages had been shot to death in reprisal for guerrilla attacks on Union soldiers. Governor Thomas E. Bramlette warned Lincoln in a letter September 3 that Federal officers' arrogant mistreatment of the people had made "thousands of bitter, irreconcilable opponents—at least three quarters of the people—and they would vote against the President's reelection." The huge majority for the Democrats in Kentucky should dispel the myth that Lincoln was really loved by the people of his native state.

As it turned out, Lincoln made a very smart move when he refused to rearrest Vallandigham. The president, a most astute politician, figured that the eloquent Copperhead would cause division among the Democrats, and it proved correct. Vallandigham thought he had scored his greatest triumph when he rammed into the party platform his fateful declaration that the war was a "failure" and that the Democrats would seek peace without victory.

New York's promoters of the McClellan campaign also resented the way their governor, Horatio Seymour, had coyly played with the "peace" bloc in quest of the presidential nomination at Chicago. Seymour lost his bid for reelection in November.

Bemoaning the Democrats' defeats, John Van Buren, son of President Martin Van Buren, exclaimed: "Seymour is a damned fool. He spoiled everything at Chicago and has been the cause of most of the disasters of the Democratic party. If Seymour and Vallandigham had been kicked out of the national convention, it would have been a good thing for the party."

✦ • ✦

Meeting with his cabinet November 11, President Lincoln took his August 23 memorandum out of his desk and read the note aloud. "You will remember," he told the cabinet, "that this was written at a time (six days before the Chicago nominating convention) when as yet we had no adversary and seemed to have no friends. I then solemnly resolved on the course of action above. I resolved, in case of the election of General McClellan, being certain that he would be the candidate, that I would see him and talk matters over with him.

"I would say, 'General, the election has demonstrated that you are stronger, have more influence with the American people than I. Now let us together, you with your influence and I with all the executive powers of the government, try to save the country. You raise as many troops as you possibly can for this final trial, and I will devote all my energies to assisting you and finishing the war.'"

Secretary Seward commented: "And the General would answer, 'Yes, yes,' and the next day when you saw him again and pressed these views upon him he would say, 'Yes, yes,' and so on forever, and he would have done nothing at all."

"At least," Lincoln said, "I should have done my duty and have stood clear before my own conscience."

McClellan accepted his defeat with good grace. He had known it would be a hard fight, but he had wanted to wage it to change the war from a conflict of extermination and abolition to a struggle on Christian principles to restore the Union. Now the voters had spoken and he had no regrets.

He resigned his army commission and, with his wife and their daughter, sailed for Europe. Once commander of all the Union armies, he now could not even claim the rank of private. His military career was over. On December 3, 1864, this "old soldier" observed his thirty-eighth birthday.

Chapter Thirty-Nine

The Last Nail in Slavery's Coffin

PRESIDENT LINCOLN'S DECISIVE reelection victory gave him a new opportunity to achieve his long-cherished dream—to abolish human slavery throughout the United States through the only clearly legal way—an amendment to the Constitution. Lincoln, who personally hated slavery, had to follow a long and winding road to his goal because of the political realities and the peril that the Union faced in the early months of the war.

His primary purpose, as he often said, was to save the Union, and all other issues had to be secondary to that. He had to hold the border slave states—Missouri, Kentucky, and Maryland—in the Union. If he had openly advocated abolition in 1861 or 1862, all three probably would have gone over to the Confederacy, and Lincoln believed it would then have been impossible to defeat such a large confederacy, nor could he have raised an army large enough to win the war.

As Union armies sliced their way through the South, many slaves left plantations and sought shelter in military camps, so the army became, de facto, an instrument of abolition. General Butler astutely observed that the war itself was steadily ending slavery, as shown by the drastic drop in the prices of slaves on the remaining Southern markets.

Northern voters, who had been either hostile or indifferent toward abolition before, gradually began to realize that every black man enlisted in the army could take the place of a white man. Lincoln said in 1864 that, without the nearly 200,000 black men in the ranks, he could not carry on the war for three weeks. So public opinion in the North eventually came around to Lincoln's point of view.

On April 8, 1864, the Thirteenth Amendment ending slavery everywhere in the United States sailed through the Senate, with its radical Republican majority, by the lopsided vote of thirty-eight to six. It also achieved a favorable vote of ninety-five to sixty-six in the House of Representatives June 15 but failed to reach the required two-thirds majority. It was blocked by the Democrats. Nearly all the Democrats in the House voted against it. So the deadlock continued into the presidential election campaign.

Lincoln could rightfully claim that his reelection amounted to a popular mandate for abolition because he ran openly on the platform adopted by the Union, or Republican, convention in Baltimore, which declared in ringing terms:

"Resolved, that, as slavery was the cause, and now constitutes the strength, of this Rebellion, and as it must be always and everywhere hostile to the principle of republican government, justice and the national safety demand its utter and complete extirpation from the soil of the Republic. ...

"We are in favor, furthermore, of such amendment to the Constitution to be made by the people in conformity with its provisions, as shall terminate and forever prohibit the existence of slavery within the limits of the jurisdiction of the United States."

In accepting his nomination, the president specifically approved the platform plank, which called for the "complete extirpation" of slavery throughout the nation. The Democrats had no such plank in their platform, and their presidential candidate, McClellan, stressed that the Democrats desired nothing except the restoration of the Union. So there was a clear-cut issue in the campaign. Lincoln favored abolition, McClellan opposed it. Lincoln won. Therefore, slavery must go.

Lincoln, as an able lawyer, knew full well that his Emancipation Proclamation, based on his assumed war powers, probably could not be legally effective after the war was over. Also, it might not survive a postwar challenge in the courts. Therefore the time had come to drive the last nail into slavery's coffin.

So, when Congress reconvened in December 1864, Lincoln urged in his annual message that the Thirteenth Amendment be finally enacted without further delay. He observed that the next Congress, with its larger Republican majority, "almost certainly will pass the measure if this does not. Hence there is only a question of *time* as to when the proposed amendment will go to the states for their action. And, as it is to so go at all events, may we not agree that the sooner the better?"

Lincoln did not question "the wisdom or patriotism" of those who had blocked the measure in the House, but he reminded them that "it is the voice of the people now, for the first time, heard upon the question."

The shrewd political manipulator in the White House realized that appeals to reason would not be enough to achieve the necessary two-thirds majority in the House. The Democrats, angry and dispirited by their defeat at his hands, were in no mood to give him a victory. Furthermore, many of them sincerely opposed abolition and saw no reason to change their principles. So, to switch enough Democrats' votes, Lincoln would have to practice the arts of persuasion.

Congressman James Sidney Rollins, a Missouri conservative, recorded his own experience at the hands of the arm-twisting president. Calling Rollins to the White House, Lincoln said:

> You and I were old Whigs, both of us followers of that great statesman, Henry Clay, and I tell you I never had an opinion upon the subject of slavery that I did not get from him. I am very anxious that the war should be brought to a close at the earliest possible date, and I don't believe this can be accomplished as long as those fellows down South can rely upon the border states to help them; but if the members from the border states would unite, at least enough of them to pass the Thirteenth Amendment to the Constitution, they would soon

see that they could not expect much help from that quarter and be willing to give up their opposition and quit their war upon the government; that is my chief hope and main reliance to bring the war to a speedy conclusion.

The vote on the amendment in the House, he said, "is going to be very close; a few votes one way or the other will decide it." Rollins replied that, although he represented perhaps the strongest slave district in Missouri and was himself one of the largest slave owners in his county, he would vote in favor of the amendment. Delighted with this switch, the president then pressed Rollins to see how many others in the Missouri delegation he could also bring over. Rollins promised to do his best.

Lincoln left no record of any inducements offered to recalcitrant Democrats. The president, a realist, would not hesitate to use any available weapon—money, jobs, or pressure—to achieve the great goal of wiping out slavery forever. All that can be said about votes being switched for money is that there is no written record of any payoffs. James Ford Rhodes, in his *History of the United States*, wrote: "some log rolling" had to be done. "Money could probably have been used to buy up the wavering members but it is doubtful whether any was used for this purpose."

When the House voted again on the Thirteenth Amendment January 31, 1865, the galleries were crowded and the floor was swarming with officials making last-minute appeals for votes. Noah Brooks reported to the *Sacramento Union:* Archibald McAllister, a Copperhead from Pennsylvania, sent up to the clerk a note saying he had voted against the amendment before but the failure of the recent peace missions convinced him that "nothing short of the recognition of their independence will satisfy the Confederacy," so he would vote now "against the cornerstone of the Southern Confederacy."

Alexander B. Coffroth of Pennsylvania read a speech switching his vote to "aye."

William H. Miller, another Pennsylvanian, avowed his intention to die like a consistent Democrat, fighting for slavery.

Anson Herrick, a New York War Democrat, explained his change of heart and his intention to vote for the amendment.

James S. Brown of Wisconsin, a Copperhead, followed.

Aaron Harding of Kentucky made a bitter, biting, querulous speech in which he branded as renegades such border men as Green Clay Smith, George B. Yeaman, and Lucien Anderson, all of Kentucky.

Then Martin Karbfleisch of New York delivered a long harangue.

Red-faced Robert Mallory, lingering among the Kentucky flesh-pots of slavery, pleaded for delay. But Speaker Schuyler Colfax called for an immediate vote. When the name of John Ganson, a New York Copperhead, gave back an echo of "Aye," much to the surprise of all, there was a burst of applause. ... A like burst of applause greeted the "aye" vote of Charles A. Eldridge of Wisconsin, heretofore a trouble-some demagogue in the opposition ranks.

Speaker Colfax voted "aye" and announced: "The ayes are 119, the noes 56, the constitutional majority of two-thirds having voted in the affirmative, the joint resolution has passed." It was just barely enough for victory.

Wrote Brooks:

"Instantly, there was a pause of utter silence, then a ... storm of cheers ... strong men embraced each other with tears. The galleries ... stood bristling with cheering crowds. The air was stirred with a cloud of women's handkerchiefs waving and floating.

"Cox, Pendleton, and the rest of the defeated Copperheads taking up hats and blackly stealing away.

"The final blow at the crime of slavery has been struck."

One by one, the states quickly ratified the Thirteenth Amendment, and on December 18, 1865, Secretary of State Seward certified that it had become part of the Constitution. Unfortunately, Lincoln did not live to see the glorious day that he had labored so long and so hard to bring about.

Chapter Forty

Aftermath

WHEN VICTORIOUS FEDERAL TROOPS entered Richmond as the Confederacy collapsed in April 1865, they found that nearly all the records of the Rebels' Secret Service had been burned by its mastermind, Judah P. Benjamin. The secretary of state, disguised as a French peddler who spoke no English, escaped by riding in a horse-drawn wagon to Florida. There, he used some of the gold pieces hidden in his ragged clothes to pay for his passage by boat to Havana; then a British steamer conveyed him to a safe haven in England. A British subject because of his birth in the West Indies, this brilliant lawyer, within a few years, became a star of the London bar. He lived abroad the rest of his life, having good reason to fear that, if he ever came back to the United States, a vengeful government would have hanged him.

Somehow, one important letter in Benjamin's Richmond archives survived. It was picked up by a Union soldier and published in the Official Records of the war. This most significant document provides positive proof that the Confederate commissioners in Canada fomented sabotage and a potential revolution in the North, tried to split the East from the West, and used the Democratic Party in efforts to win a compromise peace.

Jacob Thompson, the chief commissioner, sent this letter from Toronto to Benjamin on December 3, 1864. It did not arrive until February 13, 1865. It demolishes the theories of some recent writers that the "Northwest Conspiracy" never existed.

Thompson recalled that, at the outset of his mission in June 1864, he found strong support for the belief that by "a bold, vigorous and concerted movement, the three great Northwestern States of Illinois, Indiana, and Ohio could be seized and held" and "Kentucky and Missouri could easily be lifted from their prostrate condition and placed on their feet, and this in sixty days would end the war."

However, as the war dragged on and the Democrats began to think they could easily beat Lincoln, the enthusiasm for using brute force cooled. "Believing that the South would agree to a reconstruction … the politicians, especially the leading ones, conceived the idea that on such an issue, Lincoln could be beaten at the ballot box," Thompson wrote.

Thompson let George Nicholas Sanders and C. C. Clay run their parleys with Northern Democrats while he bankrolled attempts to free Confederate prisoners at Camp Douglas and Johnson's Island and to set fire to Chicago and New York. He noted that Confederate agents had started blazes in various New York City hotels in late November but that their "Greek fire" fizzled so that little damage ensued, but the raid at least "produced a great panic."

Although his major enterprises failed, Thompson contended that they caused the Federal government to keep at least 60,000 soldiers from the battlefield to "watch and browbeat the people at home." He estimated that he had spent about $300,000 and still held three drafts for $100,000 each, all from the Secret Service fund approved by the Confederate Congress. His letter provides irrefutable proof that Confederate gold financed insurrectionary and political activities in the North.

He proposed that in the future, Northern conscripts who refused to fight against the Confederacy be encouraged "to make their way south to join our service especially if our army opens up a road to the Ohio."

At the time this letter was written, December 3, Gen. John Bell Hood and his army were poised outside of Nashville and planning to open that "road to the Ohio." Hood made a terrific frontal assault upon the Union troops at Franklin, Tennessee, November 30, and forced them back to Nashville, but he wrecked his army in the process. He lost several generals, including Patrick R. "Pat" Cleburne, the feisty Irishman sometimes called "the Stonewall Jackson of the West." Hood still believed that he could capture Nashville, but defending general George Thomas collected thousands of more troops to build up an advantage of about two to one. Thomas smashed Hood's army on icy December 15–16 and chased the hungry, footsore, and ragged Rebels to Tupelo, Mississippi.

Hood's defeat, plus Sherman's devastating march through Georgia and the Carolinas, severely weakened the morale of the Southern people. The end of the Confederacy came with the surrender of their armies in April and May, 1865.

Thompson sought refuge in England for a while and eventually came home to Mississippi when wartime passions had cooled. John Cabell Breckinridge, President Buchanan's vice president, later Confederate general and secretary of war, also fled abroad and later returned to Kentucky.

Commissioner C. C. Clay was less fortunate. He was accused, along with Jefferson Davis and others, of plotting the assassination of Lincoln; Clay had left Canada and come home to Alabama months before the April 14, 1865 murder. Sure of his innocence, he surrendered to authorities, expecting a quick release. Instead, he was thrown into a cell at Fortress Monroe, Virginia, where Davis was also imprisoned. Clay suffered terribly from chronic asthma in his cold, damp casemate until his wife, by repeated appeals to President Andrew Johnson, won his release on April 17, 1866. Davis, whose wife also courageously challenged Johnson, was freed in 1867.

None of the Confederate leaders was ever brought to trial or convicted of any crime. The government's case for their involvement in Lincoln's assassination, based on testimony by various individuals who claimed to have heard the Confederates in Canada plotting the Lincoln murder with the approval of Richmond authorities, collapsed when the witnesses were exposed as liars, paid by Secretary of War Stanton and Judge Advocate General Joseph Holt. In a letter to Stanton July 3, 1866, Holt reluctantly admitted that he had hired the perjurers but claimed that they had deceived him.

President Johnson's proclamation of May 2, 1865, offering rewards for the men accused of plotting Lincoln's murder, named George Nicholas Sanders on the list and offered a $25,000 reward for his capture. Some writers have theorized that Sanders, who once called for the assassination of Napoleon III in France, may have sought Lincoln's life in revenge for the death of his own son, Reid, a prisoner of war who died in Fort Warren, Boston, in September 1864. But there is no credible evidence to prove this theory, which is based on the belief that Sanders met with John Wilkes Booth in Canada some time before the assassin committed his despicable deed.

The *New York Herald* reported that, one night in July 1865, six men hoping to collect the $25,000 reward for the capture of Sanders, broke into his home in Montreal and tried to kidnap him. But the burly, bearded politician and a few friends chased them out of the house. Sanders returned to New York City, unscathed, a few years later and never came to trial on any charge.

Capt. Thomas Henry Hines, the daring Confederate plotter of jail breaks and revolutions, escaped to Canada, where he studied law under Judge Joshua F. Bullitt. Hines later practiced law successfully in Kentucky. In 1875, the bold cavalier was elected chief justice of the Kentucky Court of Appeals.

John Breckinridge Castleman, Hines's companion in so many schemes of derring-do, spent the final months of the war as a prisoner, following his capture in Indiana. Because his captors found in his pockets the records of his payoffs to the men who went to Chicago to attack Camp Douglas in August, he was imprisoned as "a dangerous and daring spy." He had good reason to fear being executed. Not until years later did he learn that a relative had visited the White House, pleading for his life, and persuaded President Lincoln to block his execution. Castleman was eventually exiled to Canada for a short time. In 1898, the former Confederate cavalryman volunteered for service in the United States Army in the Spanish-American War. Castleman served with distinction and President William McKinley promoted the old Rebel to the rank of brigadier general.

Several prominent Democrats, whom the Republicans accused of being Copperheads and tools of the Rebel enemy, prospered in their careers after the war. George Pendleton, McClellan's running mate and peace advocate, won a seat in the United States Senate and is best known today as the author of the Pendleton Act (1883) for civil service reform. S. S. Cox, who lost his seat as an Ohio congressman in the 1864 debacle, moved to New York City and returned to Washington as a congressman from Manhattan.

Thomas A. Hendricks of Indiana, who spoke approvingly of forming a Northwest Confederacy, had a long career in the United States Senate. Hendricks became vice president when Grover Cleveland recaptured the White House for the Democrats in 1884 by defeating James G. Blaine. Gen. "Black Jack" Logan, who helped to save Illinois for the Republicans in 1864, was their candidate for the vice presidency and lost to Hendricks.

General McClellan, to his great surprise, was nominated for governor of New Jersey by the Democrats in 1877 and was easily elected in a display of public esteem, which partially compensated for his defeat by Lincoln. With the same executive skills he had displayed as commander of the Federal armies early in the war, he provided the state with an efficient, conservative nonpartisan regime for three successful years.

Clement Vallandigham had no success in regaining public office but rebuilt his law practice in Dayton. In 1871, while he was handling a loaded gun used as evidence in a murder trial, the gun accidentally fired and killed him. As the author of the "war failure" plank in the Democrats' 1864 platform, Vallandigham left his party with a legacy that doomed it to a series of defeats for a generation. The Republicans never tired of "waving the bloody shirt," charging that every Rebel who killed a Union soldier was a Democrat, that the Democrats had opposed the war that brought about the glorious salvation of the Union and freed the slaves. Except for Grover Cleveland's two terms, the Democrats did not break the Republicans' lock on the White House until Woodrow Wilson's victory in 1912.

The Democrats' collusion with the Confederates in shaping the party's 1864 platform presented a deadly parallel to the Hartford Convention of December 1814, at which the Federalists denounced the second war against Great Britain. That blunder sounded the death knell of the Federalist Party; the Whigs, who opposed the war with Mexico in 1846–48, also died a few years later.

That wily old politico, William Henry Seward, reasoned from these facts that "no party can survive an opposition to a war." He predicted that the Democrats "will be trying to forget years hence that they ever opposed" the Civil War.

The secretary of state recalled that, when he began his political career, "I had to carry affidavits to prove I had nothing to do with the Hartford Convention." "Now," he said, "that party that gained eminence by the folly of the Federalists in opposing the war have the chalice commended to their own lips."

A year before McClellan's defeat by Lincoln, Seward told John Hay: "The Copperhead spirit is crushed and humbled. The Democrats lost their leaders when Toombs and Davis and Breckinridge forsook them and went South; that their new leaders, the Seymours, Vallandighams and Woods, are whipped and routed. So that they have nothing left. The Democratic leaders are either ruined by the war or ... have saved them from the ruin of their party by coming out on the right side."

Thus, the Democrats paid a steep price for criticizing the Lincoln administration's management of the Civil War. Many party members bitterly opposed the war itself, denouncing it as an illegal misuse of Federal powers to coerce the Southern states.

The Democrats in 1864 bet that their alliance with the Confederates for a compromise peace would assure them victory in the battle for the White House. They made a great mistake and doomed themselves to exile from national power for many years. If they had been smarter, they would have heeded Seward's sage advice: "No party can survive an opposition to a war."

Abbreviations

B and L: *Battles and Leaders of the Civil War*. Robert U. Johnson and Clarence C. Buel, eds., 4 vols. New York, Century, 1888.

CWL: *The Collected Works of Abraham Lincoln*. Abraham Lincoln. Roy C. Basler, ed., 9 vols. New Brunswick, NJ: Rutgers Univ. Press, 1952–1955.

DAB: *Dictionary of American Biography*. Allen Johnson and Dumas Malone, eds. New York: Scribner's, 1936.

HL: Huntington Library

LC: Library of Congress

NA: National Archives and Records Administration

OR: U.S. War Department, *The War of the Rebellion: A Compilation of the Official Records of the Union and Confederate Armies*. 128 vols. Washington, DC: U.S. Government Printing Office, 1880–1901.

ORN: U.S. Naval War Records Office, *Official Records of the Union and Confederate Navies in the War of the Rebellion*. 30 vols. Washington, DC: U.S. Government Printing Office, 1894–1922.

Russell, *My Diary*: *My Diary, North and South*. William Howard Russell. London: Bradbury and Evans, 2 vols., 1863.

Strong, *Diary*: *The Diary of George Templeton Strong*, Vol. 3: *The Civil War, 1860–1865*. George Templeton Strong. Allan Nevins and Milton H. Thomas, eds. New York: Macmillan, 1952.

Welles, *The Diary*: *The Diary of Gideon Welles*. Gideon Welles. John T. Morse, Jr., ed., 3 vols. Boston: Houghton Mifflin, 1909–1911. Revised edition, Howard Beale, ed., 3 vols. New York: Norton, 1960.

Notes

Preface Notes
Page

ix "McClellan's Military Adventures": *New York Times*, Sept. 3, 1864.

ix "McClellan had been chosen": Ibid.

x "There must be some way to end this wretched business": Gilmore, *Recollections of Abraham Lincoln*, 230.

x "Do these peacemongers, who go to Canada": *Cincinnati Commercial*, Aug. 16, 1864, quoting the *Rochester (NY) Democrat*.

x Lincoln's comments on C. C. Clay's proposed Democratic platform: CWL, 7:459–60.

xi "Indeed, I have so many papers ...": Jacob Thompson to Judah P. Benjamin, from Toronto, Dec. 3, 1864, OR, series 1, vol. 43:930.

Chapter One
Page

1–2 McClellan biographies: The most authoritative biography of McClellan is Stephen W. Sears, *George B. McClellan, the Young Napoleon*. McClellan published his autobiography in 1887: *McClellan's Own Story*. Campbell, *McClellan: A Vindication of the Military Career of General George B. McClellan*, is "a lawyer's brief" in the general's defense. Other informative biographies are: Eckenrode and Conrad, *George B. McClellan, the Man Who Saved the Union*; Hassler, *General George McClellan*; Michie, *General McClellan*; and Myers, *A Study in Personality*.

2 "I find myself": McClellan to Ellen McClellan, July 27, 1861, McClellan Papers, LC.

2 "I almost think": Ibid., Aug. 2, 1861.

2–3 "As I hope one day": Ibid., Aug. 10, 1861.

3 "I feel that God has placed": Ibid.

3 "He is a very squarely-built": Russell, *My Diary*, 2:268, 327.

3 "Stout little captain of dragoons": Ibid., 269.

4 McClellan's arrests of Maryland legislators: Frederick W. Seward, son of the secretary of state, published a detailed account of the arrests in *Reminiscences of a War-Time Diplomat and Statesman*, 175–78. See also Edward McPherson, *The Political History of the United States of America During the Great Rebellion*, 153; Sprague, *Freedom Under Lincoln*, 185–91.

4 Lincoln's threat to "bombard" Maryland cities: Van der Linden, *Lincoln*, 315.

4–5 "My Lord, I can touch a bell": Marshall, *American Bastile*, xiii.

5 George Hubbell, crippled newsboy, arrest: Sprague, *Freedom Under Lincoln*, 168–69; OR, series 2, vol. 2:60, 76.

5 "The war has a four-fold object": Marshall, *American Bastile*, 143.

5 James W. Wall's arrest: Ibid., 139–52.

5 Senator Wall's election was hailed by the *Cincinnati Enquirer* in these words: "Col. Wall was one of the first victims thrown into the Administration Bastile in New York. ... He is an able, bold and eloquent man, and has been opposed to the war from the start. He is just the man for Senator." *Chicago Tribune*, Jan. 25, 1863.

5 For Senator Gwin's life: see Thomas, *Between Two Empires*, 275–76, who relates that Gen. U. S. Grant, in his successful 1863 Vicksburg campaign, wrecked Dr. Gwin's Mississippi plantation, and Federal troops destroyed a lifetime collection of personal papers. Dr. Gwin and his daughter, Lucy, escaped. They sailed to Paris aboard a blockade runner out of Wilmington and joined Mrs. Gwin and daughter, Carrie. The couple's son, Willie, after serving in the Confederate army, joined them in the French capital for the duration of the war.

6 The adventures of Senator Jones are narrated in Parish, *George Wallace Jones*. Formerly revered as one of Iowa's first senators, Jones suffered ostracism as a pro-Southern pariah in his home town, Dubuque. As wartime hatreds faded, he regained his popularity. When he returned to the Senate as a visitor in 1892, Congress awarded him a pension of $20 a month for his services in two wars—as a ten-year-old drummer boy in 1814 and as an aide de camp in the Black Hawk War of 1832. He died at Dubuque in 1896, at age ninety-two.

6 "Brummagem Bonaparte": Russell, *My Diary*, 2:395, Nov. 5, 1861. Webster's defines "brummagem" as "spurious ... cheaply showy: tawdry." The word is derived from Birmingham, England, a source of seventeenth-century counterfeit coins.

6 Lincoln "an idiot" and Scott "in his dotage": McClellan to Ellen McClellan, Aug. 16, 1861, McClellan Papers, LC.

6 "The supreme command": Hay, *Lincoln and the Civil War in the Diaries and Letters of John Hay*, 33.

Chapter Two
Page
7–8 S. L. M. Barlow's biography, DAB, vol. 1, pt. 1:613–15.

9 "Help me to dodge the nigger": McClellan to Barlow, Nov. 8, 1861; Barlow to McClellan, Nov. 11, 1861, Barlow Papers, HL.

9 "The war which was made ... ": Russell, *My Diary*, Dec. 11, 1861, Boston edition 584–5.

9–10 Barlow's invitation to Stanton to join his law firm: Thomas and Hyman, *Stanton*, 133.

10 "Such quarrels should be fostered": Barlow to Stanton, Nov. 21, 1861, Barlow Papers, HL.

10 "I think the General's true course": Thomas and Hyman, *Stanton*, 133.

10 "A most unexpected piece of good fortune": McClellan to Barlow, Jan. 18, 1862, Barlow Papers, HL.

10 "A firm, consistent Union man": Barlow to August Belmont, Jan. 17, 1862, Barlow Papers, HL.

10 "He is just the man we want": Fessenden, *The Life and Public Services of William Pitt Fessenden*, 1:299.

Chapter Three
Page

11 "The champagne and oysters on the Potomac must be stopped": Stanton to Dana, Jan. 24, 1862, Dana, *Recollections of the Civil War*, 5.

11 Welles' comment that McClellan "said he did not wish the presidency": Welles, *Diary*, Sept. 8, 1862, 1:117.

12 Horace Greeley's claim that McClellan refrained from killing potential Virginia voters: Greeley elaborated on this theme in *The American Conflict*, 1:629; 2:247.

13 "Very ugly" matter: *McClellan's Own Story*, 195–96; T. Harry Williams, *Lincoln and the Radicals*, 117–18.

13 "The president is all right": McClellan to Barlow, Mar. 16, 1862, McClellan Papers, LC.

13 McClellan's disgrace with Lincoln: Ward to Barlow, Mar. 16, 18, and 22, 1862, Barlow Papers, HL.

13 Stanton's attacks on McClellan: Browning, *The Diary of Orville H. Browning*, Apr. 2, 1862, 1:538–39.

13–14 Cabinet officers' concerns about Stanton: Welles, *Diary*, 1:127, 128, 203.

14 "There is a good deal of evidence that his brain is diseased": Strong, *Diary*, May 28, 1862, 3:227.

14 "Stanton is certainly three parts lunatic": Ibid., Aug. 16, 1862, 3:246.

14 Stanton's dagger: Flower, *Edwin McMasters Stanton*, 34.

14 Nevins, *The War for the Union*, writes about Stanton, 2:35: "A vein of hysteria amounting to partial insanity had repeatedly appeared in his early career. After his brother's suicide he had to be guarded against the same act; the loss of his baby daughter had thrown him into a frenzy. ... Numerous military men, including Grant, thought him both morally and physically timid. ... Donn Piatt, a writer and government official during the Cival War, said Stanton was rendered fiercely aggressive by 'disease that overwhelmed his nervous system.'"

14–15 "McDowell told me": Franklin to McClellan, Apr. 7, 1862, McClellan Papers, LC. Quoted in *McClellan's Own Story*, 151.

15 "I think the time is near": Lincoln to McClellan, May 24, 1862. CWL, 5:235–36.

15–16 Key–Cobb peace talks: OR, series 1, vol. 11, pt. 1:1051–60.

16 "I shall make the first battle": McClellan to Ellen McClellan, June 15, 1862, *McClellan's Own Story*, 405.

16 "Under cover of his heavy guns": Lee to Davis, June 5, 1862, Freeman, *R. E. Lee*, 2:82.

16–17 "I have lost this battle": McClellan's telegram to Stanton, June 28, 1862. Moore, ed., *The Rebellion Record*, 11:587–88.

17 "It was not war, it was murder": *B and L.*, vol. 2, 394.
17 "A thousand thanks": Lincoln to McClellan, July 6, 1862, CWL, 5:307–08.
17 "We shall hive the enemy yet": Moore, ed., *The Rebellion Record*, 12:594–95. "Hive" apparently is a colloquial expression from Lincoln's early days in Illinois.
17 "Try just now to save the army": Lincoln to McClellan, July 2, 1862, OR, series 1, vol. 11, pt. 3:286.

Chapter Four
Page
20–21 Harrison's Landing letter: McClellan to Lincoln: "Confidential," July 7, 1862, Lincoln Papers, LC.
21 "Address to the Democracy of the United States": Gray, *The Hidden Civil War*, 93.
22 "The introduction of Pope": Welles, *Diary*, 1:107.
22 "Had he lived in the time of the Saviour": McClellan to Ellen McClellan, July 13, 1862, McClellan Papers, LC.
22–23 So many brave men "have fallen victims": McClellan to Barlow, July 15, 1862, Barlow Papers, HL.
23 "The President told me that Gen. Halleck": Browning, *The Diary of Orville Hickman Browning*, July 25, 1862, 1:563.
24 Text of McClellan's protest to Halleck: Campbell, *McClellan*, 323.
24 The order "will not be rescinded": Halleck to McClellan, Aug. 6, 1862, OR, series 1, vol. 12, pt. 2:9–11.
24–25 "They need to get rid of McClellan": General Heintzelman's diary, Aug. 11, 1862, quoted in Williams, *Lincoln and the Radicals*, 156.
25 "All the successes and sacrifices": Brevet Maj. Gen. William W. Averell, "With the Cavalry on the Peninsula," B and L, 2:433.
25 "A huge blunder": Headley, 56.
25 McClellan's desperate efforts to win approval for his last ditch move against Richmond are noted by Fishel, *The Secret War for the Union*, 189.
25 "Lamming away at Pope": McClellan to his wife. Aug. 10, 1862, McCllellan Papers, LC.
25 McClellan left in command of nothing: McClellan to Ellen McClellan, Aug. 29, 1862, *McClellan's Own Story*, 530.

Rhodes, *History of the United States from the Compromise of 1850 to the Final Restoration of Home Rule in the South in 1877*, 4:117, wrote that, in fairness to McClellan, it should be stated that his plan for striking Richmond when there were only 30,000 troops left defending it, probably would have succeeded. "The bulk of the Army of Northern Virginia was in Gordonsville or its vicinity," Rhodes wrote. "It was on this very day that McClellan tried to have a telegraphic connection with Halleck, when he intended to beg for permission to throw his 81,000 soldiers upon Richmond."

Because his men and most of his officers were devoted to him, Rhodes added, "it is not improbable that he would have taken Richmond and held it, the gunboats maintaining communication until the whole energy of the government had been turned to his support. ... But Halleck would consent to no alteration of his plan."

Campbell maintains that Halleck was not general in chief in fact, that Stanton was actually in command, in *McClellan*, 291.

"There can be little doubt that the decision to withdraw the Army of the Potomac from the Peninsula played right into the hands of the enemy," Hassler contends in *General George McClellan*.

"The Union army was to pay a stern price in blood and treasure before another blue-clad army again got as close to Richmond."

Confederate Gen. Richard Taylor believed that McClellan was right. "The true line of attack was on the south side of the James, where Grant was subsequently forced by the ability of Lee," in 1864, Taylor wrote in his book, *Destruction and Reconstruction*, 88.

Chapter Five
Page

26 The "booty" seized by the Confederates at Pope's supply base: Henderson, *Stonewall Jackson and the American Civil War*, 2:131.

26 "Bag the whole crowd": Pope's dispatch, *New York Times*, Sept. 1, 1862.

26 "We fought a terrific battle": Ibid.

27 "Well, John, we are whipped again": Hay, *Lincoln and the Civil War in the Diaries and Letters of John Hay*, 46.

27 "I beg of you to assist me in this crisis": Halleck to McClellan, Aug. 31, 1862, OR, series 1, vol. 11, pt. 1:102–03.

27 Stanton and Chase would rather lose Washington than keep McClellan: Blair made this charge Apr. 3, 1879. It was quoted in *McClellan's Own Story*, 545, and repeated by Campbell, *McClellan*, 333.

27 Chase said McClellan ought to be shot: Welles, *Diary*, 1:102

28 Capt. William H. Powell's description of McClellan's welcome back to command: B and L, 2:489–90.

28 George Kimball's account of "Little Mac is back!": Ibid., 550.

28 "Again, I have been called upon to save the country": McClellan to Ellen McClellan, Sept. 5, 1862, McClellan Papers, LC.

28–29 "I feel that our army": Strong, *Diary*, Sept. 13, 1862, 3:255.

29 It was like an army of rag-pickers: *New York Times*, Sept. 23, 1862.

29 "McClellan is an able general": Lee, quoted by Confederate Maj. Gen. John G. Walker, B and L, 2:606.

30 "This was a fearful situation": General Longstreet, B and L, 2:669. Burnside's procrastination was "The greatest mistake of the day": Palfrey, *The Army in the Civil War*, 5: 107–11.

31 "Dear Mother and Father": *New York Herald*, Sept. 28, 1862.

31 "Our victory is complete": McClellan to Halleck, Sept. 19, 1862, OR, series 1, vol. 19, pt. 2:330.

31 "God in His mercy a second time": McClellan to Ellen McClellan, Sept. 20 and 22, 1862, McClellan Papers, LC.

McClellan also deplored Burnside's delay, commenting to Ellen, Sept. 29, 1862: "I ought to treat Burnside *very* severely and probably will; yet I hate to do it. He is very slow; is not fit to command more than a regiment. If I treat him as he deserves he will be my mortal enemy hereafter." *McClellan's Own Story*, 616.

32 Longstreet notes a "miracle" in the defeat of "the conquering army of the South." Longstreet, *Manassas to Appomattox*, 239, 283.

32 *The New York Times*, heretofore a sharp critic of McClellan, said his Antietam battle "will rank in history as one of the greatest and most sanguine of modern times" and added: "It is clear that General McClellan

fought it with great coolness, tenacity and soldierly skill and is fairly entitled to the honors of the day."

32 James Ford Rhodes, a historian never partial toward McClellan, gave him
full credit for defeating Lee, and much more. He wrote in *History of the
United States from the Compromise of 1850 to the Final Restoration of Home
Rule in the South in 1877*, 4:154–56: "Let us note the change of feeling in
the North from depression before South Mountain to buoyancy after
Antietam; let us reflect that a signal Confederate victory in Maryland
might have caused the Northern voters at the approaching fall elections to
declare for the peace that Jefferson Davis would offer from the head of
Lee's victorious army; and that, without McClellan's victory, the
Emancipation Proclamation would have been postponed and might never
have been issued."

32 J. Thomas Scharf, in *History of Maryland from the Earliest Period to the
Present Day*, 3:493–516, provides a detailed account of Lee's invasion of
Maryland and the battle of Antietam. Describing the ragged Rebels who
were either barefooted or had their feet wrapped in rags or raw hides, he
commented: "It was no unusual sight to see tracks of blood on the turnpike left by a marching regiment. The present writer, on the retreat from
Maryland in 1862, counted forty-nine men without shoes in a regiment of
two hundred."

Chapter Six
Page

33 Lincoln's vow to God: Welles, *Diary*, 1:143.

34 McClellan to Aspinwall, Sept. 26, 1862: Civil War Papers, HL.

34 "I guess he is right": McClellan to Ellen McClellan, Oct. 5, 1862,
McClellan Papers, LC.

34 "[T]hat the reason why the Rebel army had not been destroyed":
Montgomery Blair to McClellan, Sept. 27, 1862, Ibid.

34 Lincoln's dismissal of Major Key: Welles, *Diary*, Sept. 24, 1862, 1:146.

34 "Particularly if you had … ambitions to the presidency": Montgomery
Blair to McClellan, Sept. 27, 1862, McClellan Papers, LC.

35 Francis Preston Blair's advice to McClellan: Blair to McClellan, Sept. 30,
1862, Ibid.

35 "[D]iscussions by officers and soldiers": McClellan's General Orders No.
63, Oct. 7, 1862, Lincoln Papers, LC.

35 McClellan "conspiracy": Hay, *Lincoln and the Civil War in the Diaries and
Letters of John Hay*, Sept. 26, 1862, 51.

35 Senator Wilson's tale of officers plotting a coup: Welles, *Diary*, Sept. 10,
1862, 1:118.

35 "[T]he most alarming kind of talk": Strong, *Diary*, Sept. 13, 1862, 3:255.

35 "We have among us plenty of rotten old Democrats": Ibid., 3: 256.

35 "Abe Lincoln is far from easy in his mind": Ibid., Sept. 24, 1862, 3:259.

35–36 August Belmont's letter to Thurlow Weed, July 20, 1862: August Belmont,
Letters, Speeches and Addresses of August Belmont, 80, 81. Also see Perry
Belmont, *An American Democrat: The Recollections of Perry Belmont* for
many references to his father, August Belmont.

36 "I incline to think that the real purpose": McClellan to Ellen McClellan,
Oct. 2 and 3, 1862, McClellan Papers, LC.

36 "McClellan's bodyguard": Nicolay and Hay: *Abraham Lincoln*, 6:175.

36 "The President was very affable": McClellan to Ellen McClellan, Oct. 2 and 5, 1862. McClellan Papers, LC.

36 "General, you have saved the country": McClellan, *McClellan's Own Story*, 627–28.

36 "The President directs": Halleck to McClellan, Oct. 6, 1862, OR, series 1, vol. 19, pt. 1:72.

37 "Sinister rumors of peace intrigue": Welles, *Diary*, Oct. 18, 1862, 1:176.

37 Lincoln suspects McClellan "playing false": Hay, *Lincoln and the Civil War in the Diaries and Letters of John Hay*, 218.

Chapter Seven
Page

38 The Confederates "boldly determined": Halleck's annual report, Nov. 25, 1862, OR, series 1, vol. 16, pt. 1:5.

39 Battle of Perryville: Cincinnati dispatch printed in the *Chicago Tribune*, Oct. 14, 1862. Also "Bragg's Invasion of Kentucky," by Confederate Lt. Gen. Joseph Wheeler, B and L, 3:11–13. Officers' reports on Perryville, OR, series 1, vol. 16, pt. 1:1021–31. Bragg's report, Ibid., 1088.

39 Bragg's proclamation: OR, series 1, vol. 52, pt. 2:362–65.

39 Bragg "dispatched" by Davis to appeal to the Northwest: *New York Herald*, July 31, 1864. Nelson, *Bullets, Ballots and Rhetoric*, says Davis "prepared" this proclamation and a similar one presented by General Lee to the people of Maryland, 18.

39–40 Governor Morton's letter to Lincoln, predicting a bloody new civil war to keep Ohio, Indiana, and Illinois from seceding: Morton to Lincoln, Oct. 27, 1862. In Gray, *The Hidden Civil War*, 116–17.

Chapter Eight
Page

41 Stanton's order, Aug. 8, 1862: OR, series 2, vol. 11:221–73.

42 Congressman S. "Sunset" Cox's criticisms of arbitrary arrests: Cox, *Three Decades of Federal Legislation*, 223–25.

42 "From ten to twenty thousand:" Marshall, *American Bastile*, 753.

42 Neely cites Marshall's book for details of the worst cases of injustice in his magisterial book *The Fate of Liberty*, 53.

42 "They have been utterly arbitrary": Strong, *Diary*, Oct. 30, 1862, 3:269.

43 Slidell's report to Napoleon III: Willson, *John Slidell and the Confederates in Paris*, 84.

43 "The whole community is honeycombed": Strong, *Diary*, Oct. 23, 1862, 3:267.

43 For details of the 1862 New York governor's race see Alexander, *A Political History of the State of New York*, 3:37–51. Alexander gives the election result as Seymour, 207,663; Wadsworth, 196, 492.

44 General Wadsworth "one of those abolition intriguers": *New York Herald*, Sept. 27, 1862.

44 Greeley's denunciation of Seymour: *New York Tribune*, Oct. 18, 1862.

44 Clay's call for Seymour to hang: *New York Herald*, Oct. 14, 1862.

44 "It looks like general abandonment": Strong, *Diary*, Nov. 5, 1862, 3:271–72.

44 "Seymour is governor. God help us!": Ibid., 271.

44 "The resurrection to political life and power": Ibid., Oct. 29, 1862, 268.

45 "General McClellan has been superseded": *New York Herald*, Nov. 9, 1862.

45–46 "The order depriving me of the command": *McClellan's Own Story* cited by Gorham, *Life and Public Services of Edwin M. Stanton*, 2:73.

46 McClellan sacrificed "to appease the ebony fetish": Rep. S. S. Cox, Dec. 15, 1862, *Congressional Globe*, 37th Cong., 3rd sess., 94–100.

46 "The man who forced the President": Kendall, *Letters Exposing the Mismanagement of Public Affairs by Abraham Lincoln, and the Political Combination to Secure his Re-election*, 38–39.

Chapter Nine
Page

47 Lord Lyons to Lord Russell, Nov. 17, 1862: Edward McPherson, *Political History of the United States*, 11–16.

48 "We would not be surprised": *New York Herald*, Apr. 3, 1863. *The New York Times* revived the story about Democrats' "intrigues with our foreign enemies," Sept. 2, 1864.

49–50 Lincoln's message to Congress, Dec. 1, 1862: CWL, 5:530–37; text of Lincoln's message, OR, series 3, 2:889–997. Senator Browning called Lincoln's ideas for colonizing free slaves "a hallucination," Browning, *The Diary of Orville Hickman Browning*, Dec. 1, 1862, 591.

50 Lincoln's proclamations "disastrous" to Republicans: Browning, *The Diary of Orville Hickman Browning*; "disastrous," 589; Fessenden's remarks, 588; Browning to Lincoln, 589; Ewing's comments, 592.

51 "Mr. President it was not a battle": Curtin to Lincoln, Dec. 1862, Sandburg, *Abraham Lincoln*, 1:630.

51 "He is, I have no doubt, perplexed to death": S. Noble to Rep. Elihu B. Washburne, Dec. 25, 1862, Washburne Papers, LC.

51 "It would not surprise me if he were to destroy himself." Justice Benjamin B. Curtis, Jan. 1, 1863, Gray, *The Hidden Civil War*, 130.

51 "[U]selessly sacrificed": Strong, *Diary*, Dec. 18, 1862, 3:281.

52 Senator Wilkinson's attack on Seward: Fessenden, *The Life and Public Services of William Pitt Fessenden*, 1:231.

52 "They wish to get rid of me": Browning, *Diary*, 600, 604.

52 "[T]here would be a rebellion in the North": Ibid., Dec. 31, 1862, 607.

Chapter Ten
Page

53 Near mutiny of Illinois soldiers: OR, series 1, vol. 17, pt. 2:836–37.

53 "Strange utterances": Wirt Adams to Brig. Gen. Hébert, Jan. 15, 1863, Ibid.

54 "The soldiers would be excited": *New York Herald*, Jan. 11, 1863.

54 McClellan's tour of New England: Stephen W. Sears, *George McClellan*, 350.

54–55 The Delmonico dinner and its aftermath: *New York Evening Post*, Feb. 7, 9, 10, 14, 1863. A detailed account is in Silverman, *Lightning Man*, 396–98.

55 Lincoln's overtures to Seymour through Weed: Barnes and Weed, eds., *The Life of Thurlow Weed*, 2:428.

55 "This war should have been averted": *Daily Express*, Lancaster, PA, Jan. 7, 1863.

56 "I differ widely with my party": Weed, *The Life of Thurlow Weed*, 1:432.

56 "The opponents of the administration": Blaine, *Twenty Years of Congress*, 1:489.

56 "As cold as ice and as hard as iron": White, *The Life of Lyman Trumbull*, 203.

56 Vallandigham's speech Jan. 14, 1863: *Congressional Globe*, 37th Cong., 3d sess., 1863, Appendix, 52–60. Its title: "The Constitution, Peace and Reunion."

57 Criticism of Vallandigham's speech: *Chicago Tribune*, Jan. 15, 1863.

57 "I am for peace": Former Illinois Gov. John Reynolds, letter to the *Crisis*, Columbus, OH, Dec. 17, 1862, quoted by Gray, *The Hidden Civil War*, 115.

57 "The minds of all our friends": J. F. Ankeny, Freeport, IL, to Rep. Elihu Washburne, Feb. 3, 1863, Washburne Papers, LC.

57–58 "For God's sake, give us …:" George Hamilton, Galena, IL, to Washburne, Jan. 18, 1863, Ibid.

58 "Rebel Democrats …": Amos Miller, Rockford, IL, to Washburne, Jan. 12, 1863, Ibid.

58 Joseph Medill, Chicago, to Washburne, Jan. 14, 1863, Ibid.

Chapter Eleven

Page

59 "[T]he fire in the rear … the Democracy": Pierce, *Memoirs and Letters of Charles Sumner*, 4:114.

59 "Seemed bent on mischief": Browning, *Diary*, Jan. 9, 1863, 611.

60 "The Illinois legislature": *Chicago Tribune*, Jan. 15, 1863.

60 "The feeling in the city": Ibid., Jan. 10, 1863.

60 "The main topic of conversation": Ibid., Jan. 21, 1863.

60 "If this country does not go to the devil": C. H. Ray to Rep. Washburne, Feb. 10, 1863, Washburne Papers, LC.

60 "[A] wild, rampant, revolutionary body": Yates to Morton, Jan. 19, 1863, quoted in Hesseltine, *Lincoln and the War Governors*, 316.

61 Richardson elected to the U. S. Senate: Lusk, *Politics and Politicians*, 151.

61 Resolution for Louisville peace convention: Ibid., 154.

61 Stalled by tie in the Senate: Ibid., 158.

61 Indiana senators: Hendricks and Turpie were elected by 85 to 62 on a joint vote of the two houses of the Indiana legislature Jan. 14, 1863. Hendricks urged the Northwest to "take care of her own interests," Jan. 8, 1862, Foulke, *Life of Oliver P. Morton*, 1:176.

62 Bright, Hendricks, and Turpie run the Indiana legislature: *Chicago Tribune*, Jan. 14, 1863, quoting the *Cincinnati Commercial*.

62 "The Democratic scheme": Morton to Stanton, Feb. 9, 1863, Stanton Papers, LC.

62 A vivid description of Morton is in Foulke, *Life of Oliver P. Morton*, 1:51.

63 "[T]he scheme of the Northwestern secession": *Chicago Tribune*, Jan. 16, 1863.

63 "The assassination of Governor Morton": Ibid.

63 "The Southern part of Illinois" has "whang doodles": Ibid.

63–64 Morton's detailed account of the legislature's attempt to strip him of control over the Indiana militia: *Congressional Record*, 44th Cong., 1st sess., May 3, 1876, 2900–03.

64 Cameron says Morton saved Indiana from going into the Confederacy: Ibid.

65 "When the Legislature first met": *Chicago Tribune*, Jan. 24, 1863.

Chapter Twelve

Page

66 "Of course it was not for this": Lincoln to Hooker, CWL, 6:78–79.

67 "They are permitted to visit": OR, series 2, vol. 3:499.

67 "Columbus Turned Over to Secesh": Ibid., 500.

67 "Cheers for Jeff Davis": *Chicago Tribune*, May 12, 1863.

67 General Burnside's Order No. 38: OR, series 1, vol. 23, pt. 2: 237.

68 Vallandigham's Mount Vernon speech and arrest: OR, series 2, vol. 5:633–46.

69 "A reverse to the Union arms": *National Intelligencer*, Washington, DC, reprinted by the *Chicago Tribune*, May 6, 1863.

69 "My God, my God": Thomas, *Abraham Lincoln*, 370.

70 Vallandigham's trial: OR, series 2, vol. 5: 633–46.

70 Vallandigham's protest: Ibid, 645.

70 New York Democrats' protests: Ibid., 654–56.

70 The Albany Resolves were published in Edward McPherson, *The Political History of the United States of America During the Great Rebellion*, Lincoln's reply, 163–67.

70 Randall analysis, "The Vallandigham Case": James G. Randall, *Lincoln*, 212–38.

70 Congressman Cox's rope and bell: Cox, *Three Decades of Federal Legislation*, 236.

71 "He says if we can only hold out": Jones, *A Rebel War Clerk's Diary*, June 22, 1863, 1:358–59.

71 Burnside's order closing the *Chicago Times*: James G. Randall, *Lincoln*, 233–36.

71 Mayor Sherman's reelection: *Chicago Tribune*, Apr. 22, 1863.

71 Horace Greeley, *The American Conflict*, 2:496, wrote that the fierce opposition to Vallandigham's arrest and banishment to the Confederacy made "the Democratic party more decidedly, openly, palpably, antiwar than it had hitherto been."

Chapter Thirteen

Page

72–73 Fernando Wood's speech at New York peace rally, June 3, 1863: *New York Times*, June 4, 1863; *Chicago Tribune*, June 9, 1863. See also, Pleasants, *Fernando Wood of New York*.

72 Description of Wood: *Sacramento Union*, Apr. 20, 1864.

73 A. G. Niven's remarks: *New York Times*, June 4, 1863.

73 "It is impossible to accuse the man of principle": Kirkland, *The Peacemakers of 1864*, 31.

74 Ben Wood "tall, well shaped": *Philadelphia Inquirer*, Aug. 15, 1863.

74 "The Great Dead Rabbit": Ibid.

74 Fernando Wood's letter to Lincoln, Dec. 8, 1862: Edward McPherson, *The Political History of the United States of America During the Great Rebellion*, 296–97.

74 Lincoln's reply: CWL, 5:517–18.

75 Mozart and Tammany factions "placing their houses in order": *New York Herald*, May 16, 1863.

75–76 Thurlow Weed's efforts to woo McClellan: Weed, *The Life and Autobiography of Thurlow Weed*, 2:428–29.

76 McClellan's reply: Ibid.

76 "S. L. M. Barlow & Co. are making a cat's paw": Strong, *Diary*, July 6, 1863, 3:330.

77 Ohio Democrats' convention: *Chicago Tribune*, June 12, 1863.
77 "[H]e would have had no chance": Ibid.
77 "I believe if Jeff Davis": Ibid., June 18, 1863.
77 Franklin Pierce's leadership of the New Hampshire peace faction: Franklin Pierce Papers, LC.
77 Connecticut Democrats' nomination of Thomas Seymour: Gray, *The Hidden Civil War*, 146.
78 Lee's letter to Davis, June 10, 1863: Lee, *The Wartime Papers of R. E. Lee*, 507–09.

Chapter Fourteen
Page
80–81 A vivid account of the New York draft riots by Morgan Patrick in *The Bulletin of the Society d'Europe*, Seabrook, N.H., Nov.–Dec. 1991; Asbury, *The Gangs of New York*, 108–157. British Lt. Col. Arthur James Lyon Fremantle witnessed the New York riots. He saw innocent negroes being chased with cries of "Kill all niggers!" Fremantle, *The Fremantle Diary*, 240–41.
82 Horace Greeley's narrow escape: Asbury, *The Gangs of New York*, 130.
82 "The fury of the low Irish women": Strong, *Diary*, July 13, 1863, 3:336.
82 "You can have no idea": Lieber to Holt, July 17, 1863, Holt Papers, LC.
82 "Lincoln, this Nero": Patrick, "The New York Draft Riots," 5.
82–83 Attacks on blacks: Asbury, *The Gangs of New York*, 127–32; Nevins, *The War for the Union*, 3: 121–25.
83 Colonel O'Brien "beaten into jelly": *Chicago Tribune*, July 15, 1863.
83 "For more than three hours": Asbury, *The Gangs of New York*, 140.
84 "We have *awful* good news": Jones, *Rebel War Clerk's Diary*, July 18, 1863, 1:382–83.
84 Southerners ridiculed: *New York Herald*, July 14, 1863.
84 Followers of the Wood brothers were ringleaders: *New York Post* in Pleasants, *Fernando Wood of New York*, 141.
84 Fernando Wood's response: *Congressional Globe*, 38th· Cong., 1st sess., 2075.
84–85 "Cunning and dangerous men": *New York Times*, Oct. 17, 1863.
85 Secretary Welles commented bitterly in his diary July 16, 1863: "Governor Seymour, whose partisans constituted the rioters, and whose partisanship encouraged them, has been in New York talking namby-pamby. This Sir Forcible Feeble is himself chiefly responsible for the outrage." Welles, *Diary*, 1:372–73.

Chapter Fifteen
Page
86–87 Horatio King's discovery of antiwar feeling in Maine: letter to Joseph Holt, Aug. 18, 1863, Holt Papers, LC.
87 "If we travel through the towns and villages": Noah Brooks' dispatch from Washington, Sept. 23, 1863, in Brooks, *Selections from the Writings of Noah Brooks*, 229.
87 Charges of plots for "a great rebellion of the North": *Chicago Tribune*, Aug. 8, 1863.
88 "Seymour was too timid": Ibid.
88 "I sincerely believe that Seymour": Christian Kribben to Col. Robert N.

Renick, St. Louis, from New York, Aug. 16, 1863, OR, series 2, vol. 7: 280–82.

88 "Vallandigham is the representative man": Ibid.

89 "The convicted traitor, Vallandigham": *Chicago Tribune,* July 30, 1863.

89 "You may as well attempt to raise the dead": Morton in the *Cincinnati Gazette* quoted in the *Indiana State Sentinel,* Oct. 13, 1863.

89–90 Ohio campaign songs: *The Vallandigham Song Book for the Times.*

90 J. B. Wright quotes dying Confederate colonel on Vallandigham: A dispatch from Cincinnati, Oct. 2, 1863, *Chicago Tribune,* Oct. 8, 1863.

90 "Victory of Gigantic Proportions!" *Chicago Tribune,* Oct. 15, 1863.

91–92 Text of McClellan's letter endorsing Judge Woodward: *Congressional Globe,* 38th Cong., 1st sess., Mar. 5, 1864: 101–02.

92 Kentucky election tactics: Hesseltine, *Lincoln and the War Governors,* 321.

92 Army Saves Maryland for Republicans: Dozer, *Maryland,* 457–63.

93 "I feel very indifferent about the White House": McClellan to his mother, Dec. 6, 1863, McClellan Papers, LC. Quoted by Sears, *The Civil War Papers of George B. McClellan,* 563.

Chapter Sixteen

Page

94 A photograph of Lincoln's May 8, 1863, letter to Hooker, Hanchett, "Lincoln's Assassination Revisited," The letter, OR, series 1, vol. 25, pt. 2:449. But, as Hanchett noted, "it is conspicuously absent from Lincoln biographies and Civil War histories." Depicting Lincoln as an advocate of arson hardly fits the traditional portrait of the kindly, martyred president.

95 The Kilpatrick–Dahlgren raid is chronicled in OR, series 1, vol. 33:168–224. Secretary of War Seddon summarized it in his Apr. 28, 1864, report to President Davis, OR, series 4, vol. 3:324–27. See also: Furgurson, *Ashes of Glory,* 248–58; Tidwell, with Hall and Gaddy, *Come Retribution,* 241–52.

95 "In his indignation he hung him": OR, series 1, vol. 33: 195, 221.

96 Text of Dahlgren's manifesto: Ibid., 219.

96 "If the Confederate capital has been": *Richmond Examiner,* Mar. 5, 1864.

96 Bragg's call for Yankees' executions and Lee's disapproval: OR, series 1, vol. 33:222–23.

96–97 Kilpatrick admits approving Dahlgren's orders: Ibid., 220.

97 "I happened to be in conference with the President": Benjamin to Slidell, Mar. 22, 1864, ORN, series 2, vol. 3:1070.

97 "The original papers bore no marks of alteration": Maj. Gen. Fitzhugh Lee to Adjutant General Cooper, Mar. 31, 1864, OR, series 1, vol. 33:224.

97 Lee's note to Meade: Ibid., Apr. 1, 1864, 178.

97 Meade's reply: Ibid., Apr. 17, 1864, 180.

97 General Meade's letter to his wife: Hall, "The Dahlgren Papers," 30–39.

97 "Memoranda of the War": Furgurson, *Ashes of Glory,* fn. 255.

98 The dispute over the authenticity of the Dahlgren papers has continued over the years because, when lithograph copies were made, the signature was mistakenly "touched up," so that it seemed to spell "Dalhgren." Admiral Dahlgren, seeing one of the lithograph copies, seized upon this printing error as proof that his beloved son's memory had been wronged by "a bare-faced, atrocious forgery." In a letter to the press from his flagship off Charleston, S. C., July 24, 1864, the heart-broken father wrote that his "noble boy" had been "assassinated" and "the criminals vented their cowardly rage on his cold body and gave their names and their cause for

a lie." Moore, ed., *The Rebellion Record*, 11:184.

However, Furgurson says, "Examination of the original showed that the apparent misspelling was caused by ink soaking through from the opposite side of the sheet." Although debate over the papers rages on, Furgurson concludes "the weight of the evidence suggests that they were indeed genuine."*Ashes of Glory*, 255.

James O. Hall compared the lithograph copy with the photographic copy of Dahlgren's address in the National Archives and explained the lithographer's error: "The signature on the original address was spelled correctly," Hall, "Dahlgren Papers," 37–38.

Chapter Seventeen

Page

100   "If Lincoln could be defeated": Herschel V. Johnson to Jefferson Davis, Jan. 4, 1864. Davis, *The Papers of Jefferson Davis*, 10:153.

100   Confederate appropriation for secret service works: Ibid., 154.

100   Hines's recollections: "The Northwestern Conspiracy," 437–45, 500–510, 567–74, 699–704.

100   "Hines cut a romantic figure": Castleman, *Active Service*, 139, 189.

101   "[T]ook his life in his hand": Gen. Basil Duke, Ibid., 137.

101   Captain Hines's orders: Ibid., 150; John W. Headley, *Confederate Operations in Canada and New York*, 218–21.

101   Hines as temporary major general: Castleman, *Active Service*, 150.

101   $70,000 cotton sale: Ibid., 151.

101   Text of his orders: Ibid., 150.

101   On August 27, 1865, Hines, in Toronto, wrote this on the margin of an *Atlantic Monthly* article by Edmund Kirke (James B. Gilmore) about the plot to free Confederate prisoners at Camp Douglas, Chicago: "The plan for creating a Revolution in the West by the release of prisoners was first presented by me to the authorities at Richmond in the month of February 1864. The following month I was commissioned for this purpose and furnished with everything deemed necessary for carrying this plan into execution. The military government and command were exclusively and entirely in my hands as my commission as Major General 'pro tempore' will fully prove." Horan, *Confederate Agent*, 66.

102   Alexander Hugh Holmes Stuart: Robertson, *Alexander Hugh Holmes Stuart*, 205–08.

103   Davis drew a million-dollar warrant: Davis, *The Papers of Jefferson Davis*, 10:154.

103   "Be assured, my dear friend": C. C. Clay to Davis, May 5, 1864, Ibid., 393–96.

103   Thompson's Montreal bank account: Castleman, *Active Service*, 144.

103   Confederate agents' aliases: Tredway, *Democratic Opposition to the Lincoln Administration in Indiana*, 177. Unsigned letter to "W. P. Carson," July 29, 1864, Report No. 104, House Reports, 39th Cong., 1st sess., 1864, 18.

103–104   Vallandigham's meeting with Thompson and Hines: Hines, "The Northwestern Conspiracy," 502; John W. Headley, *Confederate Operations in Canada and New York*, 222; Castleman, *Active Service*, 144–45.

104   Thompson's pay-offs to Sons of Liberty: Castleman, *Active Service*, 144–45.

105   "The belief was entertained": Thompson to Benjamin, from Toronto,

December 3, 1864, OR, series 1, vol. 43, pt. 2:930.
105 Hines's report to Seddon: Horan, *Confederate Agent*, 92. Horan says the letter was written in cipher and decoded by a War Department clerk at Richmond, the exact date unclear.
105–106 Tredway, *Democratic Opposition to the Lincoln Administration in Indiana*, 185, says Hines planned to equip an army of 37,000 men with guns from captured arsenals. After seizing the state governments of Ohio, Indiana, and Illinois, Hines planned to lead his army to General Sherman's base at Nashville with the object of forcing him to withdraw from Georgia. Tredway also says, 181, "it is evident that Holcombe at Montreal and Clay at Saint Catharines were in touch with prominent eastern men." Saint Catharines was a small town near Niagara Falls in Canada.

Chapter Eighteen
Page
107 Congressman Long's speech, Apr. 8, 1864: *Congressional Globe*, 38th Cong., 1st sess, 1499–503.
107 "A tall, well-formed man": *Sacramento Union*, Apr. 9, 1864.
108 Congressman James A. Garfield's reply: *Congressional Globe*, 38th Cong., 1st sess., 1503–05.
108 "Harris is a small, nervous man": *Sacramento Union*, May 9, 1864, dispatch Apr. 9. In May 1865, Harris was tried by a military court in Washington on charges of sheltering two paroled Confederate soldiers. He was sentenced to three years in jail and disqualified from Federal office. President Johnson remitted the sentence. Harris, so sickly in 1861, lived into his ninetieth year. He died on his Maryland estate in 1895. Harris's biography: U.S. Congress, *Biographical Directory of the American Congress, 1774–1971*, 1073.
108 Congressman Long's biography: U.S. Congress, *Biographical Directory of the American Congress*, 1303; Congressman Garfield's biography, Ibid., 986
108–109 Harris's speech: *Congressional Globe*, 38th Cong., 1st sess., 1515–19; *Sacramento Union*, May 9, 1864.
109 Expulsion motion tabled, seventy-one to sixty-nine: Apr. 14, 1864, *Congressional Globe*, 38th Cong., 1st sess., 1634–35.
109 Ouster and censure votes: Strong, *Diary*, Apr. 10, 1864, 3:427.
109 Letter from General Rosecrans about secret organizations: OR, series 1, vol. 34:505–06.
110 "The population of Kentucky is seven-eighths Confederate": Edward F. Hoffman's report, OR, series 2, vol. 7:272.
110 Hoffman joins the secret order of "The Star": Ibid., 267.
110 "The ladies here costume themselves": Ibid., 311.
110 *Cincinnati Enquirer* "the great focus of evil:" Ibid., 337.
111 "[C]onservative Union men" in Chicago want General Lee to win: Ibid., 277.
111 "Numerous cold-blooded assassinations" in Missouri: Ibid., 237.
111 General Carrington's warnings: Ibid., 340–42; his reports, Ibid., 228–305.

Chapter Nineteen
Page
113 "Grant has shown great skill": John Tyler Jr. to Maj. Gen. Sterling Price, commanding district of Arkansas, from Lee's headquarters in Hanover

County, Virginia, June 7, 1864. OR, series 1, vol. 51, pt. 2:993–95.

113 "The number of 'dead beats'": Noah Brooks, *Sacramento Union,* June 7, 1864.

113 "Regiments are returning home": Thurlow Weed to Joseph Parks, Apr. 23, 1864. Weed, *The Life of Thurlow Weed and Autobiography of Thurlow Weed,* vol. 2, 443.

113 "The commercial metropolis of the Union": *Sacramento Union,* May 3, 1864.

113 "It was openly proclaimed on the Street:" *New York Times,* May 7, 1864.

113 The Official Records contain voluminous letters of officials, North and South, concerning deserters and "skulkers" from the armies. Examples: Desertions in South Carolina: OR, series 4, vol. 2:769–77; Alabama, Ibid., 726–27; Mississippi, Ibid., 856–59; North Carolina, Ibid., 783–85, 794–96. Also OR, series 1, vol. 51, pt. 2:709–17 and series 1, vol. 18:880–95.

114 "Grant has been badly whipped": Unsigned letter to Vallandigham from Cincinnati, May 29, 1864, OR, series 2, vol. 7:358–59.

114 "The Germans are deserting": Ibid., 359.

114 The "Dutch" corps of German Americans, led by General Franz Sigel, did not win distinction in the battles of second Bull Run and Chancellorsville. Sigel was removed from command after the corps' retreat in the battle of New Market, Virginia, May 15, 1864.

115 "Today the nation will be degraded by the nomination of Lincoln": N. Cahill to Vallandigham, June 6, 1864, OR, series 2, vol. 7:363.

115 McClure, *Lincoln and Men of War-Times,* provides the most persuasive first-hand evidence that Lincoln personally maneuvered the process of dumping Hamlin and replacing him with Johnson while officially pretending to have nothing to do with it. As a Pennsylvania delegate to the Baltimore convention, McClure had expected to vote for Hamlin and had little respect for Johnson—"he was the last I would have chosen." Governor Andrew Curtin and former Senator Simon Cameron had long headed feuding factions in Pennsylvania Republican politics. Yet the president persuaded Cameron to back Johnson and later sold the idea to McClure, an intimate friend of Curtin, 104–18.

115 "Neither of us supposed that the other was acting in the special confidence of Lincoln," McClure recalls. The author also says Henry J. Raymond worked secretly with Seward and Thurlow Weed to help Johnson by heading off his closest rival, former Senator Daniel S. Dickinson of New York. McClure, *Lincoln and Men of War-Times,* 104–18.

115–116 McClellan's West Point speech: Stephen W. Sears, *George B. McClellan,* 363.

Chapter Twenty
Page

117–118 William Thorpe's report on Vallandigham's speech, Hamilton, Ohio, June 15, 1864: Thorpe to Col. J. P. Sanderson, from St. Louis, June 18, 1864, OR, series 2, vol. 7:320–25.

118 "If V. had been disturbed": Hoffman to Sanderson, June 20, 1864, Ibid., 719.

118 "If they ever dreamed": Ibid., 721.

118–119 Vallandigham's speech, Hamilton, Ohio: Ibid., 328–32.

119 Vallandigham "not only a consummate demagogue": Ibid., 376.

119 Carrington's warning to Stanton, June 17, 1864: Ibid., 376.

119 "[T]hey have more arms and ammunition": Ibid., 729.

120 "[M]uch hacked and battered," Ibid., 725.

120 Vallandigham "will do good here": *New York Tribune,* June 17, 1864.

120 "Mr. Lincoln knew": Schuyler Colfax's explanation: *Cincinnati Commercial,* Aug. 23, 1864; *New York Tribune,* Aug. 31, 1864; *Sacramento Union,* Oct. 1, 1864.

121 "I wish they had kept Vallandigham": McClellan to Barlow, June 17, 1864, Barlow Papers, HL.

121 *Indianapolis Journal,* June 18, 1864, revealed: "It is not generally known, but is nevertheless true, that Vallandigham is the highest officer in the secret organization designating itself as 'the Sons of Liberty.' The style of his office is that of 'Grand Commander.'"

121 Carrington's warning to McClellan, June 18, 1864: McClellan Papers, LC.

121 "You may be sure": McClellan to Carrington, July 2, 1864, Ibid.

121 "I feel now perfectly free": McClellan to Manton Marble, June 25, 1864, Marble Papers, LC.

121 The *Sacramento Union,* June 22, 1864, welcomed the prospect of Vallandigham disrupting plans to nominate McClellan at the Chicago convention: "The more artful leaders of the Copperhead party would as soon see satan himself at Chicago as the candid advocate of the abasement and division of the republic, and he has been selected by a district convention to go there and disturb the plans of the 'conservative war' men."

Chapter Twenty-One
Page

122 General Early provided his own account of his raid in B and L, 4:492–500. Osborne has a detailed narrative of the daring adventure in *Jubal ,* 261–92. See also Nicolay and Hay, *Lincoln,* 9:158–83 and Scharf, *History of Maryland from the Earliest Period to the Present Day,* 3: 627–40.

122 Confederates' extortion of cash from Hagerstown and Frederick: Dozer, *Portrait of the Free State,* 458; Scharf, *History of Maryland from the Earliest Period to the Present Day,* 3:618–25.

123 "Get down, you damn fool": James M. McPherson repeats the Oliver Wendell Holmes tale in *Battle Cry of Freedom,* 757. Furgurson, who is skeptical about that yarn, tells a different version in *Freedom Rising,* 317.

123 Tip-off by "Darst": OR series 1, vol. 51, pt. 2:1000–01.

123 "I had, therefore, reluctantly": Early, B and L, 4:497.

124 Lincoln disgusted: Hay, *Lincoln and the Civil War in the Diaries and Letters of John Hay,* July 14, 1864, 216.

124 "They might have captured Washington": Welles, *Diary,* July 11, 1864, 2:73.

124 "Poltroons and cowards": July 25, 1864, Ibid., 84.

124 "I do not consider": Lincoln to Stanton, July 14, 1864, CWL, 7: 439–40.

124 Parody of "Maryland, My Maryland!": *Indianapolis Daily Journal,* July 20, 1864.

125 "I believe if he would unbosom himself": Montgomery Blair to Barlow, May 1, 1864. Barlow to Blair, May 3, 1864, Barlow Papers, HL; McClellan to Barlow, May 3, 1864, McClellan Papers, LC.

125 "Through the good offices": Nicolay and Hay, *Lincoln,* 9:248–49.

125 Montgomery Blair persuades his father to go to New York, see McClellan, and talk him out of politics, "and to take command in the Valley, given afterwards to Sheridan": Myers, *A Study in Personality: General George B.*

McClellan, 433, William E. Smith, *The Francis Preston Blair Family in Politics*, 2:280–81.

125 Blair letter Oct. 5, 1864, *National Intelligencer*.

125 "No true man should refuse it": McClellan to Francis Preston Blair Sr., July 22, 1864, quoted by Stephen W. Sears, *George B. McClellan*, 366.

Chapter Twenty-Two
Page

127 The life story of George Nicholas Sanders is derived from several sources including: Castleman, *Active Service*, 133–38; Van der Linden, *Lincoln*, 17–19, 36–38, 57–59; and Tidwell, with Hall and Gaddy, *Come Retribution*, 129, 204, 331–34.

129 "Louis Napoleon should be put to death": journal entry, Sept. 19, 1855, Anna Sanders papers, LC.

130 "[A] Red of the most sanguinary hue": Ibid., Aug. 2, 1855.

130 Sanders's reply: "Nothing": Ibid., Aug. 1, 1855.

130 Halstead's word portrait of Sanders, "a burly, piratical looking person": Halstead, *Caucuses of 1860*, 10.

131 "[A] played-out political hack": *New York Times*, Apr. 1861; defense by his son, Reid, Ibid., Apr. 17, 1861.

131 Confederates in Canada: photograph of Sanders, Hines, Castleman, and George St. Leger, Tidwell, with Hall and Gaddy, *Come Retribution*, facing 240.

131 "George Sanders has gone on to see Mr. V": Jacob Thompson's letter from Montreal to Confederate chieftains in Richmond, June 9, 1864. Copy, in long hand, is in National Archives.

131 Sanders "obtained control": Castleman, *Active Service*, 135–37.

132 "[W]e could control the Chicago convention": Sanders to Jefferson Davis, from Montreal Mar. 7, 1865. Letter published in the *New York Herald*, July 8, 1865.

133 Sanders "plotting and scheming": Ibid., July 18, 1864.

133 Sanders entertains Northern Democratic politicians at Niagara Falls, Canada: J. P. Holcombe lists various important Democrats in the parleys in his report to Judah P. Benjamin at Richmond, Nov. 16, 1864, ORN, series 1, vol. 2:1234–35.

134 Dean Richmond: "The fighting must be stopped" and he is mentioned for the presidency: *New York Tribune*, July 22, 1864.

134 "[T]ricksters and adventurers": *Philadelphia Inquirer*, July 21, 1864.

134 Sanders, "the Kentucky bloviator": *New York Times*, July 21, 1864.

135 "You have shed so much blood": C. C. Clay to Judah P. Benjamin, Aug. 11, 1864, OR, series 4, vol. 3: 584–87.

135 "The Great Conspiracy": *Philadelphia Press*, Aug. 5, 1864.

135 "The darling dream of a Confederacy": Ibid.

135 Confederate commissioners' draft propositions: *New York Times*, July 22, 1864.

136 "If the Democratic party of the Northern states": *Philadelphia Inquirer*, July 21, 1864.

136 James Gordon Bennett's analysis of the designs of the Confederate "conspirators": *New York Herald*, July 31, 1864.

136–137 "[T]he Rebels at the Clifton House": *Rochester Democrat* dispatch quoted in the *New York Herald*, July 21, 1864.

Chapter Twenty-Three

Page

138 "The McClellan wing of the Democracy": George Nicholas Sanders to Jefferson Davis, Mar. 7, 1865, published in the *New York Herald,* July 8, 1865.

139 Jewett "an unmitigated ass": *Philadelphia Inquirer,* July 26, 1864.

139 Greeley "a fanatic, crazed, muddle-headed": Gilmore, *Personal Recollections of Abraham Lincoln and the Civil War,* 102–103.

139 "Having just left Hon. George Sanders": Jewett to Greeley, July 5, 1864; Horner, *Lincoln and Greeley,* 296–97.

139 "Our bleeding, bankrupt, almost dying country": Greeley to Lincoln, July 7, 1864, Ibid., 297.

139 "It may save us from a northern insurrection": Nicolay and Hay, *Abraham Lincoln,* 9:185–87.

139 "If you can find any person": Lincoln to Greeley, July 9, 1864, Horner, *Lincoln and Greeley,* 300.

139 "I am authorized to say": Sanders to Greeley, July 12, 1864, Ibid., 301.

140 "I have now information": Greeley to Lincoln, July 13, 1864, Ibid.

140 "I was not expecting you to send me a letter": Lincoln to Greeley, July 15, 1864, Horner, *Lincoln and Greeley,* 303.

140 Greeley's failure to tell the Confederates about Lincoln's terms: Ibid., 303.

140 "[T]hey shall be exempt from arrest": Ibid., 303–305.

140 "I am disappointed": Lincoln to Greeley, July 16, 1864, OR, series 3, vol. 4:496.

140 Greeley to Clay and Holcombe, July 17, 1864: Horner, *Lincoln and Greeley,* 305.

140–141 Clay's report on the Greeley peace mission: Clay to Benjamin from St. Catharine's, Aug. 11, 1864, OR, series 4, vol. 3:483–87.

141 "[W]e are, however, in the confidential employment": Clay and Holcombe to Greeley, July 18, 1864, Horner, *Lincoln and Greeley,* 306.

141 Lincoln's manifesto: "To whom it may concern": OR, series 3, vol. 4:503–04.

141 "[A] seedy looking Rebel": Hay, *Letters of John Hay,* 1:215–17.

141 Holcombe "false-looking": Ibid.

141–142 Reply of Clay and Holcombe to Greeley, July 21, 1864: Horner, *Lincoln and Greeley,* 312–14.

142 The "actual object": *Philadelphia Press,* Aug. 22, 1864.

143 "All the Democratic presses": Clay to Benjamin, Aug. 11, 1864, Horner, *Lincoln and Greeley,* 312–14.

143 "Greeley curses all fools": Ibid.

143 "Greeley is so rotten": Welles, *Diary,* 2:111–12.

143 "I am surprised": Bates, *The Diary of Edward Bates,* July 22, 1864,

143 "It is lamentable": *New York Post,* July 25, 1864.

143 "That shuffle-gaited, peripatetic old Greeley": *New York Herald,* July 25, 1864.

143 "Greeley and Jewett": *New York World,* July 25, 1864.

143 "That dancing windbag of popinjay conceit": *Cincinnati Commercial,* July 25, 1864.

144 "Well, I'll tell you about that": Tarbell, *The Life of Abraham Lincoln,* 2:198, 317.

144 Kirkland, *The Peacemakers of 1864,* 84, wrote that, because of the Confederates' claim of bad faith dealings, Lincoln stood revealed as either inept or vacillating or else "positively dishonest."

Chapter Twenty-Four

Page

145 Kirke's (James R. Gilmore) account, "Our Visit to Richmond," *Atlantic Monthly*, Sept. 1864, 372–73.

146 Benjamin sent his version of the parley in a "circular" from Richmond, Aug. 25, 1864. It appears in ORN, series 2, vol. 3:1190–94. One copy was addressed to James M. Mason "commissioner to the Continent, Paris," former Confederate envoy to Great Britain.

148–149 Lincoln's memorandum, charging that Confederate Commissioner Clay had proposed a draft of the Democratic Party's peace plank: CWL, 7:459–60.

150 Lincoln to Abram Wakeman, New York, July 25, 1864: Ibid., 460.

Chapter Twenty-Five

Page

151–152 "If peace be not granted, then it shall be war": Thompson's report to Benjamin, Horan, *Confederate Agent*, 93; also Hines, "The Northwest Conspiracy,"

152 "Thus it was that the movements": Castleman, *Active Service.*, 147.

152 Thompson's subsidies for "peace" rallies: Thompson to Benjamin, Dec. 3, 1864, OR, series 1, vol. 43:930–36.

152 "A convention of traitors": *Chicago Tribune*, July 14, 1864.

152 "Violent and Treasonable Speeches": *New York Herald*, Aug. 23, 1864.

153 Felix Stidger's adventures as the Federal spy who exposed the Indiana revolutionary plot are detailed in his own memoirs, *Treason History of the Order of Sons of Liberty, Succeeded Knights of the Golden Circle, Afterward Order of American Knights.* Also see Pitman, ed., *The Trials for Treason at Indianapolis,* the transcript of the trials.

153 "He told me that the forces of Indiana": Stidger, *Treason History*, 37.

153 Dr. Bowles' description: William J. Davis, ed., *The Partisan Rangers of the Confederate States Army*, 431.

153 "The work" to begin in August: Jones, *A Rebel War Clerk's Diary*, 2:259.

154 Dodd says "I will leave the country": Stidger, *Treason History*, 100.

154 Stidger's meeting with Governors Morton and Bramblette: Ibid., 101–102.

154 Judge Bullitt's arrest: Ibid., 107; also Pitman, ed., *The Trials for Treason at Indianapolis,* testimony, 23–24.

155 Bingham's refusal to call Indianapolis mass meeting: His testimony, Ibid., 101–102.

155 The Indiana plot and the state Democratic leaders' decision to squelch it, are detailed in Foulke, *Life of Oliver P. Morton*, 1:399–417.

155 "The devil's to pay": Ibid., 404. Despite his ties to the Sons of Liberty, Kerr served as Speaker of the U.S. House of Representatives, 1875–1876.

156 "I also learn on undoubted authority": *Chicago Tribune*, Aug. 22, 1864, quoting the *Cincinnati Gazette*.

156 "Well, it's too late": Davis, ed., *The Partisan Rangers of the Confederate States Army*, 432.

156 "Freeman, Bowles is the only soldier": Ibid., 433.

156 "I believe fully": Ibid., 434.

156 Discovery of the "Sunday school books" in Indianapolis: *Chicago Tribune*, Aug. 28, 1864.

157 Morton's charge that the weapons were financed by Confederate gold:

Foulke, *Life of Oliver P. Morton,* 1:409–11. Also *Indianapolis Journal* account reprinted, *Philadelphia Press,* Aug. 28, 1864.

157 Col. Adam Johnson blinded, taken prisoner: Davis, ed., *The Partisan Rangers of the Confederate States Army,* 173. Also *Louisville Journal,* Sept. 3, 1864. Col. Johnson, later brigadier general, rose above the great handicap of his blindness. After the war, he settled in Texas, raised a family, and became a successful businessman.

Chapter Twenty-Six
Page

158 "I never saw him more dejected": McClure, *Lincoln and Men of War-Times,* 113–14.

158 Thurlow Weed, Lincoln's reelection "an impossibility": Weed to Seward, Aug. 22, 1864, CWL, 7:514 n.

158 "You think I don't know": letter from J. K. Herbert to Butler from Washington, DC, Aug. 11, 1864, Butler, *Private and Official Correspondence,* 5:35.

158–159 "I am in active correspondence": Henry J. Raymond to Lincoln, Aug. 22, 1864, CWL, 7: 517–18 n.

159 "Mothers, sisters, wives": Gen. John H. Martindale to Butler from Rochester, MN, Aug. 16, 1864, Butler, *Private and Official Correspondence* 5:54.

159 "Nine-tenths of the whole American people": Greeley to Lincoln, Aug. 9, 1864, Horner, *Lincoln and Greeley,* 319.

160 James Parton wrote to General Butler from New York, Aug. 19, 1864, about meeting ex-President Franklin Pierce, who said "a truce and a negotiation would result in reunion. He spoke darkly of private information that much encouraged him." Butler, *Private and Official Correspondence,* 5:80.

160 Profile of Judge Jeremiah S. Black: DAB, 1, pt. 2:310–13. His son, Chauncey F. Black, edited his *Essays and Speeches of Jeremiah Black,* 1885.

160 Black's reminiscences, published by Frank A. Burr, *Philadelphia Press,* Aug. 7, 14, 21, 28, 1881.

160 Black's mission to the Confederates in Canada, who were sure that he was an agent of Stanton: Castleman, *Active Service,* 149–50; also Hines, "Northwest Conspiracy," 501.

160 Stanton feared cabinet members "would be treated with contumely and violence": Ibid.

160–161 Black says Stanton "desired" Thompson to visit Richmond: Clay to Benjamin, Sept. 12, 1864, OR, series 4, vol. 3:636–37.

161 "Mr. Stanton was not averse, therefore, to some negotiation": Hines, "The Northwest Conspiracy," 501.

161 "Agreeably to the wish expressed by you": Black to Stanton from York, PA, Aug. 24, 1864, Black Papers, LC, contain the full text of this letter.

162 "You go for an armistice": Stanton to Black, Gorham, *Life of Stanton,* 2:153.

162 "There have been men base enough": Lincoln's remarks to former Wisconsin Governor Alexander Randall and Judge J. T. Mills, as the judge recorded them in the Grant County, Wisconsin, *Herald,* in August 1864, are recorded in Edward McPherson's *The Political History of the United States of America During the Great Rebellion,* 424, and the *New York Post,* Sept. 6, 1864. The diary of Judge Mills is in CWL, 7:606–08.

163 "The rebels have now in their ranks": Gen. Grant to Congressman Elihu Washburne, Aug. 16, 1864; *Chicago Tribune,* Sept. 10, 1864.

164 Henry J. Raymond's proposed peace commission to Jefferson Davis: Nicolay and Hay, *Abraham Lincoln*, 9:218–19.

164 "Hell is to pay": Nicolay to Hay, Aug. 25, 1864, Helen Nicolay, *Lincoln's Secretary*, 212.

164 The dump Lincoln plot: Oates, *With Malice Toward None*, 396.

165 "Mr. Lincoln is already beaten": Horner, *Lincoln and Greeley*, 351.

165 "I have seen and talked with": J. W. Shaffer to General Butler, New York, Aug.17, 1864, Butler, *Private and Official Correspondence*, 5:67–68.

165 "The country has gone to hell!": Ibid., 67.

Chapter Twenty-Seven

Page

166 The *Philadelphia Inquirer*, July 22, 1864, defined the Democratic Party's factions and interest groups.

166 New York Democratic convention's decisions: Alexander, *A Political History of the State of New York*, 3:191.

167 "There is but one voice": Cox to Marble, July 25, 1864, Marble Papers, LC.

168 Congressman Long's welcome in Ohio: *Cincinnati Commercial*, July 9, 1864.

168 Thomas Seymour "a vain, brainless man": Ibid., July 13, 1864.

168–169 August Belmont's biography: Belmont, *An American Democrat*, 1–128; also Katz, *August Belmont;* DAB 1, pt. 2:169–70.

169 Belmont's ties to John Slidell: Willson, *John Slidell and the Confederates in Paris*, 21.

169 "Mutual Admiration Association": *New York Times*, Aug. 22, 1864.

169 Mass meeting for McClellan: *New York Tribune*, Aug. 11, 1864.

169 Syracuse peace rally: *Cincinnati Commercial*, Aug. 19, 1864; *New York Times*, Aug. 19, 1864.

170 O. P. Rookes' report from Syracuse appeared in a letter to the *Syracuse Journal*, Aug. 19, 1864, reprinted in the *Daily Missouri Democrat*, St. Louis, Sept. 6, 1864.

170 "The majority of the delegates": *Sacramento Union*, Aug. 1, 1864.

171 "The conviction now seems to be almost universal": Barlow to Marble, Aug. 21, 1864, Marble Papers, LC.

171 Barlow tells Marble "to head off" a Frémont nomination: Barlow to Marble, Aug. 24, l864, Ibid.

172 "We have all sorts of rumors as to bargains and tricks": Ibid. "Guthrie" refers to James Guthrie, Kentucky railroad tycoon, the McClellan group's favorite for the vice presidency.

172 "I think you will be able to counteract": Barlow to Marble, Aug. 24, 1864, Marble Papers, LC.

172 "The rebels in Canada prefer": *New York Herald*, Aug. 30, 1864.

Chapter Twenty-Eight

Page

173 Two slightly "tight" delegates: *Cincinnati Commercial*, Aug. 31, 1864.

174 "The city is swarming like a huge beehive": *Chicago Tribune*, Aug. 27, 1864.

174 Convention of "red noses": *Philadelphia Press*, Aug. 27, 1864.

174 Crowded saloons: *Chicago Tribune*, Aug. 27, 1864.

174 "Sunday morning dawning on a vast mob": *Sacramento Union,* Oct. 11, 1864.
174 "A perfect saturnalia": *Philadelphia Press,* Aug. 29, 1864.
174 "Thousands of short boys": *Daily Missouri Democrat,* Aug. 30, 1864.
175 "These courageous men": Castleman, *Active Service,* 154.
175 "There is a feverish anxiety": *New York Times,* Aug. 30, 1864.
175 "There are now nine thousand": *Sacramento Union,* Sept. 10, 1864.
175 Most members of the order were Democrats: Hines to Secretary Seddon, Castleman, *Active Service,* 157.
176 "It was understood": Ibid., 158.
176 "[A]ppalled" by the actual demand: Ibid.
176–177 "Captain Hines agreed": Ibid.
177 "In accordance with your orders": Undated letter in NA, evidently after the Democratic convention, Ibid.
178 Plot to free Rebel prisoners: Castleman, *Active Service,* 160, quoted the *Atlantic Monthly* (July 1865) article about "The Chicago Conspiracy." Hines and Castleman recount their Chicago adventures, "The Northwest Conspiracy," 569–74.
178 Stephen Z. Starr refutes prison raids "a myth": Starr, *Colonel Grenfell's Wars,* 142–43.
178 Frank L. Klement minimizes the importance of the Democrats' secret societies in his book *The Copperheads of the Middle West* (Chicago 1960), 161–69. Starr refutes Klement's claims that the antiwar movement was "nothing more than a somewhat exaggerated manifestation of ordinary political partisanship," and adds "nothing could be further from the truth." Starr, after analyzing Klement's thesis, comments that it is "a point of view which, with the greatest respect for Dr. Klement's scholarship, the author is unable to accept." Starr, *Colonel Grenfell's Wars,* 142.

Chapter Twenty-Nine
Page
179 "By God, McClellan shall be nominated": *New York Tribune,* Aug. 29, 1864.
179 "[P]ins so fixed": *Cincinnati Commercial,* Aug. 29, 1864.
179 "He is all their own": *Philadelphia Press,* Sept. 5, 1864.
179 "Do you see that portly … ": Ibid.
179–180 "He stands with his hands in his breeches pocket": *Daily Missouri Democrat,* Aug. 30, 1864.
180 "[A] man of ponderous make-up": *Cincinnati Commercial,* Aug. 29, 1864.
180 "He would make, beyond doubt": *New York Tribune,* Aug. 22, 1864.
180 "He had little education": DAB 8, pt. 1:582–83.
180 Dean Richmond wants to "end this damned war": *Philadelphia Inquirer,* Aug. 24, 1864.
181 "'Little Mac' is run by the bloated aristocrats": *Chicago Tribune,* Aug. 29, 1864.
181 "[A] tough, uncouth specimen": *Cincinnati Commercial,* Aug. 29, 1864.
181 "By God, sir": Ibid.
181 Fernando Wood "as sleek and slimy as ever": Ibid.
182 *New York Daily News* takes $25,000 in Confederate cash: *New York Times,* Aug. 25, 1864; Castleman, *Active Service,* 146.
182 "He is a short, heavily built": *Cincinnati Commercial,* Aug. 30, 1864.
182 "He had stepped out to take a sherry cobbler": Ibid.
182 Seymour "blows hot and cold": Belmont to Barlow, Aug. 26 and 27, 1864, Barlow Papers, HL; Katz, *August Belmont,* 129.

182 "[C]onvincing the doubters": Barlow to Marble, Aug. 24, 1864, Marble Papers, LC.
182 "[W]e cannot carry this state or Pennsylvania with Seymour": Ibid.
183 "I am almost used up by excitement": Barlow to Marble, no date, Ibid.
183 "All going well": Belmont to Barlow, Barlow Papers, HL; Katz, *August Belmont*, 131–32.
183 "It is plain to me": Barlow to McClellan, Aug. 28, 1864, McClellan, *The Civil War Papers of George McClellan*, 584.
183 "If we win": Ibid.
183 Vallandigham's speech "gave the opportunity": *New York Tribune*, Aug. 31, 1864.
183 "The truth is, the masses": *Daily Missouri Democrat*, Aug. 30, 1864.
184 Dick Dodd and "midnight assassins": *Chicago Tribune*, Aug. 27, 1864.
184 James B. Wilson testified at the treason trial in Indianapolis. Pitman, ed., *The Trials for Treason at Indianapolis*, 144–49.
184 "They could search Hell over": These and many other incendiary remarks by speakers on the Chicago streets were detailed in a Republican campaign pamphlet, *The Chicago Copperhead Convention*. Most of them were copied from the *Chicago Times*, a Democratic newspaper.
185 Sanderson, "What is this war for?" *Indianapolis Daily Journal*, Sept. 12, 1864.
185 Paine, "Do the people want a draft?" *The Chicago Copperhead Convention*.
185 This war is carried on "for the nigger": *Indianapolis Daily Journal*, Aug. 31, 1864.
185 Hendricks, "hurl the smutty old tyrant": *Cincinnati Commercial*, Aug. 31, 1864.
185 Senator Richardson's oratory: Ibid.
185 W. W. O'Brien predicts "Old Abe" to be kicked out: *The Chicago Copperhead Convention*.
185 Cox, "Abraham Lincoln has deluged the country with blood": Ibid.
185 Allen, "The people will soon rise": Ibid.
186 McClellan called Lincoln's "dog": *Daily Missouri Democrat* and *Cincinnati Commercial*, Sept. 2, 1864.
186 "Before God, gentlemen": *Daily Missouri Democrat*, Sept. 1, 1864.

Chapter Thirty
Page
187 "[C]razy as bedbugs": Noah Brooks, *Sacramento Union*, Oct. 11, 1864.
187 "The farmers of the rural districts": *Chicago Tribune*, Aug. 30, 1864.
187 "Dixie" the favorite tune of the convention: *Daily Missouri Democrat*, Sept. 6, 1864.
188 "He has a rather Broadway look": *Philadelphia Press*, Aug. 29, 1864.
188 "We are not here as War Democrats": *New York Times*, Aug. 30, 1864.
188–189 "'McClellan and Peace' are to be blazoned": *Daily Missouri Democrat*, Aug. 29, 1864.
189 C. L. Weller's imprisonment: *Sacramento Union*, July 26, 28, and Aug. 16, 1864.
189 "They will not let the shedding of blood cease": *Washington Evening Star*, Aug. 30, 1864 and *New York Tribune*, Aug. 31, 1864.
189–190 Full text of the Democrats' platform: Greeley, *American Conflict*, 2:668.
190 "Stop the war for a month": *Chicago Tribune*, Aug. 30, 1864.
191 "[M]ost vociferous applause": *Sacramento Union*, Oct. 11, 1864.

191–192 Speech by Congressman Harris attacking McClellan: Ibid.

192 "[E]very third man in the convention is armed": *New York Tribune*, Aug. 30, 1864.

192 "[P]ins so fixed": *Cincinnati Commercial*, Aug. 29, 1864.

192 "Instantly, the pent-up feelings of the mob": *Sacramento Union*, Oct. 11, 1864.

192, 194 For Vallandigham's guarantee of being named secretary of war, see C. C. Clay's post-convention letter to Judah Benjamin from Canada, Sept. 12, 1864, OR, series 4, vol. 3:636–39.

194 "Mirabile dictu": *Daily Missouri Democrat*, Aug. 30, 1864.

194 George Pendleton "smart and sharp": Brooks, *Washington, D.C. in Lincoln's Time*, 304.

194 Nichols, *Franklin Pierce, Young Hickory of the Granite Hills*, 247, describes Guthrie, when treasury secretary, as a giant, more than six feet tall, with a very sturdy build, "a veritable picture of strength and endurance.

"He was plain, rather unattractive, and presented a sleepy-looking appearance which his soft drawl accentuated. His movements were slow, as he had been lamed in a fight in his youth, but he was really energetic and determined, peremptory, rapid in execution and decision and sometimes obstinate.

"He had made a fortune in a number of enterprises including railroads, but had little experience in politics outside of the Kentucky legislature.

"His tall figure, with a broad-brimmed Quaker hat, was a familiar sight in the vicinity of the Treasury. Sound business sense reigned in that office while he occupied it."

194 "So help me God": *Chicago Tribune*, Nov. 3, 1864.

195 Wickliffe "the leader of the Rebel wing": *The Chicago Copperhead Convention*.

195 "[T]o open Lincoln's prison doors": *Daily Missouri Democrat*, Sept. 1, 1864.

195 "[A] putty head": *Sacramento Union*, Oct. 11, 1864.

195 "[A] kangaroo ticket": *Daily Missouri Democrat*, Sept. 1, 1864.

195 "The Peace-Sneaks Got All": *Chicago Tribune*, Sept. 1, 1864.

Chapter Thirty-One
Page

196 For profiles of Seward: Van Deusen, *William Henry Seward*, 7–12; Seward, *Reminiscences of a War-Time Statesman and Diplomat*, 28–30.

197 "Atlanta is ours and fairly won": Lewis, *Sherman, Fighting Prophet*, 409; Sherman, *Memoirs of General William T. Sherman, by Himself*, 2:109.

197 Seward's charge of Democrats' collusion with Confederates: *New York Herald*, Sept. 7, 1864.

199 "By heavens, we've got 'em!": Ibid.

199 "Here the Copperheads were caught": *Sacramento Union*, Oct. 10, 1864.

200 "The platform means peace": C. C. Clay to Judah P. Benjamin, Sept. 12, 1864, OR, series 4, vol. 3:636–39.

200 "I had an interview today with Gen. McClellan": James Harrison to Col. L. V. Bogy, New York, Aug. 24, 1864, NA.

201 "It is absolutely necessary": August Belmont to McClellan, Sept. 3, 1864, McClellan Papers, LC.

201 Peace plank "foisted on the convention": *New York Herald*, Sept. 4, 1864.

201 "Do not listen to your Eastern friends": Vallandigham to McClellan,

Sept. 4, 1864, McClellan Papers, LC.

201 "I could not look in the faces": McClellan's letter of acceptance, *Official Proceedings of the Democratic National Convention in 1864 in Chicago*, 60–61.

201–202 "[T]here was no chance whatever": McClellan to Cox, Sept. 15, 1864, McClellan, *The Civil War Papers of George B. McClellan*, 598.

202 "[P]latitudes floating in mucilage": Strong, *Diary*, Sept. 9, 1864, 3:484.

202 "[A]rrogant, war-spitting letter": Sanders to Jefferson Davis, Mar. 7, 1865, *New York Herald*, July 8, 1865.

202–203 "The Peace Democracy of this state": *Daily Missouri Democrat*, Sept. 12, 1864.

203 Long spurns independent nomination: Roseboom, *A History of Presidential Elections*, 201.

203 "God gave us the victory": Leonard Swett to his wife. Letter sent by Herbert Leonard Swett of Aurora, Illinois, to Ida M. Tarbell, quoted in *The Life of Abraham Lincoln*, 3:202–203.

203 "It was equally formidable and vicious": Thurlow Weed to Seward, Sept. 20, 1864, Lincoln Papers, LC.

203 General Butler spends hours with Weed: Hay, *Letters of John Hay and Excerpts from His Diary*, Sept. 29, 1864, 2:221.

204 Frémont's letter of withdrawal: Edward McPherson, *The Political History of the United States of America During the Great Rebellion*, 426.

Chapter Thirty-Two

Page

205 "Dixie, Davis, and the Devil": Silbey, *A Respectable Minority*, 166–67.

205–206 Montgomery Blair's speech: *Sacramento Union*, Oct. 24, 1864.

206 "He is one of those fellows": Senator Jim Lane speaking at Lawrenceburg, Indiana, Sept. 26, 1864. *Cincinnati Commercial*, Sept. 28, 1864.

206 "George H. Pendleton is a fine-looking man": *Daily Missouri Democrat*, Aug. 30, 1864.

206 "I could name fifty young barristers": *Philadelphia Press*, Sept. 2, 1864.

207 "An apoplexy, catarrh, or cough": Strong, *Diary*, 3: 489, Sept. 17, 1864.

207 "Suppose, in one of the powerful": *Cincinnati Commercial*, Sept. 15, 1864.

207 "If you find conciliation impossible": *The Chicago Copperhead Convention*, 15–16.

207–208 "Why, Vallandigham himself: *Sacramento Union*, Sept. 6, 1864.

208 "I was born in Ohio": Pendleton's speech at New York rally, Oct. 24, 1864. Edward McPherson, *The Political History of the United States of America During the Great Rebellion*, 422.

208 "[T]o rebuke the demagogue": *New York Times*, Sept. 4, 1864.

208 "[A] pale, sleek-headed man": *New York Herald*, Aug. 26, 1864.

208 "He is a small, dark-complexioned man": *Daily Missouri Democrat*, Aug. 27, 1864.

209 "August Belmont, the gorgeous and fastidious": *Sacramento Union*, Oct. 21, 1864.

209 Samuel Medary's refusal to place McClellan's name on his paper's masthead: *Cincinnati Commercial*, Sept. 8, 1864; *Daily Missouri Democrat*, Sept. 14, 1864.

209 The chariot of "His Democratic Majesty": *Daily Missouri Democrat*, Sept. 14, 1864, quoting the *Crisis*.

210 "The rabble think they nominated McClellan": *Chicago Tribune*, Sept. 8,

1864.

210 "George B. McClellan is simply the chattel of Sam Barlow": Ibid., Nov. 3, 1864.

210 "Why did Belmont urge the nomination of McClellan?": Ibid., Nov. 8, 1864.

211 "I am glad to hear from you": Katz, *August Belmont*, 90.

211 Jewish press defends Belmont: *The Jewish Messenger* 6, Nov. 4, 1864.

211 Belmont's lawsuit for libel: Katz, *August Belmont*, 143.

Chapter Thirty-Three
Page

213 Jefferson Davis's pep talks: Davis, *Jefferson Davis, Constitutionalist*, 6:342–43; Dyer, *The Gallant Hood*, 275; Moore, ed., *The Rebellion Record*, 11:148–49; Davis, *The Papers of Jefferson Davis*, 11: 62, 64, 85.

213 Two-thirds of Confederate soldiers AWOL: Moore, ed., *Rebellion Record*, 11:149; Davis, *Papers of Jefferson Davis*, 11:62.

213 "Let fresh victories crown our arms": *Cincinnati Commercial*, Oct. 31, 1864.

214 Sherman's March to the Sea: OR, series 1, vol. 39, pt. 3:161, 202, 595, 660.

214 "He had expected to find": Col. Henry Stone, "Repelling Gen. Hood's Invasion of Tennessee," B and L, 4: 441.

215 Confederates' plan "to cross the Ohio and attack General Thomas in the rear": Yeary, *Reminiscences of the Boys in Gray*, 168–71.

215–216 Confederate deserters' interviews: *Chicago Tribune*, Sept. 29, 1864.

Chapter Thirty-Four
Page

217 "[D]efection of the executive governments": Hay, *Lincoln and the Civil War in the Diaries and Letters of John Hay*, 229.

218 "A very large number of men": Col. James G. Jones to Brig. Gen. James G. Fry, Sept. 12, 1864, OR, series 3, vol. 4:711–12.

218 "[T]o strike terror": Foulke, *Life of Oliver P. Morton*, 1:419–20.

219 "Dodd turned a deathly pale": Stidger, *Treason History of the Order of Sons of Liberty*, 152.

219 "Treason" headline: *Troy Times*, Troy, OH, Oct. 6, 1864.

219 Stidger's testimony is detailed in his own memoirs; also in the transcript of the Indiana treason trials. Pitman, ed., *The Trials for Treason at Indianapolis*, Memoirs: 152–55; Transcript: 10–40.

219 Plot against Governor Morton and Treason Trials: Foulke, *Life of Oliver P. Morton*, 1:429–31.

219 Wesley Trantor's testimony: Pitman, ed., *The Trials for Treason at Indianapolis*, 47–48.

219 William Clayton's testimony: Ibid., 47.

219 Steven Teney's testimony: Ibid., 97.

220 Dodd's escape: Foulke, *Life of Oliver P. Morton*, 1:421.

220 General Carrington's warning to voters: Ibid., 420–21.

220 "If the rebels in arms could vote": *Indianapolis Journal*, Oct. 11, 1864.

220 Out-of-state soldiers voted in Indiana: Hesseltine, *Lincoln and the War Governors*, 379.

220 "I am deeply thankful": Hay, *Lincoln and the Civil War in the Diaries and Letters of John Hay*, 229.

221 "[T]hat disgusting compound of whisky, grease, vulgarity and cowardice":

Indianapolis Journal, Aug. 6, 1864.

221 Heffren's military careers: Ibid.
221 General Carrington's telegram: OR, series 2, vol. 7:1089.
221 "[H]alf a million dollars": *Indianapolis Journal,* Nov. 5, 1864.
221–222 "The order members were to march": Pitman, ed., *The Trials for Treason at Indianapolis,* 135.
222 "Heffren said the O. A. K": *Chicago Tribune,* Nov. 5, 1864.
222–223 Colonel Burnett's charges: *Indianapolis Journal,* Nov. 5, 1864.
223 Holt's report: OR, series 2, vol. 7:930–53.
223–224 "Judea produced but one Judas Iscariot": Holt's report, Ibid.
224 Holt's attack on the McClellan Minute Guard: Edward McPherson, *The Political History of the United States of America During the Great Rebellion,* 446.
224 Reply by Dr. R. F. Stevens: Ibid.
224 Holt's biography: DAB, 5, pt. 1:181–83.
225 "A man who, once a Democrat": unsigned letter to Holt, Oct. 15, 1864, Holt Papers, LC.
225 "Copperhead tirades;" E. W. Dennis to Holt, Oct. 24, 1864, from Canandaigua, NY, Ibid.
225 "My dear Josey": letter signed "M. K. S.", Ibid.

Chapter Thirty-Five
Page
226 Lincoln's prediction of a narrow election victory: Oates, *With Malice Toward None,* 399.
227 James Robinson's acceptance of Confederate gold: Castleman, *Active Service,* 168–71.
227 "If elected governor": Castleman, *Active Service,* 171. The original is in the Thomas Henry Hines Papers, University of Kentucky.
228 "If it was not treasonous": Long, *The Jewel of Liberty,* 106.
229 "The Democracy of the state was cheated": *Daily Missouri Democrat,* Sept. 9, 1864.
229 "In person, he is large, coarse looking and vulgar": Ibid.
229 In the battle of Corinth: *Indianapolis Journal,* Sept. 9, 1864.
230 "If you would throw the great weight": *Chicago Tribune,* Oct.12, 1864.
230 "Originally a Whig": criticism of Judd, *Chicago Tribune,* Sept. 29, 1864.
230 Defense of "Black Jack" Logan against "cowardly slanders": Lusk, *Politics and Politicians,* 175.
231 "Intriguing political tricksters": Ibid.
231–232 Logan's Carbondale speech: *Cincinnati Commercial,* Oct. 5, 1864.
233 "It is no use to deceive ourselves": Washburne to Lincoln, Oct. 17, 1864, Lincoln Papers, LC.
233 "Logan is carrying all before him": Nicolay and Hay, *Abraham Lincoln,* 9:372.

Chapter Thirty-Six
Page
234 "[M]ysterious passengers in tattered uniforms": *Chicago Tribune,* Nov. 6, 1864.
235 "What are these men here for?" Ibid.
235 "After they had drunk freely": Ibid.

235 "We are sounding no false alarm": Ibid., Nov. 7, 1864.

236 Col. George St. Leger Grenfell profile: Starr, *Colonel Grenfell's Wars*, 8–14.

236 "This city is filling up with suspicious characters": Col. B. J. Sweet to Brig. Gen. John Cook, Springfield, IL, Nov. 6, 1864, OR, series 1, vol. 45, pt. 1:1081.

236 Bettersworth revealed "the whole plan to Detective Shanks": Castleman, *Active Service*, 195.

236–237 "[I]nfamous traitor": Horan, *Confederate Agent*, 187.

237 Colonel Sweet's arrests: OR, series 1, vol. 45:1077–80.

237 Captain Hines's escape: Castleman, *Active Service*, 192–94.

237–238 "The course of Mayor Sherman": *Chicago Tribune*, Nov. 7, 1864.

238 "Every one of those raiders was a Democrat": Ibid., Nov. 8, 1864.

238 Magazine article praising Colonel Sweet: Kirke, *Atlantic Monthly*, July 1865.

238 Greeley's belief that the conspiracy was intended to "lift the siege of Richmond": Greeley, *American Conflict*, 2:687.

238–239 Colonel Sweet's official report to Washington, Nov. 23, 1864: OR, series 1, vol. 45:1077–80

239 "I sometimes pity the poor devils": *Chicago Tribune*, Nov. 3, 1864.

239 On Aug. 31, 1864, George St. Leger Grenfell wrote to William Maynard in London: "The North West states are ripe for revolt. If interfered with in their election, they will rise. … Abe Lincoln will either have made peace, or made himself a dictator within the next two months. In the latter case, the N. W. provinces secede and there comes a row. Either course aids the South." Weaks, "Colonel George Saint Leger Grenfell," 11.

Chapter Thirty-Seven

Page

240–241 "There is hardly a county in the North": *New York Times*, Aug. 27, 1864, noting *Albany Atlas and Argus* letter.

241 "[T]he miserable sweepings of the cities": *Philadelphia Press* Sept. 1, 1864.

241 "Europe is bankrupt of criminals": A. Dudley Mann to Benjamin, Aug. 20, 1864, ORN, series 2, vol. 3:1186.

241 Strong's "Dutch boy" substitute: Strong, *Diary*, Aug. 25, 1864, 3:479.

241 "The men are running mad with speculation": *Philadelphia Inquirer*, Oct. 3, 1864.

242 "Are there no means for arresting": E. B. Wolcott to Gov. James T. Lewis, Aug. 28, 1864, OR, series 3, vol. 4:684.

242 "The Democratic majority," *New York Herald*.

242 Secessionists all over New York City: *New York Herald*, May 25, 1864.

243 "The platform offended McClellan": Thurlow Weed's statement. *Cincinnati Commercial*, Oct. 19, 1864.

243 Confederates' plans for New York City violence: Headley, *Confederate Operations in Canada and New York*, 264–73.

244 "[A] vicious sentiment against the draft": Ibid.

244 Butler's use of troops to keep New York quiet on Election Day: Flower, *Edwin McMasters Stanton* 393; *New York Times*, Nov. 5, 1864.

244 August Belmont barred from voting: Strong, *Diary*, Nov. 8, 1864, 3:510.

Chapter Thirty-Eight

Page

245 Election results of 1864: Greeley, *American Conflict*, 2:671–72.

246 "25,000 votes": letter from General Butler to Wendell Phillips, Dec. 20, 1864, OR, series 3, vol. 4:1001.

246 Bonekemper, *A Victor, Not a Butcher*, 330, writes: "What is amazing is that a shift of less than one per cent of the popular vote (29,935 out of 4,031,195) could have given McClellan an additional ninety-seven electoral votes—just enough to provide him with the total 118 electoral votes needed to win the election." He presents a state-by-state chart to bolster this point.

246–247 Greeley, *American Conflict*, 2:672, shows how slim Lincoln's edge was in several key states that he carried:

	Lincoln	McClellan
Connecticut	44,693	42,288
New Hampshire	36,595	33,034
Maryland	40,153	32,739
Minnesota	25,060	17,375
Oregon	9,888	8,457
Nevada	9,826	6,594

Greeley also notes that Nevada chose three electors but one failed to appear "and his colleagues did not fill his place."

247 Flower, *Edwin McMasters Stanton*, 393, asserts that Stanton carried the election for Lincoln by dispatching troops and marshals to quell Rebel schemes for disturbances on Election Day.

247 "All the power and influence of the War Department": Dana, *Recollections of the Civil War*, 260–61

Assuming that Dana is correct, it could be said that Lincoln won *because* this was a wartime election, in which he could use the troops for his benefit. This would contradict the widely held notion that it was quite remarkable that an election could be held at all in time of war. Of course, the administration's rationale for using the soldiers at the polls was not to intimidate Democratic voters but to prevent Confederate sympathizers from helping them pull off dirty tricks, such as stuffing ballot boxes for McClellan.

247–248 "Without the soldier vote in six crucial states": Hesseltine, *Lincoln and the War Governors*, 304.

249 Lusk, *Politics and Politicians*, details Republican victories in Illinois where, he says on 163, they routed the Democrats "horse, foot and dragoon."

249–250 Ohio Democrats' big loss in congressional seats, Greeley, *American Conflict*, 2:673.

250 Lincoln's big loss in Kentucky: Greeley, *American Conflict*, 2:672; Hesseltine, *Lincoln and the War Governors*, 383.

250 "Seymour is a damned fool": Alexander, *A Political History of the State of New York*, 3:135, quoting the *New York Tribune*, Nov. 3, 1865.

251 Hay, *Letters of John Hay and Excerpts from His Diary*, 238, tells how Lincoln read his letter to the cabinet; text of the letter, CWL, 7:514.

Chapter Thirty-Nine
Page

253 Thirteenth Amendment abolishing slavery passed the United States Senate April 8, 1864: Greeley, *American Conflict*, 2:673–75.

253 "Resolved, that, as slavery was the cause": Long, *The Jewel of Liberty*, 279–80.

254 Lincoln's argument that the new Congress "almost certainly will pass" the amendment abolishing slavery: Greeley, *American Conflict*, 2:674.

254–255 Congressman Rollins' account of Lincoln wooing old Whigs to vote for the Thirteenth Amendment: Angle and Miers, *Tragic Years, 1860–65*, 2: 981–84.

255 "[S]ome log rolling": Rhodes, *History of the United States from the Compromise of 1850 to the Final Restoration of Home Rule in the South in 1877*, 5:50.

255 Dramatic last-minute vote in the House: Report by Noah Brooks in the *Sacramento Union*, Jan. 31, 1865, printed in Brooks, *Washington, D.C. in Lincoln's Time*, 408–11.

Chapter Forty
Page
257 Benjamin's escape to England and his career at the London bar are detailed in Evans's brilliant biography, *Judah P. Benjamin, the Jewish Confederate*, 292–348.

258 Jacob Thompson's December 3, 1864, report to Benjamin: OR, series 1, vol. 43:930–36.

258–259 Hood's defeat at Nashville: Horn, *The Decisive Battle of Nashville*, .

259 Clay's appeal to President Johnson, Nov. 23, 1865, OR, series 2, vol. 8:812–14.

259 Clay's release: Ibid., 899.

259 Holt's confession that he paid for perjured testimony: Holt to Stanton, July 3, 1866, Ibid., 931–45.

260 Attempt to kidnap Sanders: *New York Herald*, July 29, 1865.

260 Election of Thomas Henry Hines as chief justice, Kentucky Court of Appeals: Castleman, *Active Service*, 129

260 Castleman's arrest: Ibid., 174–81.

260 Maj. Gen. Alvin P. Hovey at Indianapolis May 25, 1865, branded Castleman "a dangerous and daring spy" and called for him to be banished to Canada: Ibid., 183.

260 Lincoln blocks Castleman's execution: Ibid., 179.

260 Castleman's Spanish-American War service: Horan, *Confederate Agent*, 290.

260–261 Senate careers of George H. Pendleton and Thomas A. Hendricks: U.S. Congress, *The Biographical Directory of the American Congress*, Hendricks 1105; Pendleton 1527; Cox 793; Vallandigham 1847.

261 McClellan as governor of New Jersey: Myers: *A Study in Personality*, 494–502.

261 Vallandigham's death, June 17, 1871: Marshall, *American Bastile*, 745–51.

261 For "bloody shirt" campaigns: See Cox, *Three Decades of Federal Legislation*, 622.

262 "[N]o party can survive an opposition to a war": Seward's dictum: Hay, *Lincoln and the Civil War in the Diaries and Letters of John Hay*, 117.

Bibliography

Manuscript Collections

In the Manuscript Division of the Library of Congress are the papers of many individuals of the Civil War era. Among the most important are the Robert T. Lincoln Papers, a large collection of letters to Abraham Lincoln as well as the president's own papers.

Other collections in the Manuscript Division of the library are the papers of the following persons:

Robert Anderson
Edward Bates
August Belmont
Judah P. Benjamin
James Gordon Bennett
Jeremiah Sullivan Black
Francis Preston Blair
Benjamin Franklin Butler
Simon Cameron
Zachariah Chandler
Salmon Portland Chase
Thomas Ewing
William Pitt Fessenden
John Hay
Joseph Holt
Andrew Johnson
Horatio King
John A. Logan
George B. McClellan

Manton M. Marble
Anna Sanders
George Nicholas Sanders
John Sherman
Edwin M. Stanton
Alexander Hugh Holmes Stuart
Jacob Thompson
Lyman Trumbull
Benjamin F. Wade
Robert John Walker
Elihu B. Washburne
Gideon Welles

The Henry E. Huntington Library at San Marino, California, is a treasure house of documents about the Civil War era. Most important are the papers of Samuel L. M. Barlow, the mastermind of the campaign to win the presidency for Gen. George B. McClellan.

Newspapers

Albany, NY, *Atlas and Argus*
Albany, NY, *Evening Journal*
Baltimore, the *South*
Baltimore Sun
Charleston, SC, *Courier*
Charleston, SC, *Mercury*
Chicago Times
Chicago Tribune
Cincinnati Commercial
Cincinnati Enquirer
Cincinnati Gazette
Columbus, OH, the *Crisis*
Fayetteville, NC, *Observer*
Indianapolis Daily Journal
Indianapolis Daily State Sentinel
Lancaster, PA, *Daily Express*
New York Herald
New York Evening Post
New York Times
New York Tribune

New York World
Philadelphia Bulletin
Philadelphia Inquirer
Philadelphia Press
Raleigh, NC, *Confederate*
Raleigh Standard
Richmond Dispatch
Richmond Enquirer
Richmond Examiner
Richmond Sentinel
Richmond Whig
Sacramento Union
St. Louis *Daily Missouri Democrat*
St. Louis *Daily Missouri Republican*
Salisbury, NC, *Carolina Watchman*
Springfield, IL, *Daily State Journal*
Troy, OH, *Times*
Washington Evening Star
Washington, DC, *National Intelligencer*

Published Letters and Diaries

Bates, Edward. *The Diary of Edward Bates, 1859–60.* Howard Beale, ed. Washington, DC: U. S. Government Printing Office, 1933. Vol. 4 of the Annual Report of the American Historical Association, 1930. Reprint, New York, Da Capo Press, 1971.
Belmont, August. *Letters, Speeches and Addresses.* New York: privately printed, 1890.
Black, Jeremiah Sullivan. *Essays and Speeches of Jeremiah Black.* Chauncey F. Black, ed. New York: Appleton, 1885.
Browning, Orville H. *The Diary of Orville Hickman Browning.* Theodore Calvin Pease and James G. Randall, eds. Springfield: The Trustees of the Illinois State Historical Society, 1927.
Buchanan, James. *The Works of James Buchanan.* John Bassett Moore, ed. 12 vols. Philadelphia: Lippincott, 1908–1911.
Butler, Benjamin F. *Private and Official Correspondence of Gen. Benjamin F. Butler during the Period of the American Civil War.* Privately issued, 1917.
Chase, Samuel Portland. *The Salmon P. Chase Papers.* John Niven, ed. 5 vols. Kent, OH: Kent State Univ. Press, 1993–1998.
Daly, Maria Lydig. *The Diary of a Union Lady, 1861–1865.* Harold Earl Hammond, ed. New York: Funk & Wagnalls, 1962.
Davis, Jefferson. *Jefferson Davis, Constitutionalist: His Letters, Papers and Speeches.* Dunbar Rowland, ed. 10 vols. Jackson: Mississipi Department of Archives and History, 1923.
_____. *Private Letters, 1823–1889.* Hudson Strode, ed. New York: Harcourt, Brace, 1966.
_____. *The Papers of Jefferson Davis.* Linda Lasswell Crist, ed. 11 vols. Baton Rouge: Louisiana State Univ. Press, 1989–2004.
Hay, John. *Letters of John Hay and Excerpts from His Diary.* 3 vols. New York: Gordian Press, 1989. Reprint of the 1908 edition.
_____. *Lincoln and the Civil War in the Diaries and Letters of John Hay.* Tyler

Dennett, ed. New York: Dodd, Mead, 1939.

Johnson, Andrew. *The Papers of Andrew Johnson.* Paul H. Bergeron, Leroy P. Graf and Ralph V. Haskins, eds. 16 vols. Knoxville: Univ. of Tennessee Press, 1956–2000.

Jones, John Beauchamp. *A Rebel War Clerk's Diary at the Confederate States Capital.* 2 vols. Philadelphia: Lippincott, 1866.

Kean, Robert Garlick Hill. *Inside the Confederate Government, the Diary of Robert Garlick Hill Kean.* Edward Younger, ed. New York: Oxford Univ. Press, 1957.

Lee, Robert E. *The Wartime Papers of R. E. Lee.* Clifford Dowdey and Louis Manarin, eds. New York: Bramhall House, 1961.

Lincoln, Abraham. *The Collected Works of Abraham Lincoln.* Roy P. Basler, ed. 9 vols. New Brunswick, NJ: Rutgers Univ. Press, 1952–1955.

_____. *The Lincoln Papers.* David C. Mearns, ed. 2 vols. Garden City, NY: Doubleday, 1948.

McClellan, George B. *The Civil War Papers of George B. McClellan.* Stephen W. Sears, ed. New York: Ticknor and Fields, 1989.

Rhodes, Elisha Hunt. *All for the Union: The Civil War Diary and Letters of Elisha Hunt Rhodes.* New York: Orion Books, 1985.

Russell, William Howard. *My Diary, North and South.* London: Bradbury and Evans, 2 vols., Boston edition, T. O. H. P. Burnham, 1863.

Strong, George Templeton. *The Diary of George Templeton Strong.* Vol. 3: *The Civil War 1860–1865.* Allan Nevins and Milton H. Thomas, eds. New York: Macmillan, 1952.

Welles, Gideon. *The Diary of Gideon Welles.* John T. Morse Jr., ed. 3 vols. Boston: Houghton Mifflin, 1909–1911. Revised edition, Howard K. Beale, ed. 3 vols. New York: Norton, 1960.

Biographies and Memoirs

Adams, Charles Francis, Jr. *Charles Francis Adams, 1835–1913: An Autobiography.* Boston: Houghton Mifflin 1916.

_____. *Charles Francis Adams, 1807–1886.* Boston: Houghton Mifflin, 1900.

Alexander, Delmar. *The Life of Gen. George B. McClellan.* New York: T. R. Dawley, 1864.

Anderson, Dwight G. *Abraham Lincoln: The Quest for Immortality.* New York: Knopf, 1982.

Auchampaugh, Philip Gerald. *James Buchanan and His Cabinet on the Eve of Secession.* Lancaster, PA: privately printed, 1926.

Bancroft, Frederic. *The Life of William H. Seward.* 2 vols. New York: Harper, 1900.

Belmont, Perry. *An American Democrat: The Recollections of Perry Belmont.* New York: Columbia Univ. Press, 1940.

Beveridge, Albert J. *Abraham Lincoln, 1809–1858.* 2 vols. Boston: Houghton Mifflin, 1928.

Blaine, James G. *Twenty Years of Congress: From Lincoln to Garfield.* 2 vols. Norwich, CT: The Henry Bill Publishing Co., 1884.

Bonekemper, Edward H. *A Victor, Not a Butcher: Ulysses S. Grant's Overlooked Military Genius.* Washington, DC: Regnery, 2004.

Bradley, Erwin Stanley. *Simon Cameron, Lincoln's Secretary of War.* Philadelphia: Univ. of Pennsylvania Press, 1966.

Brockett, L. P. *Life and Times of Abraham Lincoln, Sixteenth President of the United States.* Philadelphia: Bradley and Co., 1865.

Butler, Benjamin Franklin. *Butler's Book.* Boston: A. H. Thayer and Co., 1892.

Butler, Pierce. *Judah P. Benjamin.* Philadelphia: G. W. Jacobs, 1907.

Campbell, James Havelock. *McClellan: A Vindication of the Military Career of General George B. McClellan. A Lawyer's Brief.* New York: Neale Publishing Co., 1916.

Castleman, John B. *Active Service.* Louisville: Courier-Journal Job Printing Company, 1917.

Charnwood, Lord. *Abraham Lincoln.* New York: Henry Holt and Co., 1917.

Clay-Clopton, Virginia. A *Belle of the Fifties.* Narrated by Ada Sterling. New York: Doubleday, Page & Co., 1905.

Cole, Donald B. and John J. McDonough, eds. *Benjamin Brown French, Witness to the Young Republic: A Yankee's Journal, 1828–1970.* Hanover, NH: Univ. Press of New England, 1989.

Cox, Samuel S. *Three Decades of Federal Legislation 1855–1885.* Providence, RI: J. A. and R. A. Reid, 1886.

Current, Richard N. *The Lincoln Nobody Knows.* New York: McGraw Hill, 1958.

Curtis, George Ticknor. *Life of James Buchanan.* New York: Harper and Brothers, 1883.

Cutting, Elizabeth Brown. *Jefferson Davis, Political Soldier.* New York: Dodd, Mead, 1930.

Dana, Charles A. *Recollections of the Civil War: With the Leaders at Washington and in the Field in the Sixties.* New York: D. Appleton Co., 1898.

Davis, Jefferson. *The Rise and Fall of the Confederate Government.* 2 vols. New York: 1890; New York: Thomas Yoseloff, 1958.

Davis, Varina Howell. *Jefferson Davis: A Memoir by his Wife.* 2 vols. Freeport, NY: Books for Libraries Press, 1971.

Davis, William C. *Jefferson Davis, the Man and His Hour.* New York: Harper Collins, 1991.

_____. *Breckinridge, Soldier, Statesman, Symbol.* Baton Rouge: Louisiana State Univ. Press, 1974.

De Leon, Thomas C. *Four Years in Rebel Capitals.* Spartanburg, SC: The Reprint Co., 1975. Reprint of the 1892 edition, Mobile, AL: Gossip Printing Co.

Dix, Morgan. *Memoirs of John Adams Dix.* Compiled by his son. 2 vols. New York: Harper, 1882.

Donald, David Herbert. *Charles Sumner and the Coming of the Civil War.* New York: Knopf, 1970.

_____. *Lincoln.* New York: Simon and Schuster, 1995.

_____. *Lincoln Reconsidered.* New York: Knopf, 1958.

_____. *Lincoln's Herndon.* New York: Knopf, 1948.

_____. *"We Are Lincoln Men": Abraham Lincoln and His Friends.* New York: Simon and Schuster, 2003.

Douglas, Henry Kyd. *I Rode With Stonewall.* Chapel Hill: Univ. of North Carolina Press, 1940.

Dowd, Clement. *The Life of Zebulon B. Vance.* Charlotte, N.C.: Observer Printing and Publishing House, 1897.

Dowdey, Clifford. *Lee.* Boston: Little, Brown, 1965.

Duke, Basil W. *Reminiscences of Basil W. Duke.* Garden City, NY: Doubleday Page, 1911.

Dyer, John P. *The Gallant Hood.* Indianapolis: Bobbs-Merrill, 1950.

Eaton, Clement. *Jefferson Davis.* New York: The Free Press, 1977.

Eckenrode, Hamilton James. *Jefferson Davis, President of the South.* New York: Macmillan, 1923.

Eckenrode, Hamilton James, and Bryan Conrad. *James Longstreet, General Lee's Old War Horse.* Chapel Hill: Univ. of North Carolina Press, 1936.

_____. *George B. McClellan, the Man Who Saved the Union*. Chapel Hill: Univ. of North Carolina Press, 1941.

Elliott, Charles Winslow. *Winfield Scott, the Soldier and the Man*. New York: Macmillan 1937.

Evans, Eli N. *Judah P. Benjamin, the Jewish Confederate*. New York: The Free Press, 1988.

Fessenden, Francis. *The Life and Public Services of William Pitt Fessenden*. 2 vols. Boston: Houghton Mifflin, 1907.

Flippin, Percy S. *Herschel V. Johnson of Georgia: States Rights Unionist*. Richmond: Press of the Dietz Printing Co., 1931.

Flower, Frank Abial. *Edwin McMasters Stanton, the Autocrat of Rebellion, Emancipation and Reconstruction*. Akron, OH: Saalfield, 1905.

Foulke, William Dudley. *Life of Oliver P. Morton*. 2 vols. Indianapolis: Bowen-Merrill, 1899.

Freeman, Douglas Southall. *R. E. Lee*. 4 vols. New York: Charles Scribner's Sons, 1934.

Garrison, Webb. *The Lincoln No One Knows*. Nashville, TN: Rutledge Hill Press, 1993.

Gilmore, James R. *Personal Recollections of Abraham Lincoln and the Civil War*. Boston: L. C. Page, 1898.

Gorham, George C. *Life and Public Services of Edwin M. Stanton*. 2 vols. Boston: Houghton Mifflin, 1899.

Hale, William Harlan. *Horace Greeley, Voice of the People*. New York: Harper, 1950.

Hassler, Warren W. Jr. *General George McClellan, Shield of the Union*. Baton Rouge: Louisiana State Univ. Press, 1957.

Henderson, Lieut. Col. G. F. R. *Stonewall Jackson and the American Civil War*. 2 vols. New York: Longmans, Green, 1911.

Herndon, William H., and Jesse W. Weik. *Abraham Lincoln: The True Story of a Great Life*. Paul Angle, ed. New York: D. Appleton, 1916.

Herrick, Anson. *A Condensed Biography of Fernando Wood by a Veteran Democrat*. New York: 1866.

Holland, J. G. *Life of Abraham Lincoln*. New York: Paperback Library, 1961. Reprint of the 1865 edition.

Hood, John B. *Advance and Retreat*. Edison, NJ: The Blue and Grey Press, 1985. Reprint of the 1881 edition.

Julian, George W. *Political Recollections, 1849–1872*. Chicago: Jansen, McClurg & Co., 1884.

Katz, Irving. *August Belmont, a Political Biography*. New York: Columbia Univ. Press, 1968.

King, Horatio: *Turning on the Light*. Philadelphia: J. B. Lippincott, 1895.

King, Willard. *Lincoln's Manager, David Davis*. Cambridge, MA.: Harvard Univ. Press, 1960.

Kirwan, Albert D. *John J. Crittenden, the Struggle for the Union*. Lexington: Univ. of Kentucky Press, 1962.

Klein, Philip Shriver. *President James Buchanan*. University Park: Pennsylvania State Univ. Press, 1962.

Klement, Frank L. *The Limits of Dissent: Clement Vallandigham and the Civil War*. Lexington: Univ. of Kentucky Press, 1970.

Kunhardt, Philip B. Jr., Philip B. Kunhardt III, and Peter W. Kunh Kunhardt. *Lincoln: An Illustrated Biography*. New York: Knopf, 1992.

Lamon, Ward Hill. *Recollections of Abraham Lincoln 1847–1865*. Dorothy Lamon Teillard, ed. Washington, DC, privately published, 1911.

_____. *The Life of Abraham Lincoln, His Birth to His Inauguration as President.* Boston: J. R. Osgood and Co., 1872.

Lewis, Lloyd. *Sherman, Fighting Prophet.* New York: Harcourt, Brace, 1932.

Lindsay, David. *"Sunset" Cox, Irrepressible Democrat.* Detroit: Wayne State Univ. Press, 1959.

Longstreet, James. *From Manassas to Appomattox: Memoirs of the Civil War in America.* Philadelphia: Lippincott, 1903.

Luthin, Reinhard H. *The Real Abraham Lincoln.* Englewood Cliffs, NJ: Prentice-Hall, 1960.

Macartney, Clarence E. *Little Mac: The Life of General George B. McClellan.* Philadelphia: Dorrance, 1940.

McClellan, George B. *McClellan's Own Story.* William L. Prime, ed. New York: Charles L. Webster, 1887.

McClure, Alexander K. *Lincoln and Men of War-Times.* Philadelphia: The Times Publishing Co., 1892.

_____. *Recollections of Half a Century.* Salem, MA: The Salem Press Co., 1902.

McFeely, William S. *Grant.* New York: Norton, 1981.

McJimsey, George T. *Genteel Partisan: Manton Marble, 1834–1917.* Ames: Iowa State Univ. Press, 1971.

McWhiney, Grady. *Braxton Bragg and Confederate Defeat.* 2 vols. New York: Columbia Univ. Press, 1969.

Mai-jour (Translated May Day). General George Barnum McClellan. Militant-Homeopath to the Army of the Confederates Attacked, After His Own Mode, Through Parallels. London: John Lee Publisher, 1864.

Meadex, Robert Douthat. *Judah P. Benjamin, Confederate Statesman.* New York: Oxford Univ. Press, 1943.

Michie, Peter Smith. *General McClellan.* New York: Appleton, 1901.

Minor, Charles L.C. *The Real Lincoln.* Gastonia, NC: Atkins-Rankin, 1928.

Mitchell, Stewart. *Horatio Seymour of New York.* Cambridge, MA: Harvard Univ. Press, 1938.

Myers, William Starr. *A Study in Personality: General George B. McClellan.* New York: Appleton-Century, 1934.

Nash, Howard P. Jr. *Stormy Petrel: The Life and Times of General Benjamin F. Butler, 1818–1893.* Rutherford, NJ: Fairleigh Dickinson Univ. Press, 1969.

Nichols, Roy Franklin. *Franklin Pierce, Young Hickory of the Granite Hills.* Philadelphia: Univ. of Pennsylvania Press, 1931.

Nicolay, Helen. *Lincoln's Secretary: A Biography of John G. Nicolay.* New York: Longmans, Green, 1949.

Nicolay, John G., and John Hay. *Abraham Lincoln, a History.* 10 vols. New York: Century, 1886–1890.

Niven, John. *Gideon Welles, Lincoln's Secretary of the Navy.* New York: Oxford Univ. Press, 1973.

Oates, Stephen B. *With Malice Toward None: The Life of Abraham Lincoln.* New York: Harper and Row, 1977.

Parish, John Carl. *George Wallace Jones.* Iowa City: The State Historical Society of Iowa, 1912.

Pierce, Edward L. *Memoir and Letters of Charles Sumner.* 4 vols. Boston: Roberts Brothers, 1877–1892. Reprint: New York: Arno Press, 1959.

Pleasants, Samuel Augustus. *Fernando Wood of New York.* New York: AMS Press, 1980. Reprint of original edition: New York: Columbia Univ. Press, 1948.

Pollard, Edward A. *Life of Jefferson Davis with a Secret History of the Southern Confederacy.* Reprint of first edition by National Publishing Co.

Philadelphia, 1869.

Poore, Benjamin Perley. *Perley's Reminiscences of Sixty Years in the National Metropolis.* 2 vols. New York: AMS Press, 1971.

Pratt, Fletcher. *Stanton, Lincoln's Secretary of War.* New York: Norton, 1953.

Pryor, Mrs. Roger. *Reminiscences of Peace and War.* New York: Macmillan, 1905.

_____. *My Day: Reminiscences of a Long Life.* New York: Macmillan, 1909.

Randall, James G. *Lincoln the President.* 4 vols. New York: Dodd, Mead, 1945–1955. 4: *The Last Full Measure,* was completed by Richard N. Current.

Randall, Mary Painter. *Lincoln's Sons.* Boston: Little, Brown, 1955.

Reagan, John H. *Memoirs, with Special Reference to Secession and Civil War.* New York: Neale Publishing Co., 1906.

Richardson Leon Burr. *William. E. Chandler, Republican.* New York: Dodd, Mead, 1940.

Riddle, Donald W. *Congressman Abraham Lincoln.* Urbana: Univ. of Illinois Press, 1957.

Robertson, Alexander F. *Alexander Hugh Holmes Stuart, 1807–1891.* Richmond: The William Byrd Press, Inc., 1925.

Sandburg, Carl. *Abraham Lincoln: The War Years.* 4 vols. New York: Harcourt, Brace and World, 1939.

Schurz, Carl. *The Autobiography of Carl Schurz.* Wayne Andrews, ed. New York: Scribner, 196l.

_____. *The Reminiscences of Carl Schurz.* 3 vols. Garden City, NY: Doubleday, 1913.

Scott, Winfield. *Memoirs of Lieut. General Scott, LLB, Written by Himself.* 2 vols. New York: Sheldon and Co., 1864.

Sears, Louis Martin. *John Slidell.* Durham, NC: Duke Univ. Press, 1925.

Sears, Stephen W. *George McClellan, the Young Napoleon.* New York: Ticknor and Fields, 1988.

Seward, Frederick W. *Seward at Washington.* New York: Derby and Miller, 1891.

_____. *Reminiscences of a War-Time Statesman and Diplomat, 1830–1915.* New York: G. P. Putnam's Sons, 1916.

Seitz, Don C. *The James Gordon Bennetts, Father and Son Proprietors of the New York Herald.* Indianapolis: Bobbs-Merrill, 1928.

_____. *Braxton Bragg, General of the Confederacy.* Freeport, NY: Books for Libraries Press, 1971. Reprint of 1924 edition Columbia, SC: The State Co.

Shenton, James P. *Robert John Walker: A Politician from Jackson to Lincoln.* New York: Columbia Univ. Press, 1961.

Sherman, John. *Recollections of Forty Years in the House, Senate and Cabinet.* Chicago: Werner, 1895.

Sherman, William T. *Memoirs.* Bloomington: Indiana Univ. Press, 1875.

_____. *Memoirs of General William T. Sherman, by Himself.* Vol. 2. Bloomington: Indiana Univ. Press, 1957.

Silverman, Kenneth. *Lightning Man: The Accursed Life of Samuel F. B. Morse.* New York: Knopf, 2003.

Smith, Elbert B. *Francis Preston Blair.* New York: The Free Press, 1980.

Smith, William Ernest. *The Francis Preston Blair Family in Politics.* 2 vols. New York: Macmillan, 1933.

Starr, Stephen Z. *Colonel Grenfell's Wars, The Life of a Soldier of Fortune.* Baton Rouge: Louisiana State Univ. Press, 1971.

Stephens, Robert Grier, Jr. *Intrepid Warrior, Clement Anselm Evans.* Dayton, Ohio: Morningside House, 1992.

Stidger, Felix W. *Treason History of the Order of Sons of Liberty, Succeeded by Knights of the Golden Circle, Afterward Order of American Knights.* Chicago: privately printed, 1903.

Stillwell, Lucille. *Born to be a Statesman: John Cabell Breckinridge.* Caldwell, ID:The Caxton Printers, 1936.

Stout, L. H. *Reminiscences of General Braxton Bragg.* Hattiesburg, Miss.: The Book Farm, 1942.

Strode, Hudson. *Jefferson Davis.* 3 vols. New York: Harcourt Brace, 1955–1964.

Tarbell, Ida Minerva. *The Life of Abraham Lincoln.* 2 vols. New York: Macmillan, 1917.

Tate, Allen. *Jefferson Davis, his Rise and Fall: A Biographical Narrative.* New York: Minton, Balch, 1929.

Taylor, Richard. *Destruction and Reconstruction.* Richard B. Harwell, ed. Waltham, MA: Blaisdell Publishing Co., 1968. Reprint of the original edition published by Appleton in 1879.

Thayer, William Roscoe. *The Life and Letters of John Hay.* 2 vols. Boston: Houghton Mifflin, 1919.

Thomas, Benjamin P. *Abraham Lincoln, a Biography.* New York: Knopf, 1958.

Thomas, Benjamin P., and Harold Hyman. *Stanton: The Life and Times of Lincoln's Secretary of War.* New York: Knopf, 1962.

Thomas, Lately. *Between Two Empires, the Life Story of California's First Senator, William McKendree Gwin.* Boston: Houghton Mifflin, 1969.

_____ . *The First President Johnson.* New York: William Morrow, 1968.

_____. *Sam Ward: King of the Lobby.* Boston: Houghton Mifflin, 1965.

Thomason, John. *Jeb Stuart.* New York: Scribner's, 1930.

Trefousse, Hans Louis. *Benjamin Franklin Wade, Radical Republican from Ohio.* New York: Twayne Publishers, 1963.

Tucker, Glenn. *Zeb Vance: Champion of Personal Freedom.* Indianapolis: Bobbs-Merrill, 1965.

Turner, Justin G., and Linda Levitt Turner. *Mary Todd Lincoln, Her life and Letters.* New York: Knopf, 1972.

Vallandigham, James L. *A Life of Clement L. Vallandigham.* Baltimore: Turnbull Brothers, 1872.

Van Deusen, Glyndon G. *William H. Seward.* New York: Oxford Univ. Press, 1967.

_____. *Thurlow Weed, Wizard of the Lobby.* New York and Boston: Little, Brown, 1947.

Vandiver, Frank E. *Mighty Stonewall.* New York: McGraw-Hill, 1957.

Von Abele, Rudolph. *Alexander H. Stephens.* New York: Knopf, 1946.

Weed, Thurlow. *The Life of Thurlow Weed and Autobiography of Thurlow Weed.* Thurlow Weed Barnes and Harriet A. Weed, eds. 2 vols. Boston: Houghton Mifflin, 1883–1884.

Wert, Jeffry B. *General James Longstreet. NewYork:* Simon and Schuster, 1993.

White, Horace. *The Life of Lyman Trumbull.* Boston: Houghton Mifflin, 1913.

Williams, T. Harry. *Beauregard, Napoleon in Gray.* Baton Rouge: Louisiana State Univ. Press, 1954.

Wilson, Douglas L. *Honor's Voice: The Transformation of Abraham Lincoln.* New York: Knopf, 1998.

Willson, Beckles. *John Slidell and the Confederates in Paris, 1862–1865.* New York: Minton, Balch, 1932.

Wise, Henry Alexander. *Seven Decades of the Union.* New York: Lippincott, 1881.

Wise, John S. *The End of an Era.* Boston: Houghton Mifflin, 1901.

Wright, Mrs. D. Giraud (nee Louise Wigfall). *A Southern Girl in '61.* New York:

Doubleday, Page, 1905.
Yeary, Mamie. *Reminiscences of the Boys in Gray, 1861–1865*. Dallas, TX: privately printed, 1912.

Official Publications
U.S. Congress. *Biographical Directory of the American Congress, 1774–1971.* Washington, DC: U.S. Government Printing Office, 1971.
_____. *Congressional Globe*. Vols. 1861–1867. Washington, DC.
_____. *Report of the Joint Committee on the Conduct of the War*. 6 vols. Washington, DC: 1863–1865. Supplemental Report, 2 vols, 1866.
_____. House., 39th Cong., 2d sess. *Executive Document No. 50. Message from the President of the United States in Answer to a Resolution of the House of the 19th of December, Transmitting Papers Relative to the Case of George Saint Leger Grenfell*, January 21, 1867.
_____. House. House Reports, 39th Cong., 1st sess., 1864: Report No. 104.
U. S. Naval War Records Office. *Official Records of the Union and Confederate Navies in the War of the Rebellion*. Washington, DC: Government Printing Office, 1894–1922.
U. S. War Department. *The War of the Rebellion: A Compilation of the Official Records of the Union and Confederate Armies*. 128 vols. Washington, DC: Government Printing Office, 1880–1901.

Other Publications
Alexander, De Alva Stanwood. *A Political History of the State of New York*. 3 vols. Port Washington, NY: Ira J. Freedman, 1969. Reprint of first edition by Holt: New York, 1909.
Allen, Mary Bernard. *Joseph Holt, Judge Advocate General (1862–1875): A Study in the Treatment of Political Prisoners by the United States Government During the Civil War*. Ph.D. dissertation, Chicago, IL, 1927.
Anderson, Frank Maloy. *The Mystery of "A Public Man."* Minneapolis: The Univ. of Minnesota Press, 1948.
Angle, Paul M., and Earl Schenck Miers. *Tragic Years, 1860–1865: A Documentary History of the American Civil War*. 2 vols. New York: Simon and Schuster, 1960.
Asbury, Herbert. *The Gangs of New York, an Informal History of the Underworld*. New York: Knopf, 1928.
Barton, William E. *The Soul of Abraham Lincoln*. New York: George H. Doran, 1920.
Belden, Thomas, and Marva Robins Belden. *So Fell the Angels*. Boston: Little, Brown. 1956.
Benton, Elbert J. *The Movement for Peace Without a Victory During the Civil War*. New York: Da Capo Press, 1972. Reprint of original issued in 1918 as publication No. 99 of the Western Reserve Historical Society, Cleveland, OH.
Bernstein, Iver. *The New York City Draft Riots*. New York: Oxford Univ. Press, 1990.
Bill, Alfred Hoyt. *The Beleaguered City: Richmond 1861–1865*. New York: Knopf, 1946.
Binkley, Wilfred E. *American Political Parties, Their Natural History*. New York: Knopf, 1953.
Botts, John Minor. *The Great Rebellion, Its Secret History, Rise, Progress and Disastrous Failure*. New York: Harper and Brothers, 1866.
Bowers, Claude. *The Tragic Era: The Revolution After Lincoln*. Boston: Houghton Mifflin, 1929.

Brooks, Noah. *Selections from the Writings of Noah Brooks, Civil War Correspondent.* P. J. Staudenraus, ed. New York: A. S. Barnes. Reprint by Thomas Yoseloff, 1967.

_____ . *Washington, D.C. in Lincoln's Time.* New York: Century, 1895.

Brownlow, William Gannaway. *Sketches of the Rise, Progress and Decline of Secession.* Philadelphia: G. W. Childs, 1862.

Burgess, John W. *The Civil War and the Constitution.* 2 vols. New York: Scribner's, 1901.

Carman, Harry J., and Reinhard H. Luthin. *Lincoln and the Patronage.* New York: Columbia Univ. Press, 1943.

Catton, Bruce. *The Centennial History of the Civil War.* 3 vols. New York: Doubleday, 1961–1965.

_____. *Grant Moves South.* Boston: Little, Brown, 1960.

The Chicago Copperhead Convention, the Treasonable and Revolutionary Utterances of the Men Who Composed It. Washington, DC: The Union Congressional Committee, 1864.

Chittenden, Lucius E. *Recollections of President Lincoln and His Administration.* New York: Harper, 1891.

Clark, Allen C. *Abraham Lincoln in the National Capital.* Washington, DC: W.P. Roberts Co., 1925.

Cochran, William C. *The Dream of a Northwestern Confederacy.* Madison: The State Historical Society of Wisconsin, 1916.

Coulter, Ellis Merton. *The Civil War and Readjustment in Kentucky.* Gloucester, MA: P. Smith, 1966.

_____. *The Confederate States of America, 1861–1865.* Vol. 7: *A History of the South.* Baton Rouge: Louisiana State Univ. Press, 1950.

Craven, Avery. *The Coming of the Civil War.* New York: Scribner's, 1942.

_____. *The Repressible Conflict.* Baton Rouge: The Louisiana State Univ. Press, 1939.

Cullen, Joseph P. *The Peninsula Campaign, 1862.* Harrisburg, PA: Stackpole Books, 1973.

Current, Richard N. *Lincoln and the First Shot.* Philadelphia: Lippincott, 1963.

Davis, William C. *An Honorable Defeat. The Last Days of the Confederate Government.* New York: Harcourt, Inc., 2001.

_____, ed. *The Image of War, 1861–1865.* Vol. 1: *Shadows of the Storm,* 1961; Vol. 2: *The Guns of '62,* 1982. Garden City, NY: Doubleday.

_____. *Look Away! A History of the Confederate States of America.* New York: The Free Press, 2002.

Davis, William J., ed. *Partisan Rangers of the Confederate States Army.* Louisville, KY: George C. Fetter Co., 1904. New edition, Hartford, KY: Cook & McDowell Publications, 1979.

Dell, Christopher. *Lincoln and the War Democrats.* Rutherford NJ: Fairleigh Dickinson Univ. Press, 1975.

Dozer, Donald Marquand. *Maryland, a Portrait of the Free State.* Cambridge, MD: Tidewater Publishers, 1976.

Eaton, Clement. *A History of the Southern Confederacy.* New York: Macmillan, 1954.

_____. *The Mind of the Old South.* Baton Rouge: Louisiana State Univ. Press, 1967.

Fishel, Edwin C. *The Secret War for the Union: The Untold Story of Military Intelligence in the Civil War.* Boston: Houghton Mifflin, 1996.

Fisher, Col. Horace Newton. *The Harris Letter: Outlining Bragg's Plan of Campaign for the Invasion of Kentucky in 1862.* N.p.: Horace Cecil Fisher, 1953.

Foote, Henry S. *The War of the Rebellion.* New York: Harper, 1866.

Foote, Shelby. *The Civil War, a Narrative.* 3 vols. New York: Random House, 1958.

Forney, John W. *Anecdotes of Public Men.* 2 vols. New York: Harper, 1873.

Fremantle, Arthur James Lyon. *The Fremantle Diary,* Walter Lord, ed. Boston: Little Brown, 1954.

Furgurson, Ernest B. *Ashes of Glory, Richmond at War.* New York: Knopf, 1996.

_____. *Freedom Rising: Washington in the Civil War.* New York: Knopf, 2004.

Gray, Wood. *The Hidden Civil War: The Story of the Copperheads.* New York: Viking, 1942.

Greeley, Horace. *The American Conflict.* 2 vols. Hartford, CT: O. D. Case & Co., 1865–1866.

Hall, James O. "The Dahlgren Papers." *Civil War Times,* Nov. 1983, 30–39.

Halstead, Murat. *Caucuses of 1860.* Columbus, OH: Follett, Foster and Co., 1860.

Hanchett, William. "Lincoln's Assassination Revisited." *Lincoln Herald,* Spring 1997.

Headley, Joel Tyler. *The Great Rebellion: A History of the Civil War in the United States.* 2 vols. Hartford, CT: American Publishing Co., 1866.

Headley, John W. *Confederate Operations in Canada and New York.* New York: Neale Publishing Co., 1906.

Hendrick, Burton J. *Lincoln's War Cabinet.* Boston: Little, Brown, 1966.

_____. *Statesmen of the Lost Cause.* Boston: Little, Brown, 1939.

Henry, Robert Selph. *The Story of the Confederacy.* Indianapolis: Bobbs-Merrill, 1943.

Hesseltine, William B. *Lincoln and the War Governors.* New York: Knopf, 1948.

Hines, Thomas H. "The Northwest Conspiracy." *Southern Bivouac* 2, June 1886-May 1887: 437–445, 500–510, 567–574, 699–704.

Horan, James D. *Confederate Agent: A Discovery in History.* New York: Crown, 1954.

Horn, Stanley F. *The Decisive Battle of Nashville.* Baton Rouge: Louisiana State Univ. Press, 1956.

Horner, Harlan Hoyt. *Lincoln and Greeley.* Urbana: Univ. of Illinois Press, 1953.

Hurlbert, William Henry. *McClellan and the Conduct of the War.* New York: Sheldon, 1864.

Johnson, Allen, and Dumas Malone, eds. *Dictionary of American Biography.* New York: Scribner's, 1936.

Johnson, Robert U., and Clarence Buel, eds. *Battles and Leaders of the Civil War.* 4 vols. New York: Century, 1888.

Jones, J. William. *The Davis Memorial Volume: Our Dead President, Jefferson Davis, and the World's Tribute to His Memory.* Atlanta: H. C. Hudgins, 1890.

Kendall, Amos. *Letters Exposing the Mismanagement of Public Affairs by Abraham Lincoln and the Political Combination to Secure His Re-Election.* Washington, DC: The Constitutional Union Office, 1864.

Kirke, Edmund (James R. Gilmore). "Our Visit to Richmond." *Atlantic Monthly,* July 1864, 372–83. "The Chicago Conspiracy." *Atlantic Monthly,* July 1865.

Kirkland, Edward Chase. *The Peacemakers of 1864.* New York: Macmillan, 1927.

Klement, Frank L. *The Copperheads in the Middle West.* Chicago: Univ. of Chicago Press, 1960.

_____. *Dark Lanterns: Secret Political Societies, Conspiracies and Treason in the Civil War.* Baton Rouge: Louisiana State Univ. Press, l984.

Kunhardt, Dorothy Meserve, and Philip B. Kunhardt, Jr. *Twenty Days.* New York: Harper and Row, 1965.

Leech, Margaret. *Reveille in Washington,* 1860–1865. New York: Harper, 1941.

Lewis, Lloyd. *Myths After Lincoln.* New York: Harcourt, Brace, 1929.

Long, David E. *The Jewel of Liberty: Abraham Lincoln's Re-Election and the End of Slavery.* Mechanicsburg, PA: Stackpole Books, 1994.

Long, E. B., with Barbara Long. *The Civil War Day by Day, 1861–1865.* Garden City, NY: Doubleday, 1971.

Lusk, D. W. *Politics and Politicians: A Succinct History of the Politics of Illinois from 1856 to 1884.* Springfield, IL: H. W. Rokker, 1884.

McKellar, Kenneth. *Tennessee Senators as Seen by One of Their Successors.* Kingsport, TN: Southern Publishers, Inc., 1942.

McLaughlin, Andrew C. *A Constitutional History of the United States.* New York: Appleton-Century, 1935.

McPherson, Edward. *The Political History of the United States of America During the Great Rebellion, 1860–1865.* New York: Da Capo Press, 1972. Reprint of original edition published in Washington, DC: Philip and Solomons, 1865.

McPherson, James M. *Abraham Lincoln and the Second American Revolution.* New York: Oxford Univ. Press, 1990.

————. *Battle Cry of Freedom: The Civil War Era.* New York: Oxford Univ. Press, 1968.

————. *Ordeal by Fire: The Civil War and Reconstruction.* New York: McGraw Hill, 1992.

Marshall, John A. *American Bastile: A History of the Illegal Arrests and Imprisonment of American Citizens During the Late Civil War.* Philadelphia: Thomas W. Hartley, 1878.

Meigs, Montgomery C. "Gen. M. C. Meigs on the Conduct of the Civil War." *American Historical Review* (Jan. 1921): 285–303.

Milton, George Fort. *Conflict: The American Civil War.* Washington, DC: The Infantry Journal, 1941.

————. *Abraham Lincoln and the Fifth Column.* Washington, DC: The Infantry Journal, 1942.

Moore, Frank, ed. *The Rebellion Record.* 12 vols. New York: D. Van Nostrand, 1861–1868. Reprint New York: Arno Press, 1977.

Morton, Joseph W. *Sparks from the Camp Fires, or Tales of the Old Veterans.* Philadelphia: Keystone, 1892.

Naglee, Henry Morris. *McClellan v. Lincoln.* Philadelphia: 1864.

Neely, Mark E., Jr. *The Fate of Liberty: Abraham Lincoln and Civil Liberties.* New York: Oxford Univ. Press, 1991.

————. *The Last Best Hope of Earth: Abraham Lincoln and the Promise of America.* Cambridge, MA: Harvard Univ. Press, 1993.

Nelson, Larry E. *Bullets, Ballots, and Rhetoric: Confederate Policy for the United States Presidential Contest of 1864.* Tuscaloosa, AL: Univ. of Alabama Press, 1980.

Nevins, Allan. *The Emergence of Lincoln.* 2 vols. New York: Scribner's, 1950.

————. *The War for the Union.* 4 vols. New York: Scribner's, 1959–1971.

Newman, Ralph G. *Lincoln for the Ages.* Garden City, NY: 1960.

Official Proceedings of the Democratic National Convention in 1864 in Chicago. Chicago: Times Steam Book and Job Printing House, 1864.

Osborne, Charles C. *Jubal: The Life and Times of General Jubal A. Early, CSA, Defender of the Lost Cause.* Chapel Hill, NC: Algonquin Books of Chapel Hill, 1992.

Palfrey, Francis W. *The Army in the Civil War.* Vol. 5: *The Antietam and Fredericksburg.* New York: Scribner's, 1885.

Patrick, Morgan. "The New York Draft Riots." 1–10, in *Bulletin of the Society d'Europe,* Seabrook, NH, November–December, 1991.

Piatt, Donn. *Memories of the Men Who Saved the Union.* New York: Belford Clark, 1887.

Pinsker, Matthew. *Lincoln's Sanctuary: Abraham Lincoln and the Soldiers' Home*. New York: Oxford Univ. Press, 2003.

Pitman, Benn, ed. *The Trials for Treason at Indianapolis, Disclosing the Plans for Establishing a North Western Confederacy*. Cincinnati: Moore, Wilstach and Baldwin, 1865.

Pollard, Edward A. *The Lost Cause*. New York: E. B. Treat, 1879.

Poore, Ben Perley, ed. *The Conspiracy Trial for the Murder of the President and the Attempt to Overthrow the Government by the Assassination of Its Principal Officers*. 2 vols. Boston: J. E. Tilton, 1865.

Rhodes, James Ford. *History of the United States from the Compromise of 1850 to the Final Restoration of Home Rule at the South in 1877*. 8 vols. New York: Macmillan 1906–1919.

Rice, Allen Thornton. *Reminiscences of Abraham Lincoln by Distinguished Men of His Time*. New York: North American Publishing Co., 1886.

Richardson, Albert B. *The Secret Service: The Field, the Dungeon, and the Escape*. Hartford, CT: American Publishing Co., 1866.

Roland, Charles P. *The Confederacy*. Chicago: Univ. of Chicago Press, 1960.

Roman, Alfred. *The Military Operations of General Beauregard in the War Between the States*. 2 vols. New York: Harper and Brothers, 1884.

Roseboom, Eugene H. *A History of Presidential Elections*. New York: Macmillan, 1957.

Safire, William. *Freedom*. Garden City, NY: Doubleday, 1987.

Scharf, J. Thomas. *History of Maryland from the Earliest Period to the Present Day*. 3 vols. Baltimore: J. B. Piet, 1879. Reprinted by Tradition Press, Hatboro, PA, 1967.

Schouler, James. *History of the United States under the Constitution*. 7 vols. New York: Dodd, Mead, 1894–1913.

Scrugham, Mary. *The Peaceable Americans, 1860–1861*. New York: Columbia Univ. Press, 1921.

Sears, Stephen W. *Controversies and Commanders: Dispatches from the Army of the Potomac*. Boston: Houghton Mifflin, 1999.

————. *Landscape Turned Red: The Battle of Antietam*. New York: Ticknor & Fields, 1983.

Silbey, Joel H. *A Respectable Minority: The Democratic Party in the Civil War Era, 1860–1865*. New York: Norton, 1977.

Smith, Page. *A People's History of the Civil War and Reconstruction*. Vol. 5: *Trial by Fire*. New York: McGraw Hill, 1982.

Southern Bivouac, a monthly Literary and Historical Magazine. Louisville, KY, 1887.

Sprague, Dean. *Freedom Under Lincoln: Federal Power and Personal Liberty Under the Strain of Civil War*. Boston: Houghton Mifflin, 1965.

Stampp, Kenneth M. *Indiana Politics during the Civil War*. Indiana Historical Collections, 21, Indianapolis: Indiana Historical Bureau, 1949.

Stanwood, Edward. *A History of the Presidency from 1788 to 1897*. 2 vols. Boston: Houghton Mifflin, 1898.

Stephens, Alexander H. *A Constitutional View of the Late War Between the States*. 2 vols. Boston: Houghton Mifflin, 1898.

Stern, Philip Van Doren. *Secret Missions of the Civil War*. Chicago: Rand McNally, 1959.

Stimpson, George: *A Book about American Politics*. New York: Harper, 1952.

Summers, Richard J. *Richmond Redeemed: The Siege at Petersburg*. Garden City, NY: Doubleday, 1981.

Swinton, William. *The Campaign of the Army of the Potomac*. New York: Charles B.

Richardson, 1866.

Tidwell, William A. *April '65: Confederate Covert Action in the American Civil War.* Kent, Ohio: Kent State Univ. Press, 1995.

Tidwell, William A. with James O. Hall and David Winfred Gaddy. *Come Retribution: The Confederate Secret Service and the Assassination of Lincoln.* Jackson: Univ. Press of Mississippi, 1988.

Tilley, John Shipley. *Lincoln Takes Command.* Chapel Hill: Univ. of North Carolina Press, 1941.

Tredway, G. R. *Democratic Opposition to the Lincoln Administration in Indiana.* Indianapolis: Indiana Historical Bureau, 1973.

The Vallandigham Song Book. Songs for the Times. Columbus, OII: J. Walter & Co., 1863

Van der Linden, Frank: *Lincoln: The Road to War.* Golden, CO: Fulcrum Publishing, 1998.

Vandiver, Frank. *Jubal's Raid: General Early's Famous Attack on Washington in 1864.* New York: McGraw–Hill, 1960.

Warren, Louis A. *Lincoln's Gettysburg Declaration: "A New Birth of Freedom."* Fort Wayne, Indiana: Lincoln National Life Foundation, 1964.

Waugh, John C. *The Class of 1846: From West Point to Appomattox: Stonewall Jackson, George McClellan and Their Brothers.* New York: Warner Books, 1994.

_____. *Re-electing Lincoln: The Battle for the 1864 Presidency.* New York: Crown, 1997.

_____. *Surviving the Confederacy: Rebellion. Ruin and Recovery—Roger and Sara Pryor During the Civil War.* New York: Harcourt, Inc., 2002.

Weaks, Mabel Clare. "Colonel George St. Leger Grenfell." *Filson Club Quarterly* (Jan. 1960) vol. xxxiv, 8–23.

Wiley, Bell Irvin. *The Life of Johnny Reb, the Common Soldier of the Confederacy.* Indianapolis: Bobbs-Merrill, 1943.

_____. *The Life of Billy Yank, the Common Soldier of the Union.* Indianapolis: Bobbs-Merrill, 1952.

Williams, Kenneth P. *Lincoln Finds a General: A Military Study of the Civil War.* 5 vols. New York: Macmillan, 1949–1959.

Williams, T. Harry. *Lincoln and His Generals.* New York: Knopf, 1952.

_____. *Lincoln and the Radicals.* Madison: Univ. of Wisconsin Press, 1941.

Wills, Garry. *Lincoln at Gettysburg: The Words that Remade America.* New York: Simon and Schuster, 1992.

Winks, Robin W. *Canada and the United States: The Civil War Years.* Baltimore: The Johns Hopkins Press, 1960.

Zornow, William Frank. *Lincoln and the Party Divided.* Norman: Univ. of Oklahoma Press, 1954.

JAN 0 2 2008

973.7 V284
Van der Linden, Frank.
The dark intrigue :